MATERNAL THINKING

"A major step in the translation of women's common skills into literary language, helping to bring women's resources into the public political tool kit of humankind." *The Boston Globe*

"An original book that deserves a broad hearing. Ruddick has shared her brave and generous thinking in a way that could lead to real changes. . . . It can help all of us—men and women—see the complex task of mothering more clearly, and to realize that its concrete way of thinking should be more prevalent in public and official practice. Maternal thinking can be the alternative to a long-dominant mode of thought which tends to distance and destroy the very realities for which mothers—and all of us—care." *Cross Currents*

"I find Ruddick's descriptions of mothering to be both accurate and inspiring. . . . She succeeds in giving mothering the respect and self-esteem that it deserves. But Ruddick does more—she establishes it as the foundation for an important political movement." *Peace Review*

MATERNAL

THINKING

TOWARD

A POLITICS

OF PEACE

SARA RUDDICK

Ballantine Books • New York

TO WILLIAM RUDDICK

Library of Congress Catalog Card Number: 89-91494

ISBN: 0-345-36611-5

This edition published by arrangement with Beacon Press, Boston.

Cover design by James R. Harris

Cover painting: Pablo Picasso, *Portrait of Dora Maar* (detail), 1936.
Private Collection, Paris. Giraudon/Art Resource.

Manufactured in the United States of America

First Ballantine Books Edition: June 1990

10 9 8 7 6 5 4 3 2 1

Contents

Acknowledgments

OVER THE YEARS that I have been writing about mothering, war, and reason, many people have generously supported my work, including some who disagree with its political aims and philosophical presuppositions. I would like to thank especially for their various kinds of engagement with my enterprise Mary Belenky, Robert Berman, Blythe Clinchy, Carol Cohn, Pamela Daniels, Louise DeSalvo, Dorothy Dinnerstein, Patrice Diquinzio, Nancy Goldberger, Sandra Harding, Adrienne Harris, Nancy Hartsock, Virginia Held, Alison Jaggar, Ynestra King, Genevieve Lloyd, Jane Roland Martin, Elizabeth Minnich, Nel Noddings, Lucius Outlaw, Rayna Rapp, Amélie Rorty, Elizabeth Spelman, Susan Squier, Amy Swerdlow, Joyce Trebilcot. Margaret Walker, William Werpehowski, and Terry Winant.

Carol Gilligan's writing has been indispensable to mine and I am grateful for her interest and encouragement. Jean Bethke Elshtain has been a lively critic and warmly supportive promoter of my work. Frieda Kurash has helped assuage the anxieties of authorship and has taught me new ways to think about mothering and children. I have relied upon Maureen Reddy's steady supply of bibliographic references and upon her penetrating, often hilarious, commentaries on literature and politics. For as long as feminism has been central to my life, I have profited from intense discussions with Evelyn Fox Keller about feminist theory and practice and have become accustomed to watching my thinking improve in her presence. In several collaborative endeavors and numerous conversations, Carol Ascher has helped me to sharpen my ideas and to clarify my feelings. For thirty-five years Marilyn Young has kept me writing, offering witty and intelligent counsel and trying to extricate me from the political and social scrapes I land in. One of the most trenchant critics of violence, and occasionally its most thoughtful defender, she has shaped my thinking about particular wars and warmaking. In the five years I have been writing this book, I have discussed the issues of mothering, women's voices, and nonviolence with my colleague Jane Lazarre; my intellectual debt to her writing and conversation is incalculable; without her confidence in my project I would not have been able to continue.

For creating an atmosphere in which it is possible to break conservative academic habits and ask peculiar questions, I thank the faculty and students at the Eugene Lang College of the New School for Social Research. I am grateful to the Lang administration for leaves that allowed me to finish this book.

At a crucial point in my writing, Aryeh Kosman arranged an invigorating and recuperative year at Haverford College. I am grateful to students and faculty of Haverford and Bryn Mawr Colleges for their energetic intellectual and political conversations during that year and especially to my cohorts in various feminist projects, Elaine Hanson, Anne McGuire, and Maureen Reddy.

My editor at Beacon, Joanne Wyckoff, waited patiently for a manuscript to appear and edited it with spirit and insight. Barbara Flanagan proved once again to be a sensitive and indefatigable copy editor. Tom Fischer, Beacon's managing editor, well deserves his reputation for combining tact and competence.

For careful readings of early or current versions of particular chapters of this book, I thank Adrienne Harris, Temma Kaplan, Eva Kittay, Joan Rothschild, and Margaret Walker. Carol Cohn, Evelyn Keller, Jane Lazarre, Elizabeth Spelman, and Marilyn Young commented on, and greatly improved, the manuscript as a whole; Carol Ascher and William Ruddick read the whole and read revisions with the eye of a copy editor, the mind of a logician, and the heart of a friend. Susan Suleiman provided the title. Sara Krulwich took the only picture I have liked and it has lasted for two books.

Although in these pages I occasionally take an irreverent attitude toward traditional families, I depend upon my own. My father was my childhood intellectual companion; although in later years he was puzzled by my work, he took pride in its completion. During the last few years, which have included his critical illness and death and two critical illnesses of our mother, my brother Christopher Loop has proved that family feeling and cooperative responsibility can survive the sharpest political differences.

Barbara Owen has taken a gratifying sisterly pride in my work. In the midst of family crises she has appreciated and protected my need for time to write and was never too busy to talk through confused feelings, sharing love and relieving worries and guilt.

As children, Hal and Lizza Ruddick made thinking about mothering both necessary and possible; now as students of history and labor organizers they criticize my ideas with a thoroughness and confidence no friend would dare. I am inspired by their high-spirited efforts to live both morally and happily, and by similar struggles of so many other young people of their generation — students, my friends' children, and my children's friends. Among these many "children," I would like to mention especially Nina Schulman and Corinna Owen.

As always, William Ruddick has listened to my most unformed ideas with attentive respect and insisted that we make together time for me to set them down. We have shared in a daily way philosophical and feminist questions and, for the whole of our children's lives, the tasks of mothering and the challenges of maternal thinking. Although he writes about parents, children, and moral issues in a quite different style, I believe that this book is his as much as it is mine.

In this book, I speak as a mother but what I say and my desire to say it reflects my experience as a daughter. The protective care and careful love I received from my mother as a child seem continuous with the model of courageous and cheerful resilience she bequeathes to me now. Although I consciously write with her grandchildren and their future in mind, in remembering mothering and honoring mothers, I have taken what my mother calls "a long walk into the past." I now appreciate vividly the ways her work animates mine.

A Note on Usage

THROUGHOUT HISTORY and still today women assume disproportionately the responsibilities of caring for children. Therefore, even though mothering work is as suitable to men as to women, I use feminine grammatical forms whenever I refer to mothers. I mean no disrespect to the many men who now undertake the responsibilities, pleasures, and tasks of caring for children. Although biological sexual division is not as sharply dimorphic as linguistic custom suggests, children are labeled and label themselves as either female or male. In this book, as in life, a child is a he or she, not s/he or her/his. In speaking of children, I have tried to vary feminine and masculine forms evenhandedly and never intend to suggest that one sex is either more valuable or more "generic" than the other.

PART I

Thinking About Mothers Thinking

Love's Reason

MY LIFE HAS been shaped by a love affair with Reason. When I felt awkward or left out as a child or beset by lustful and envious fantasies, I clung to Reason in the most obsessive manner, determined to be faithful despite my "wild," unpleasant feelings. And Reason rewarded me, promising that if I took refuge in books and held fast to the Rational, I would someday control "irrational," unruly desires or at least, from Reason's perch, belittle them. Somewhat later, as I battled with my devoted and intimidating lawyer father, Reason gave me arguments. My voice might be tense, I might even cry, but with Reason on my side I could manage my love and my fear. Soon I went to a women's college where I was encouraged to adopt Reason's values and imitate His style.

In college I realized that not only did Reason protect me from social and emotional imbroglios, He — or it, as I was learning to say — offered me worldly possibilities. In the service of Reason, I could avoid the humdrum world of wives and mothers, instruct people in Reason's ways, and get paid for it. Perhaps I could conceive Reason's children: my roommate and I made lists of the books we would someday write. Meanwhile, however impersonally imagined, the romance continued. Sitting in a narrow aisle of the Gothic college library reading Bertrand Russell's lectures on logical atomism in aging volumes of *The Monist,* I was in thrall to the aroma of the books, the feel of the pages, the philosophy itself, so utterly transcendent of particular meaning, so very English, so far from the fantasies and fights I'd left behind in Ohio. I read *Gaudy Night,* fell in love with Harriet Vane's desire for *pure* intellectual work and with Reason's emissary Peter Wimsey. I took down my prints of van Gogh and El Greco and copied passages from Spinoza to paste on my wall — determined to persevere in my own being, to grasp my life *sub specie aeternitatis.* In 1957 I set out for graduate school to study philosophy.

Ten years later, Ph.D. in hand, I hovered anxiously on the margins of academic life. "Trying to write" was a preoccupying activity, although I rarely put words to paper and I finished virtually nothing. After college, I never participated easily in philosophical discussion and had come to avoid professional meetings altogether. Yet I still depended on Reason's arguments and its promise to control irrational desires. And occasionally, teaching young people Plato, Spinoza, or Wittgenstein, I would feel the old romance stirring. If I could not live happily with Reason, I could not quite live without Him/it either. How had such a passionate affair gone so wrong?

Although I didn't know it then, my personal alienation was in large part caused by the sexual politics in which Reason was enmeshed. In my generation, women's attempts to reason were typically met with contempt, still wounding even when too subtle to name. Those women who managed to hold on to their intellectual ambitions often suffered from outrageous discrimination and almost always from self-doubt. It is not surprising that I lost heart amidst the late sixties emissaries of Reason — masculine, professional, and usually arrogant, if also often kind. But the failure of my passion was also partly the responsibility of Reason Himself and of the grounds of my love. Reason, at least as Western

philosophers had imagined Him, was infected by — and contributed to — the pervasive disrespect for women's minds and lives
from which I suffered. For a woman to love Reason was to risk
both self-contempt and a self-alienating misogyny.

In my childhood, indeed straight through high school, Reason
had brought me facts, histories, and stories — Shakespeare's plays
all jumbled up with the causes of the first world war and the
nervous system of frogs. It did not occur to me that it was less
rational or more "womanly" to love Shakespeare best. But in
college I became aware of the division between hard reason (philosophy) and something softer (literature) and something harder
still (science). And, in that context, I learned that literature was
thought to be effeminate and that both men and women worried
about toughening it up, that the philosophy teacher who taught
existentialism (the only woman in the department) was as soft as
existentialism itself but that hard philosophy provided a ticket to
a masculine world.

It was philosophy's Reason that abetted my desire to free myself
from the fate of wife-and-mother with its messy, fleshly children
and dull duties. I remember memorizing that part of the *Symposium*
where Plato suggests that the right use of sexual desire leads away
from any particular desired body and toward love for abstract
Beauty. I would have sympathized with his remark that it is "vul-
gar" men who "turn to women as the object of their love, and
raise a family."[1] Plato believed that the worst possible model for
a young man was "a woman, young or old or wrangling with
her husband, defying heaven, loudly boasting, fortunate in her
own conceit, or involved in misfortune or possessed by grief and
lamentation — still less a woman that is sick, in love, or in labor"[2]
While I was certainly not about to take a woman for a model,
there was always a danger that in an emotional, uncontrolled moment I might turn "womanly." I took it as a warning that in order
to talk with (male) philosophers before he died, Socrates had to
send the women away.

When we went inside we found Socrates just released from his chains,
and Xantippe — you know her! — sitting by him with the little boy

[their son] on her knees. As soon as Xantippe saw us she broke out into the sort of remark you would expect from a woman: "Oh Socrates, this is the last time you and your friends will be able to talk together!" Socrates looked at Crito. "Crito," he said, "Someone had better take her home."[3]

To cast one's lot with reason meant staying with the men, on the right side of power. Philosophers have often suggested that people of superior rationality are justified in excluding and dominating others. Aristotle[4] puts the matter plainly: free men and women are superior to slaves because the former are reasonable while the latter have only enough rationality to hear and obey orders. Similarly, free women are rightfully subordinate to free men. Although the free woman, unlike the slave woman or man, has some deliberative capacity, in her this capacity is weakly developed; she cannot govern herself but must submit to the deliberative capacity of men. In a similar vein, Aquinas justified the rule of men over their kinswomen:

Good order would have been wanting in the human family if some were not governed by others wiser than themselves. So by such a kind of subjection woman is *naturally* subject to man, because in man the discretion of reason predominates. [Emphasis added.][5]

I was sufficiently alienated from anything womanly that I didn't yet realize that Reason would justify someone's subordinating *me;* on the contrary, I delighted in the social status Reason conferred. The arguments that made it possible for me to hold my own with my father helped me to win prizes. Like many philosophers, I learned to argue people down and to use the charge of irrationality to dismiss or intimidate. Moreover, I lived in a country where allegedly superior "rationality" was explicitly used to justify the class and racial privileges from which I profited. The injustice — and the irrationality — of these uses of rationality were conveniently obscured in the long shadow cast by the mythically impersonal, "transcendant" Man of Reason.

The ticket to staying with men on the right side of power was objectivity, self-control, and detachment. As the feminist philosopher Susan Bordo remarks, speaking specifically of Descartes: "The key term [that defines reason] is detachment: from emotional life, from the particularities of time and place, from personal quirks and prejudices, and, most centrally, from the object itself" — from whatever and whomever Reason knows.[6] Descartes's vision of a Reason defined in terms of "correct method" and founded on certainty reassured me largely because it circumvented both social privilege and personal conflict. The better I reasoned, the farther I would move from myself, from social responsibility, and from any particular — and therefore subjective and confusing — loves.

Reason seemed to serve me well so long as I was protected from the patriarchal mores of professional and domestic life. In a women's college I could stay with the men — at least as a daughterly student and reader. Reason never really controlled fantasy or passion. On the other hand, He was not threatened by the politics, friendships with women, and confused family feelings from which I had successfully detached Him. But in graduate school I was confronted simultaneously with the masculinity of professional life and with my own love for a flesh-and-blood man. Because my lover, soon to be my husband, was a philosopher and therefore Reason's emissary, I tried to serve Reason through him, shaping my life to his ambitions. But my lover also provoked feelings that Reason labeled "feminine," and that I no longer wanted Him to judge, even if feeling and femininity disqualified me from Reason's pursuits. I had so long associated Reason with both masculinity and detachment that it sometimes seemed necessary to dissociate my *self* from Him entirely. Then I had children and another "irrational" passion, a grittier, more troubling one but equally consuming. Although I was the wife-and-mother I had feared becoming, I still often tried to stay with the men. But increasingly I felt a fraud and also disloyal to the other mere women-and-mothers with whom I spent much of my time.

It was not only "womanly" passion that threatened Reason's calm; dispassionate transcendence was failing in the streets as well as in the living room. Shortly after I arrived at graduate school, I picketed Woolworth's in support of sit-ins in the South; pregnant with my son, I took part in my first antiwar protest. For the most part I stayed busy with domestic and teaching duties, taking part in demonstrations that others planned. But neither I nor my students and friends could ignore the violences that men of reason rationally justified, nor could we transcendentally apprehend oppression, or in my case privilege, "under the aspect of eternity".[7] While teaching or studying alone, I might still be at home with Reason. But even the remnants of my attachment were undermined in virtually every seminar and professional meeting; too many philosophers, cashing in on Reason's promise, "rose above" the social divisions from which they profited. In the worst case, a few of them coolly justified violence with Reason's arguments.

Reason was failing me — as a lover, mother, and citizen. As Western philosophers had idealized it, Reason was meant to be detached and impersonal, at best irrelevant to particular affections and loyalties. I needed to act on passion and be responsible to love. Ideally, Reason both justified domination and transcended the political uses to which it was put; I needed to confront the sexual and social politics of Reason, if only to speak self-respectfully to my children. I still treasured Spinoza's identification — which was also an injunction — of the individual as one who perseveres in its own being. But now my being was not my "own," nor did I want it to be. An argument that didn't draw on love and sustain it in action was worse than no argument at all.

I might, in my disappointment, have turned against Reason. Whenever I reasoned actively or was successful in Reason's world, I felt detached from the passions in which my life was rooted. Since setting out to work meant leaving love behind, I wanted to slay the Man of Reason I depended on. Still intimidated and internally silenced by philosophical ideals of rationality, I was like the scientists whom Evelyn Fox Keller imagines, walking "a path bounded on one side by inauthenticity and the other by subversion".[8] Yet however rebellious I felt, I did not doubt, and I do not now, that as destructive as Western ideals of Reason may be, the capacity to reason is a human good. I know what a pleasure it is to learn, experiment, imagine, discover, design, and invent. There is real strength in steady judgment, self-reflectiveness, clear speech, and attentive listening. These are activities of reason and they are human blessings. I have never been persuaded that there is anything precious, or specifically bourgeois, or merely Western, or exclusively masculine about the human needs and pleasures of reason.

If I could not reject Reason, could I honor Reason differently? If I could no longer serve the Reason I had known, was it possible to reconceive a reason that strengthened passion rather than opposing it, that refused to separate love from knowledge? In the past, women who have criticized prevailing ideals of reason or failed to measure up to them have been called irrational. Would it be possible to reverse this judgment, finding fault not in women but in the ideals? Or, more daringly, were there alternative ideals of reason that might derive from women's work and experiences, ideals more appropriate to responsibility and love? Virginia Woolf claimed that alternative ideals might arise from the very differences between women and men that Reason meant to transcend:

"We" — meaning by "we" a whole made up of body, brain and spirit, influenced by memory and tradition — must still differ in some respects from "you," whose body, brain and spirit have been so differently trained and are so differently influenced by memory and tradition. Though we see the same world, we see it through different eyes.[9]

Suppose, as Margaret Anderson suggests, that culture as men have created it "is assumed to present the entire and only truth. . . . [Then] women's culture . . . is invisible, silenced, trivialized, and wholly ignored."[10] Could it be that "women are *even now* thinking in ways which traditional intellection denies, decries or is unable to grasp,"[11] as Adrienne Rich asked in 1976?

Faced with these new and disturbing questions, I did not give up the ideals of Reason in which I'd been trained. I proceeded in an abstract, detached manner, asking first: What is the relation of thinking to life? Here I turned to the men I had studied, particularly Wittgenstein, Winch, and Habermas. All thinking, they had seemed to teach me, arises from and is shaped by the practices in which people engage. What then, I asked, is a woman's practice? Of the many activities assigned to women, I chose one: the work of mothering is central to many women's lives and indirectly affects the thinking of countless others who as daughters, sisters, or friends identify with mothers. If women were now thinking in ways we had yet to grasp, then these ways would be at least partly reflected in the thinking to which mothering gives rise — maternal thinking.

I began my first essay on maternal thinking by quoting a Victorian rendition of maternal love, written, like so many sentimental tributes, by a son:

> There was a young man loved a maid
> Who taunted him. "Are you afraid,"
> She asked, "to bring me today
> Your mother's head upon a tray?"
>
> He went and slew his mother dead,
> Tore from her breast her heart so red,
> Then toward his lady love he raced,
> But tripped and fell in all his haste.
>
> As the heart rolled on the ground
> It gave forth a plaintive sound.
> And it spoke in accents mild:
> "Did you hurt yourself, my child?"[12]

Many of the wishes and fears in this poem were familiar. Women are cast as rivals for the men they love. For the sake of masculinity and "normality," "good" mothers allow their sons to express contempt for their mother's feelings, if not for their lives. Moreover, mothers are said to be masochistic and bored. No wonder that they sacrifice their minds and hearts. It is only damage to *children* that counts: "Did you hurt *yourself*, my child?"

This poem appealed to me, however, for its unfamiliar twist. In the version I had discovered (I've since learned that there are others) the lady asks for her lover's mother's head; evidently she fears and respects maternal thinking. The son follows the conventional wisdom, believing that it is maternal passion his lover needs to control. Most mothers, and certainly I myself, had shared the judgment of the son. The passions of maternity are so sudden, intense, and confusing that women themselves remain ignorant of the perspective, the thought, that develops from mothering. As a young mother, the only "maternal thinking" with which I was familiar was thinking *about* mothers and children by "experts" who hoped to be heard by mothers rather than to hear what mothers had to say. However disenchanted I became with Reason, it did not occur to me that there was an intellectual life that had anything to do with mothering. I "thought" only when I had time to myself, put my children out of my mind, and did philosophy. Now, however, armed with my detached philosophical questions, I considered and interviewed the head of "the mother." But who was I, armed with questions posed by the Man of Reason? Could it be that it was my head there on the ground?

Certainly as a mother I had found myself thinking. For years I had engaged in spirited reflection about children's lives with other mothers — sometimes friends, often casual acquaintances. Now, nearing forty, I and a few close friends found ourselves preoccupied with our children's conflicts and changes and with the ways our own choices, disappointments, and pleasures affected our children. We were asking how we could become, during these hard times, "good enough" mothers. We were not reflecting for the sake of reflection; we needed answers — by bedtime, by teacher conference time, by the time we had to accept or reject a job offer in a distant city. Though we desperately needed to act, it was abundantly clear that our nighttime conclusions simply yielded the next afternoon's questions. We started again, with each other and in long internal dialogue.

Could this "chattering," so unlike the philosophy in which I was trained, be "thinking"? Did I, did we, through endless telephone calls and late night coffees, create themes of a "discourse"? Could what we thought and the way we thought be put to use?

I began to answer these questions by providing a respectable conceptual context in which the idea of maternal thinking made sense. My initial attempt to develop distinctions and a vocabulary for maternal thinking is represented, in amended form, in Chapter 1. In this chapter, I devise a very general description of maternal work in terms of the demands to which the worker responds. These demands shape, and are in turn shaped by, the metaphysical attitudes, cognitive capacities, and identification of virtues that make up maternal thinking. As I try to make sense of the idea of maternal thinking, I am motivated by loyalty to mothers' experiences, including my own. But I reflect abstractly, alluding only to banal and largely uncontested facts — for example, that children need protection to survive.

Even the most abstract scheme has its particular social history and its political consequences. In Chapter 2 I take up three frequent objections to the way in which I talk about maternal work and thinking: that I idealize mothering, ignore both fathers and female birthgivers, and obscure the differences and oppressive divisions among mothers. In responding to these objections, my aim is to clarify the politics that motivate my project.

To say that mothering gives rise to a certain type of thinking says nothing about which attitudes, capacities, and values arise, or why. I address this vexing question in Chapters 3, 4, and 5. There the epistemological climate changes as I draw explicitly on my own experience of mothering and try to entice readers into reflecting on theirs.

I proceed stepwise from the general and abstract to the more concrete and particular with a detour for contentious argument about the project as a whole. Throughout, my aim is to articulate distinct ways of thinking about the world — for example, about control, vulnerability, "nature," storytelling, and attentive love. Although I speak often of maternal temptation and failure, I have engaged in my project because I believe the particular maternal ways of thinking that I have identified are valuable.

Throughout parts I and II, I consider maternal thinking, with its distinctive flaws and virtues, as one discipline among others. It is only in part III that I make more ambitious claims. There I take maternal thinking to be an engaged and visionary standpoint from which to criticize the destructiveness of war and begin to invent peace. Mothers are often militarist and usually support the war policies of their states. Nonetheless, I will argue, maternal thinking and practices are important resources for developing peace politics. But for the moment, I claim only that maternal thinking exists and that, whatever a reader's politics, is worthy of respectful consideration.

CHAPTER ONE

Maternal Thinking

IN RECENT DECADES several philosophers have elaborated a "practicalist" conception of "truth." They have argued negatively that there is no truth by which all truths can be judged nor any foundation of truths nor any total and inclusive narrative of all true statements. Positively they have claimed that distinctive ways of knowing and criteria of truth arise out of practices. I use this general philosophical view — which makes no mention of either women or mothers — to describe the relation between mothering and thinking. I therefore begin by outlining very briefly certain tenets of practicalism that I assume.[1]

Thinking and Practice

From the practicalist view, thinking arises from and is tested against practices. Practices are collective human activities distinguished by the aims that identify them and by the consequent demands made on practitioners committed to those aims. The aims or goals that define a practice are so central or "constitutive" that in the absence of the goal you would not have that practice. I express this intrinsic dependency when I say that to engage in a practice means to be committed to meeting its demands. People more or less consciously create a practice as they simultaneously pursue certain goals and make sense of their pursuit. Understanding shapes the end even as the practical pursuit of the end shapes the understanding. Horse racing, for example, is defined by the goal of winning a race by means of riding a horse over a finish line. In a particular culture, horse racers refine their concept of the race and the means of victory as questions about meaning or policy arise. A horse racing riderless past the wire, and a jockey slowing her mount in the interests of its beauty are not engaged in horse racing. Natural science is defined by its goal of understanding nature's workings so that they may be explained, predicted, and, in so far as possible, controlled. Central to scientific control is replication by experiment. A chemist who created only beautiful reactions, invented her results, or was uninterested in replicating a reaction would not be doing chemistry.

Individuals need not be enthusiastic or honorable participants to be said to engage in a practice. A rider who drugs her horse is cheating in horse racing but she is still racing her horse. Although an individual scientist hates her work and writes up her experiments with one eye on "General Hospital," she nonetheless, by dint of her activity, acknowledges that the idea of scientific truth is dependent on replication by experiment. To engage in a practice is, by definition, to accept connections that constitute the practice. To be recognized as a jockey or a scientist means to evince or to pretend a commitment to crossing the finish line or replicating by experiment.

The goals that constitute a practice determine what counts as reasonable within it. Practices in some ways surprisingly alike and in others strikingly divergent give rise to reasons that can be compared and contrasted. Scientific reasoning, for example, is distinct from, though in many of its elements similar to, religious, historical, mathematical, and psychoanalytic reasoning.

To say that thinking depends on practice means that thought is social in at least two senses. First, concepts are defined by shared aims and by rules or means for achieving those aims. An individual may race a horse across a finish line or conduct an experiment. Individuals nonetheless make sense of their activities to themselves by means of concepts and values that are developed socially. Thinking itself is often a solitary activity; its cooperative forms are the dialogue or conversation, not the chorus. Yet the language of solitary thinking is necessarily public in the sense that it is governed by public criteria of meaning and truth. One can think alone, but one cannot "think" "Monday is read asparagus" or "I am Napoleon." Of course, someone could invent an idiosyncratic meaning for the phrase "Monday is read asparagus," but if it is to have any sense, that sense must be sharable. One can claim — as many people have — to be Napoleon; but, except for Napoleon himself, the only public sense of the claim makes it necessarily false.

More important, on the practicalist view, thought does not transcend its social origins. There is no truth to be apprehended from a transcendental perspective, that is, from no perspective at all. Practicalists reject a recurrent philosophic fantasy of finding a language free from the limits of any language in which to speak of the limits of all language. Limit and perspective are intrinsic to language and to thought, not a deficiency of them. In particular, practicalists have been suspicious of attributing to science a privileged relation to reality and making scientific knowledge the paradigm of intellectual accountability against which all other ways of knowing are tested. Science, like any other kind of thinking, presupposes communities of participants, shared goals, and an agreement that some methods of reaching goals are appropriate while others are not. In scientific inquiry, observation is inseparable from theory, and both are inseparable from a commitment to the restraints of experimental inquiry. Both theory and experiment depend on agreement, shared language, and shared actions. Similarly, psychoanalytic, critical, or historical thinking depends on the community of participants in which it arises and their truths are tested by shared criteria.

Truth is perspectival, relative to the practices in which it is made. To say that true statements are relative in this sense does not mean that their truth is a matter of the opinion of communities of speakers. The statement that Mount Baldy is ten feet high is false, whatever any like-minded group of people may think. The point is that it is possible to make the false statement (and the alternative true one) because some people have identified mountains and invented a vocabulary of measurement. To speak, name, and measure means to act in social contexts in which geography and height matter to us. It is true that Margaret Thatcher was reelected prime minister of Great Britain, no matter how much a group of her opponents might wish otherwise, but that truth is dependent on a whole set of institutions in which the meaning of "elect" and "prime minister" have been constituted.

It is only within a practice that thinkers judge which questions are sensible, which answers are appropriate to them, and which criteria distinguish between better and worse answers. The philosopher Peter Winch puts the practicalist point using religious language as an example:

Job is taken to task for having gone astray by having lost sight of the reality of God; this does not, of course, mean that Job has made any sort of theoretical mistake, which should be put right, perhaps, by means of an experiment. God's reality is certainly independent of what any man may care to think, but what that reality amounts to can only be seen from the religious tradition in which the concept of God is used, and this use is very unlike the use of scientific concepts, say of theoretical entitie. The point is that it is *within* the religious use of language that the conception of God's reality has its place, though, I repeat, this does not mean that it is at the mercy of what any man cares to say; if this were so, God would have no reality.[2]

In sum, any discipline will distinguish true from false, will take some matters on faith, others on evidence, will judge evidence inadequate or faith misplaced. The practicalist's point is that the criteria for truth and falsity, the nature of evidence, and the role of faith will vary with the practice, whether the practice be religious, scientific, critical — or maternal.

Maternal Practice

Maternal practice begins in a response to the reality of a biological child in a particular social world. To be a "mother" is to take upon oneself the responsibility of child care, making its work a regular and substantial part of one's working life.

Mothers, as individuals, engage in all sorts of other activities, from farming to deep sea diving, from astrophysics to elephant training. Mothers as individuals are not defined by their work; they are lovers and friends; they watch baseball, ballet, or the soaps; they run marathons, play chess, organize church bazaars and rent strikes. Mothers are as diverse as any other humans and are equally shaped by the social milieu in which they work. In my terminology they are "mothers" just because and to the degree that they are committed to meeting demands that define maternal work.

Both her child and the social world in which a mother works make these demands. "Demands" is an artificial term. Children demand all sorts of things — to eat ice cream before dinner, stay up all night, take the subway alone, watch the latest horror show on TV. A mother's social group demands of her all sorts of behavior — that she learn to sew or get a high school degree, hold her tongue or speak wittily in public, pay her taxes or go to jail for refusing to do so, sit ladylike in a restaurant or sit in at a lunch counter. A mother will decide in her own way which of these demands she will meet.

But in my discussion of maternal practice, I mean by "demands" those requirements that are imposed on anyone doing maternal work, in the way respect for experiment is imposed on scientists and racing past the finish line is imposed on jockeys. In this sense of demand, children "demand" that their lives be preserved and their growth fostered. In addition, the primary social groups with which a mother is identified, whether by force, kinship, or choice, demand that she raise her children in a manner acceptable to them. These three demands — for *preservation, growth,* and *social acceptability* — constitute maternal work; to be a mother is to be committed to meeting these demands by works of preservative love, nurturance, and training.

Conceptually and historically, the preeminent of these demands is that of preservation. As a species, human children share prolonged physical fragility and therefore prolonged dependence on adults for their safety and well-being. In all societies, children need protective care, though the causes and types of fragility and the means of protection vary widely. This universal need of human children creates and defines a category of human work. A mother who callously endangers her child's well-being is simply not doing maternal work. (This does not mean that she is a bad person. She may sacrifice maternal work out of desperation or in a noble cause.)

The demand for protection is both epistemological and practical. Meeting the demand presupposes a minimal attentiveness to children and an awareness that their survival depends upon protective care. Imaginatively grasping the significance of children's biological vulnerability is necessary but not sufficient for responding to them. The perception that someone is in need of care may lead to caring; but then again it may lead to running away. In the settings where I first encountered polliwogs and goldfish (usually in jars and bowls where I'd managed to put them), they were exceedingly vulnerable. When I was young, I saw that these little creatures were vulnerable and I cared for them. Much later, when I was dealing with my children's attachment to them, I found the vulnerability and total unpredictability of goldfish merely an annoyance. I cared for them because I cared for my children but, given the total inadequacy of our caring, I would have been delighted if my children had forgotten them altogether. Now I almost never think about goldfish and never want to care for one the rest of my life.

Given the passions that we have for children, comparing them to goldfish may seem frivolous. When you *see* children as demanding care, the reality of their vulnerability and the necessity of a caring response seem unshakable. But I deliberately stress the optional character first of perceiving "vulnerability" and then of responding with care. Maternal responses are complicated acts that social beings make to biological beings whose existence is inseparable from social interpretations. Maternal practice begins with a double vision — seeing the fact of biological vulnerability as socially significant and as demanding care. Neither birth nor the actual presence of a vulnerable infant guarantees care. In the most desperate circumstances mothers are more apt to feed their babies than to let them sicken and starve. Yet when infants were dependent solely on mothers' milk, biological mothers could refuse the food their children needed, for example, sending them away to wet-nurses, although this was known to have a high risk of illness and even death.[3] To be committed to meeting children's demand for preservation does not require enthusiasm or even love; it simply means to see vulnerability and to respond to it with care rather than abuse, indifference, or flight. Preserving the lives of children is the central constitutive, invariant aim of maternal practice; the commitment to achieving that aim is the constitutive maternal act.

The demand to preserve a child's life is quickly supplemented by the second demand, to nurture its emotional and intellectual growth. Children grow in complex ways, undergoing radical qualitative as well as quantitative change from childhood to adulthood. They experience intense emotions and varieties of changing, complex sexual desire. As they grow they develop more or less useful ways of coping with other people and their own feelings — adaptive strategies and defenses against anxiety, fear, shame, and guilt. Children's minds also develop gradually, their cognitive capacities and uses of memory becoming different in kind as they move from early childhood through adolescence. In one sense, children grow "naturally," provided favorable conditions for growing. On the other hand, each child grows in her or his distinctive, often peculiar way. Children's desires, defenses, and goals can be hurtful to others and to themselves; their cognitive and emotional development is easily distorted or inhibited. They "demand" nurturance.

This demand to foster children's growth appears to be historically and culturally specific to a degree that the demand for preservation is not. To be aware of children's need for nurturance depends on a belief, prevalent in my social milieu, that children have complicated lives, that their minds and psyches need attending. But even in social groups I know firsthand, some people — in my experience more often men — claim that if children are protected and trained, growth takes care of itself. On the other hand, it is difficult to judge what mothers themselves really believe about the conditions of growth. Some mothers who say that children simply grow and need little nurturance nonetheless act in ways that indicate they believe their children are complex and needy beings.

To say that the demand to foster growth is culturally and historically specific does not mean that the complexity of children's lives is primarily a cultural creation. In cultures dramatically different from middle-class North American culture — where, for example, there are no notions of "adolescence" or "cognitive development" — children's growth is still complex. Only some cultures, and some people within a culture, may believe, as I do, that children's spiritual and intellectual growth requires nurturance. But what I believe, I believe about all children. When others claim that children are simple, naturally growing beings whose growth does not require attentive nurturance, we disagree in our beliefs about *all* children's needs. To believe that only the children of one's own or similar cultures are complex — that their complexity is essentially a cultural creation — is a familiar form of racism. Certainly, some children exist in conditions in which they can do no better than "simply" survive. It seems grotesque to speak of the complex psychological needs of children who are dying of famine. Yet those children, in my view, are as complicated and demanding of nurturance as any others. Where terror or deprivation reduces children to the most basic need for simple survival, they are nonetheless fragile, complicated human creatures who have been so reduced.

In the urban middle-class cultures I know best, mothers who believe that children's development is sufficiently complex to require nurturance shoulder a considerable burden. Many people other than mothers are interested in children's growth — fathers, lovers, teachers, doctors, therapists, coaches. But typically a mother assumes the primary task of maintaining conditions of growth: it is a mother who considers herself and is considered by others to be primarily responsible for arrested or defective growth. The demand to nurture children's growth is not as ineluctable as the demand to ensure their survival. Mothers often find themselves unable to deal with the complexities of their children's experience because they are overwhelmed simply tending to their children's survival or are preoccupied by their own projects or are simply exhausted and confused. Children survive nonetheless.

The third demand on which maternal practice is based is made not by children's needs but by the social groups of which a mother is a member. Social groups require that mothers shape their children's growth in "acceptable" ways. What counts as acceptable varies enormously within and among groups and cultures. The demand for acceptability, however, does not vary, nor does there seem to be much dissent from the belief that children cannot "naturally" develop in socially correct ways but must be "trained." I use the neutral, though somewhat harsh, term "training" to underline a mother's active aims to make her children "acceptable." Her training strategies may be persuasive, manipulative, educative, abusive, seductive, or respectful and are typically a mix of most of these.

A mother's group is that set of people with whom she identifies to the degree that she would count failure to meet their criteria of acceptability as her failure. The criteria of acceptability consist of the group values that a mother has internalized as well as the values of group members whom she feels she must please. Acceptability is not merely a demand imposed on a mother by her group. Indeed, mothers themselves as part of the larger social group formulate its ideals and are usually governed by an especially stringent form of acceptability that nonmothers in the group may not necessarily adhere to. Mothers want their children to grow into people whom they themselves and those closest to them can delightedly appreciate. This demand gives an urgency — sometimes exhilarating, sometimes painful — to mothers' daily lives.

In training their children, mature and socially powerful mothers find opportunities to express their own values as well as to challenge and invigorate dominant creeds. Often, however, a mother is ambivalent about her group's values and feels alienated or harassed by the group's demands on her and her children. Mothers are usually women, and women typically, though to varying degrees, have less power than men of their group. Many mothers are, at least at the beginning of their work, young women. Although they consider failing the group as their own failure, this assessment may be less motivated by moral self-definition than by fear or a need for social survival. If a group demands acceptable behavior that, in a mother's eyes, contradicts her children's need for protection and nurturance, then the mother will be caught in painful and self-fragmenting conflict. Nonetheless, however alienated they feel, mothers seem to recognize the demand to train their children as an ineluctable demand made on them as mothers.

In addition to preservation, growth, and social acceptability there may well be other demands that constitute maternal practices. Certainly there are other ways to categorize maternal commitment. But without any claim to exhaustiveness, I take the goals of preservation, growth, and social acceptability as constitutive of maternal practice.

Although in my view all social groups demand training, all mothers recognize their children's demand to be protected, and all children require some kind of nurturance, it may well be that some cultures do not recognize "children" or "mothers" in my sense of the terms. The concept of "mother" depends on that of "child," a creature considered to be of value and in need of protection. Only in societies that recognize children as creatures who demand protection, nurturance, and training is there a maternal practice that meets those demands. Social historians tell us that in many cultures, it was a normal practice to exploit, neglect, or abuse children.[4] What I call "maternal practice" is probably not ubiquitous, even though what I call "children" exist everywhere.

In any culture, maternal commitment is far more voluntary than people like to believe. Women as well as men may refuse to be aware of or to respond to the demands of children; some women abuse or abandon creatures who are, in all cultures, dependent and vulnerable. All mothers sometimes turn away, refuse to listen, stop caring. Both maternal work and the thinking that is provoked by it are decisively shaped by the possibility that any mother may refuse to see creatures as children or to respond to them as complicated, fragile, and needy.

Among those cultures who do recognize children, perceptions of their fragility and adult responses to it vary enormously and may be difficult for outsiders to understand. As anyone knows who listens to mothers, commonality of childhood demands does not preclude sharp disagreement about children's "nature" and appropriate maternal responses to it. Comparing and contrasting differing strategies of maternal work goes on among mothers all the time. When it is generous and thoughtful, this collective, self-reflective activity is a source of critical and creative maternal thinking.

To protect, nurture, and train — however abstract the schema, the story is simple. A child leans out of a high-rise window to drop a balloon full of water on a passerby. She must be hauled in from the window (preservation) and taught not to endanger innocent people (training), and the method used must not endanger her self-respect or confidence (nurturance). In any mother's day, the demands of preservation, growth, and acceptability are intertwined. Yet a reflective mother can separately identify each demand, partly because they are often in conflict. If a child wants to walk to the store alone, do you worry about her safety or applaud her developing capacity to take care of herself? If you overhear your son hurling insults at a neighbor's child, do you rush to instill decency and compassion in him, or do you let him act on his own impulses in his need to overcome shyness? If your older child, in her competitive zeal, pushes ahead of your younger, smaller child while climbing a high slide, do you inhibit her competitive pleasure or allow an aggressiveness you cannot appreciate? Should her younger brother learn to fight back? And if he doesn't, is he bowing too easily to greater strength? Most urgently, whatever you do, is somebody going to get hurt? Love may make these questions painful; it does not provide the answers. Mothers must *think*.

Maternal Thinking

Daily, mothers think out strategies of protection, nurturance, and training. Frequently conflicts between strategies or between fundamental demands provoke mothers to think about the meaning and relative weight of preservation, growth, and acceptability. In quieter moments, mothers reflect on their practice as a whole. As in any group of thinkers, some mothers are more ambitiously reflective than others, either out of temperamental thoughtfulness, moral and political concerns, or, most often, because they have serious problems with their children. However, maternal thinking is no rarity. Maternal work itself demands that mothers think; out of this need for thoughtfulness, a distinctive discipline emerges.

I speak about a mother's thought — the intellectual capacities she develops, the judgments she makes, the metaphysical attitudes she assumes, the values she affirms. Like a scientist writing up her experiment, a critic working over a text, or a historian assessing documents, a mother caring for children engages in a discipline. She asks certain questions — those relevant to her aims — rather than others; she accepts certain criteria for the truth, adequacy, and relevance of proposed answers; and she cares about the findings she makes and can act on. The discipline of maternal thought, like other disciplines, establishes criteria for determining failure and success, sets priorities, and identifies virtues that the discipline requires. Like any other work, mothering is prey to characteristic temptations that it must identify. To describe the capacities, judgments, metaphysical attitudes, and values of maternal thought presumes not maternal achievement, but a *conception* of achievement.

Maternal thinking is one kind of disciplined reflection among many, each with identifying questions, methods, and aims. Some disciplines overlap. A mother who is also a critic may learn something about "reading" a child's behavior from reading texts or learn something about reading itself from her child. A believer's prayer or a historian's sense of causal narrative or a scientist's clear-eyed scrutiny may enliven maternal attentiveness, which in its turn may prepare a mother for prayer, historical insight, or experiment. Disciplines may, on the other hand, be undertaken quite separately without conflicting. An engineer may find the particular kind of reasoning required by engineering almost entirely different from that required by mothering, and each may provide welcome relief from the other. Even though people's behavior is limited by the disciplines they engage in, no one need be limited to a single discipline. No person because she is a woman, no woman or man because they are mothers, should be denied any intellectual activities that attract them. A scientist cannot disregard evidence for the sake of beauty, but she may care differently at different times about both. If a mother is called on to decide an appropriate punishment for a child's misbehavior or to weigh the possible success of a medical treatment against its serious pain, she cannot compose a sonata in response. There is a time for composing and a time for maternal thinking and, on happy days, time for both.

Mothers meeting together at their jobs, in playgrounds, or over coffee can be heard thinking. This does not necessarily mean that they can be heard being good. Mothers are not any more or less wonderful than other people — they are not especially sensible or foolish, noble or ignoble, courageous or cowardly. Mothers, like gardeners or historians, identify virtues appropriate to their work. But to identify a virtue is not to possess it. When mothers speak of virtues they speak as often of failure as of success. Almost always they reflect on the *struggles* that revolve around the temptations to which they are prey in their work. What they share is not virtuous characteristics but rather an identification and a discourse about the strengths required by their ongoing commitments to protect, nurture, and train.

Identifying virtues within maternal thinking should not be confused with evaluating the virtue of maternal thinking itself. Though no less thoughtful, no less a discipline than other kinds of thinking, maternal thinking is also not free from flaws. For example, as I will show later, in training children, mothers often value destructive ways of thinking and misidentify virtues. This means that mothers not only fail but in certain respects mischaracterize what counts as success and failure.

If thinking arises in and is tested by practice, who is qualified to judge the intellectual strength and moral character of a practice as a whole? It is sometimes said that only those who participate in a practice can criticize its thinking. Accordingly, it might be argued that it is not possible to evaluate maternal thinking without practicing maternal work or living closely and sympathetically with those who do. When mothers engage in self-criticism, their judgments presuppose a knowledge of the efforts required to respond to children's demands that those unpracticed in tending to children do not have. Maternal criticisms are best left to those who know what it means to attempt to protect, nurture, and train, just as criticism of scientific or — to use a controversial example — psychoanalytic thinking should be left to those who have engaged in these practices.

There are moral grounds for critical restraint. People who have not engaged in a practice or who have not lived closely with a practitioner have no right to criticize. Although any group might make this claim, the point is particularly apt for maternal thinkers. Mothers have been a powerless group whose thinking, when it has been acknowledged at all, has most often been recognized by people interested in interpreting and controlling rather than in listening. Philosophically minded mothers have only begun to articulate the precepts of a thought whose existence other philosophers do not recognize. Surely, they should have time to think among and for themselves.

In the practicalist account of reason, there is also a powerful epistemological check on criticism. Critical vocabularies and standards are themselves embedded in practices from which they arise. Even principles of logical consistency and coherence do not stand outside of practices, although any practice can be assessed in their terms. To many outsiders, contemporary physics, Christian theology, and theories of nuclear defense abound in contradiction. But as experiences with scientists, believers, and defense intellectuals suggest, the intellectual and practical contradictions are interpreted and their weight measured not by the outside observer but by practitioners reflecting on their shared aims.

This is not to say that even an outsider's charge of inconsistency is without force. Unless self-deceived or ignorant of the contradictions their thinking displays, most people find the experience of self-contradiction both disorienting and demoralizing. Indeed, political and philosophical critics charge people with contradictory thinking in the expectation of provoking them to change. I, for example, hope that maternal thinkers will be affected by my claims that certain concepts of maternal thinking that arise from training are inconsistent with other maternal concepts and that preservative love is at least *prima facie* incompatible with maternal militarism (see Chapters 5, 6, and 8). But although my respect for consistency is not connected to mothering, my particular identification of contradictions within maternal thinking arises from my experience of maternal practice, and the effect of my criticism can be measured only by mothers' responses.

One should not, however, conflate epistemological restraint with critical silence. The practical origins of reason do not preclude radical self-criticism. Indeed, developing vocabularies and standards of self-criticism is a central intellectual activity in most practices. More important, although all criticism arises from some practice or other, interpractice criticism is both possible and necessary for change. It is common sense epistemologically that alternative perspectives offer distinctive critical advantages. A historian, medical ethicist, and peace activist — especially if they themselves were conversant with science — might claim to have a better sense than a scientist not only of the limits but also of the character of scientific discipline. Militarists criticize maternal thinkers for insufficient respect for abstract causes, while peacemakers criticize them for the parochial character of maternal commitment.

Interpractice criticism is possible and often desirable; yet there is no privileged practice capable of judging all other practices. To criticize is to act on one's practical commitments, not to stand above them. Maternal thinking is one discipline among others, capable of criticizing and being criticized. It does not offer nor can it be judged from a standpoint uncontaminated by practical struggle and passion.

CHAPTER TWO

Talking About "Mothers"

I HAVE TALKED about mothers and mothering for several years to academic and nonacademic audiences, to women alone and to women and men together. Sometimes it has been difficult to present — even as a lively hypothesis for collective reflection — the idea that a distinctive kind of thinking arises from the work of mothers. Frequently questioners will be quite explicit: "I like what you say, if only you could say it without talking about mothers." "The idea of maternity is sentimental and reactionary." "Talking about mothers leaves me out" (said by women and men). More often, these people express an unease that I cannot name.

This chapter addresses three apparent implications of the ways I speak of "mothers" that have troubled audiences over the last several years. First, despite my intentions to speak realistically, and though I know full well the malign effects on mothers and children of sentimentalizing motherhood, I am often heard as "idealizing" mothers. Second, to talk of mothers, rather than more abstractly of nurturance or more generically of parents, seems to some people to exclude men and many women from a work and thinking that they claim to share. Third, the very idea of *maternal* thinking ignores differences among mothers and the oppressions that some but not all mothers suffer. In reflecting on these three resistances to my project, I do not mean to anticipate objections or to still dissent, but rather to make open discussion more likely. I hope to clarify the meaning I give to "mothering" and to explain why I still speak of mothers the way I do despite the likelihood of idealization and ethnocentrism and despite the temptation — often my own as well as my listeners' — to speak more generally of nurturance or more generically of parents and other caretakers.

Idealization and Maternal Power

It is hard to speak precisely about mothering. Overwhelmed with greeting card sentiment, we have no realistic language in which to capture the ordinary/extraordinary pleasures and pains of maternal work. War, poverty, and racism twist a mother's best efforts. These are not sorrows brought on by mothering; they are socially caused and politically remediable. Yet when children are assaulted by social evils that could be prevented, though a mother herself may be helpless to prevent them, mothering becomes cruel and bitter work. In many societies, the ideology of mother*hood* is oppressive to women. It defines maternal work as a consuming identity requiring sacrifices of health, pleasure, and ambitions unnecessary for the well-being of children.

These are not sacrifices intrinsic to maternal work and indeed they are often balanced, even in impoverished or oppressed groups, by the pleasures children bring in tolerably good times. To suggest that mothers, by virtue of their mothering, are principally victims is an egregiously inaccurate account of many women's experience and is itself oppressive to mothers. For many women, mothering begins in a fiercely passionate love that is not destroyed by the ambivalence and anger it includes. Many mothers develop early a sense of maternal competence — a sense that they can and will care for their children. Often they are socially rewarded for their work by the shared pleasure and confirmation of other mothers, by the gratitude and pride of grandparents, and frequently by the intense, appreciative love of their mates. At home mothers frequently have more control over the details of their work than many other workers do. Many mothers, whatever their other work, feel part of a community of mothers whose warmth and support is hard to match in other working relationships. When their children flourish, almost all mothers have a sense of well-being.

But no children flourish all of the time. Even the luckiest children are often ill, lonely, mean, dispirited, or afraid. The emotional and physical pains of their children are anguishing for mothers, inducing a sense of helplessness and guilt. Nor do mothers, typically, take an easy pleasure in their own competence. On the best days, a mother can only do her best, and her best often, in the long run, does not seem quite "good enough." Mothers succumb to the temptations inherent in their work — possessiveness, parochialism, fearfulness, cheery denial, high-mindedness, self-righteousness, self-sacrifice, and a rage for order that frightens even mothers themselves, to name only a few temptations. Mothers infuriate their children and disappoint themselves.

In writing as in living, it is difficult to describe the pleasures of motherhood without sentimentality, to discuss the inevitable pain without false pathos, to balance the grim and the satisfying aspects and to speak of each honestly. Partly because I write about mothers' "struggles," especially the struggle to be nonviolent, I stress the aggressive elements of maternal practice. Once, when I insisted that mothers dominate, humiliate, hate, and hit, a listener complained that I made mothering sound like "war, not love." The "peacefulness" with which mothers are credited is usually a sweet, appeasing gentleness that gives peace a bad name while alienating almost anyone who had a mother or is one. Maternal peacefulness is a way of fighting as well as of loving, as angry as it is gentle. Nonetheless, mothers are not, as a constitutive part of their work, engaged in war, even though battles with, on behalf of, and between their children are a prominent aspect of their life. Moreover, if mothers are not good, most of them are not routinely violent either, as the survival of their children attests.

There is also a somberness in my account of mothers that comes, I believe, from a concern with maternal *thinking*. According to the philosopher C. S. Peirce, we think when we are disturbed, and the aim of our thinking is to recover our equilibrium. If it is conflict and trouble that spur thought, then to describe a work to articulate its thinking means looking for its disturbances among its routines. To identify the disburbances of maternal work requires attending to the unhappy moments of children's as well as mothers' lives. As I highlight those moments in a mother's or a child's life that make maternal thinking urgent, I myself am disturbed by my emphasis on children's pain and mothers' confusion and ambivalence. I turn from writing to look at children and mothers on the street and realize that I have accentuated unhappiness in humanly ordinary, and therefore ordinarily happy, lives.

When talking to mothers — some of whom are feminists — I am often thought to be cynical; among feminists — some of whom are mothers — I am more often thought idealistic. And, indeed, I can hear myself making mothers sound reliably better than we are. To the extent that mothers are embattled, I am on their side, and my passion shows, whatever words I use. On the other hand, because I am a mother I know the demoralizing, mind-numbing effects of sentimental descriptions of good mothering.

An idealized figure of the Good Mother casts a long shadow on many actual mothers' lives. Our days include few if any perfect moments, perfect children perfectly cared for. Self-doubts are compounded by others' promptings. "Experts" can undermine the most self-respecting woman's confidence when her child is delinquent, "underachieving," or simply sad. Fathers, grandparents, even best friends can seem like judges. Most painfully, children make clear the unhappiness we cause them, as indeed they should. Many mothers who live in the Good Mother's shadow, knowing that they have been angry and resentful and remembering episodes of violence and neglect, come to feel that their lives are riddled with shameful secrets that even the closest friends can't share.

The idealized Good Mother is accompanied in fear and fantasy by the Bad Mother. Paradoxically, a mother herself may welcome the idea of the Bad Mother as a protection against her own sense of badness. The Really Bad Mother's evils are specific, avoidable, and worse than her own. Sometimes, a competitive mother will describe her neighbor as "bad" in order to claim a superiority of which she is uncertain. But, however comforting for the moment, the Bad Mother ends up unnerving those who would depend on her. Guilty secrets fester; a "superior" mother's children have their unhappy days. The mother who took comfort in another's greater badness finds in herself the same "evil."

There are probably as many versions of "bad" mothers as there are cultures in which women are held responsible for raising children. A particular bogey that has interested me is Mom, the bad mother who appeared after World War II and who was contrasted with Mother, the "truly mature, maternal woman." Mom was made famous by the social critic Philip Wylie. She also appeared in the ruminations of psychiatrist Edward Strecker, who studied men who could not or would not fight in World War II.[1] According to Strecker, Mom needed her children so fiercely that when they went off to war she cried and "shrieked." She was insufficiently submissive to paternal authority or had too little mind of her own. Her boys, in turn, were either so mother-ruined or mother-identified that they couldn't kill. Bad mothers like Mom are frightening because they are created from familiar elements of mothering and from bad moments of any mother's day. Mom's passion for her children, overprotectiveness, and confused relation to paternal authority are all too familiar. "Some mothers recognize the symptoms [of the disease of being a Mom] and, like the real mothers they are, fight it. Others slip and another mom is added to the rolls."[2] Neither a woman herself nor her neighbor can be sure whether or in what degree she is Mother or Mom. As Strecker warns, you can't tell by looking at her; you know bad mothers by their children.

The myth that mothers are naturally good or wickedly bad inspires ignorant contempt for the actual work that mothers do. Toward the end of her book *Pink Collar Workers,* Louise Kapp Howe reports a government study conducted in 1975 that rated the difficulty of kinds of work in terms "complexity."[3] Assuming that every job required abilities to deal with data, people, and things, the report assigned a number to each category that measured the complexity of the task and therefore the skill required to perform it. The lower the number, the greater the complexity and skill. The individual numbers, designating specific abilities, were then combined to produce an overall score. One of the top scores was awarded to a surgeon, who received a 1 for data, a 0 for people, and a 1 for things, for a cumulative score of 101. This low score, reflecting high abilities, contrasts, say, with a parking lot attendant who got only 8 for data, 7 for people, and 8 for things, for an overall 878, just about the lowest score possible. Other low-ranking jobs include dog pound attendant (874), mud mixer helper (887), and shoveler of chicken offal into a container (877). What struck readers of the report was the astonishingly low rating received by jobs usually performed by women: child-care attendant (878), nursery school teacher (878), practical nurse (878). Even a midwife was considered slightly less skilled (378) than a hotel clerk (368). The description in the study of a foster mother's work captures those days when nothing much goes wrong and intense feelings are kept in check.

[She] rears children in her own home as members of family. Oversees activities, regulating diet, recreation, rest periods, and sleeping time. Instructs children in good personal health and habits. Bathes, dresses and undresses young children. Washes and irons clothing. Accompanies children on outings and walks. Takes disciplinary action when children misbehave.[4]

The foster mother's job is rated 878.

If maternal work were as easy as this contemptuous description of it suggests, anyone could do it. Yet along with popular contempt goes an apparently contrary view. It seems that the work is so difficult that whenever something goes wrong with a child, it is assumed that a mother has failed. Here is the French psychoanalyst Monique Plaza speaking about the way the mother figures in psychoanalytic discourse:

In my psychoanalytic practice with children, I am confronted with the Mother. A violent and painful confrontation. . . . It is in listening to the psychological discourses (the discourses of the "scholars," the discourse of the "practitioners") even more than in meeting women functioning as mothers that I have directly focused on the Mother. What have I heard? That mothers are often suspicious beings, beings with a sort of insatiable instinct which pushes them to smother their children. What have I seen? That traces of this instinct are searched for in (Mothers') discourse. Do they still wash their children at ten years two months? Do they pick them up at school at eight years seven months? Did they want them when they were nine months pregnant? Seven months? Do they take them into their beds? Do they accept the authority of the father? What have I read? That the madness of the child can be explained by referring to the perversion of the mother. . . . An awful Mother, worthy of a horror film. . . . I suspect the vast apparatus of hatred of the Mother of being one of the most prodigious and effective bastions of misogyny.[5]

The "vast apparatus of hatred" attributes to mothers and their work amazing power. To look realistically at maternal work or mothers, it is necessary to bring this power into focus. All power lies at least partly in the eye of the beholder. To a child, a mother is huge — a judge, trainer, audience, and provider whose will must be placated.[6] A mother, in contrast to the perception her children have of her, will almost always experience herself as relatively powerless. In the best of social systems she is beholden to the workings of "nature" whose indifference — most poignantly evident in illness, death, and damage to a child or his or her closest loved ones — can frustrate her best efforts. With the birth of her first child a mother learns that her power in respect to her children is limited. Children are born with a distinctive physical constitution and soon display a host of traits and moods that appear inborn. To deny that there is much in the character of an infant that is innate turns a relation that is to some extent determined and "natural" into one entirely subject to management and therefore subject to blame and guilt. As their children grow older, mothers can neither predict nor control the intellectual skills, moods, tastes, ambitions, friendships, sexuality, politics, or morality of their children.

Added to this unavoidable powerlessness is the fact and feeling of social impotence. Many mothers placate the will and serve the needs of a father. Especially if she lives alone, in almost all countries and certainly in the United States, a mother is apt to experience distinct forms of poverty. Whatever her domestic arrangements, her ability to determine her own and her children's lives depends on economic and social policies over which she has minimal control. Contrary to myth, mothers do not work in private. They are always in public, in doctors' offices and clinics, supermarkets and welfare offices, courthouses and schools, movie houses and amusement parks. Mothers are almost everywhere, and almost everywhere they learn of the contempt Louise Kapp Howe reports and the limits of their authority over their children. Even a child's teacher is apt to treat the mother condescendingly and belittle her advice. With other experts and professionals, from pediatricians to Selective Service officials, from welfare workers to psychiatrists, the powerlessness of mothers is notorious.

From a mother's point of view, maternal powerlessness is very real indeed. Yet adults are not hallucinating when they remember their mothers as having immense power over their physical activities and emotional lives. Especially if she is isolated with one or two children, a mother's desires, moods, and style determine a child's options. Children learn from their mother a "mother-tongue," a sense of what can be named and what must remain secret; what is unavoidably given and what can be changed; who is to be feared and whose authority is only a sham. Outlining the contours of "normal" life, it is mothers who distinguish the astonishing, outrageous, frightening, or joyous event and who decide which of a child's pains are normal or even valuable. Mothers can negotiate with or sabotage the will of the powerful, deciding what to reveal about their children and what to demand on their behalf. A mother dealing with the daily exigencies of her own and her children's lives may not *feel* powerful. There are many external constraints on her capacity to name, feel and act. But in the daily conflict of wills, at least with her children, a mother has the upper hand. Even the most powerless woman knows that she is physically powerful, stronger than her young children. This along with undeniable psychological power gives her the resources to control her children's behavior and influence their perceptions. If a mother didn't have this control, her life would be unbearable.

Not surprisingly, it is difficult for the most clear-sighted mother to keep her power and powerlessness in focus. It is a powerless woman who is powerful and whose power is exaggerated as much as it is feared. The hand that rocks the cradle has certainly not ruled the world. Real maternal power is not a stable quantity but highly variable depending on technological development, individual as well as collective economic resources, changing social and military policies, employment opportunities, housing practices, family arrangements, the mood, success, well-being, and age of her children, and, of course, her own health, energy, and non-maternal ambitions. It is exceedingly difficult to predict what will in fact damage children; damage is almost never attributable to maternal "failure" alone, but at most to maternal fallibility in a complicated and troubling family and world.

The conjunction of maternal power and powerlessness is difficult for children to comprehend. They confront and rely on a powerful maternal presence whom they inevitably resent as well as love. This powerful presence becomes powerless in front of their father, a teacher, welfare worker, doctor, judge, landlord — the world. Disappointed in their powerful mother, children can feel "wildly unmothered,"[7] forced to separate themselves from such a powerless power — indeed, forced to treat her with contempt. A daughter's sense of abandonment by a powerful mother turned powerless may be even fiercer than her brother's, since she is usually the same sex as her mother and may more easily imagine mothering as part of her adult life.

The complexity of maternal power is poignantly expressed in a woman's biological ability to give birth and, therefore, her ability to refuse to do so. In giving birth, women put themselves at some risk physically. Although cultures vary radically in the sacrifices they require of pregnant women and the services they provide for them, pregnancy and labor render a woman vulnerable to others' control. At least in the United States, the autonomy of a woman and her control over her own pregnancy are threatened in unprecedented ways by technological developments that multiply possibilities for arrogant medical intrusion ranging from forced sterilization of poor and minority women to fertility assistance and fetal surgery for the more affluent. Nonetheless, so long as only women can give birth, women also potentially have the power to give children to those they love and to their social group as well as the power to refuse to do so. This power is increased many times when contraception is safe, free, and effective and when abortion is readily available. That is, women's powers are increased by the very technological and medical interventions that threaten their autonomy.

How can mothers learn to look at maternal power so they can describe its shifts and compromises accurately? A good place to begin is to admit that power is something humans want and that mothers are, of course, human. To be powerful is to have the individual strength or the collective resources to pursue one's pleasures and projects. What mother wouldn't want the power to keep her children healthy, to prevail over people who frighten or demean them, to create hospitals, schools, jobs, day care, and work schedules that serve her maternal work and make possible lively nonmaternal projects and loves, and even to select for her children loves and ambitions that would suit them both?[8] Yet mothers are often frightened of power and deny desiring it.

After admitting that power is desirable, the next step is to look at its realities from a *maternal* perspective. This is a difficult task. Mothers were once children too. They may still hate a punishing or neglecting mother or fear maternal power or share the culture's contempt for mothers, perhaps especially their own. No adult simply outgrows childish feelings, but mothers who live in the midst of childhood passion are particularly susceptible to a return of their own childhood needs and fantasies. Moreover, mothers consciously school themselves to assume, at least temporarily, a child's-eye view, in the interest of acting effectively with and on behalf of their children. Yet it is confusing for a child when — as often happens — a mother loses an adult perspective. And if a mother cannot adopt a maternal perspective — the perspective of her own work — she will be confused about her power and about much else as well.

Until quite recently, mothers attempting to hold fast to a maternal perspective have gotten little support from artists or psychoanalysts. Novelists and poets attest to the force of a child's perceptions, a young lover's passion, or a hero's quest; with notable exceptions, they are less likely to give voice to or speak from the perspective of a mother. This is not to say that mothers are not celebrated. In women's writings there often seems to be a nostalgia for a "paradise lost," an original mother-tongue, mother-home, mother-landscape that was sacrificed to the father's symbolic, oedipal order.[9] It is not surprising that nostalgic fantasies for mothers or their bodies abound in feminist critiques of technocratic, patriarchal societies or that as *daughters,* mothers may participate in them. These fantasies are, however, children's creations. It is difficult for a mother to connect them with the busy and flawed mother-home she herself is making, so unlike the one that daughterly fantasy requires.

Psychoanalytic theories regale us with the passions of family life told from a child's point of view. Typically the "mother" is either powerfully good and bad or a silent other, a mirror in which children look to confirm *their* identity without interference from hers. To be sure, psychoanalytic theorists also romanticize maternal power, sometimes attributing to a child's earliest relation with his or her mother not only the vicissitudes of gender identity but also fundamental capacities to work and love.[10] A mother reading these theories may find her experience entirely lost in a child's perception — and analyst's naming — of her as "pre-oedipal," good or bad, a maternal body, or, most reductively, a breast. If she is not seduced into self-blame, she may find these fantasies farcical or assaultive as she reads with a mother's eye about her own "magical" breast/body/self.

Sometimes feminists have seemed to confirm the cultural silencing of mothers' voices. A few seem to share the romantic view of the mother-home outside men's languages and cultures.[11] For many other women, becoming feminist is inseparable from breaking with a tradition of oppressive maternal self-sacrifice. As peace activist Ynestra King puts the point:

The feminist movement has spoken in the voice of angry rebel daughters. Even when mothers join the movement it is often the wronged daughter in them who speaks. Each of us is familiar as daughters with maternal practice, but most of us in becoming feminists have rejected the self-sacrificing, altruistic, infinitely forgiving, martyred unconditionally loving mother — for this is how I saw my mother — have rejected that mother in *ourselves* as the part of ourselves which is complicitous in our own oppression.[12]

Fortunately, in the feminist tradition numerous writers neither fear nor romanticize mothers and their work. These feminist writers distinguish the experience of mothering from the oppressive, confining, isolating institutions of motherhood that spoil that experience for so many women. They insist that grown-up children — that is, all of us — acknowledge a mother's separate, subjective self. Speaking of a widely diverse group of Black women "[who] have found in their mothers' legacies the key to the release of their creative powers," Mary Helen Washington remarks that

the educated daughters need to open the "sealed letter" their mothers "could not plainly read," to have their mothers' signatures made clear in their work, to preserve their language, their memories, their myths.

Yet she warns and enjoins her sister critics:

Before these signatures can be read clearly, we will have to free the mother from the domination of the daughter, representing her more honestly as a separate, individuated being whose daughters cannot even begin to imagine the mysteries of her life.[13]

In *Tar Baby,* Toni Morrison's character Ondine requires of all women the same kind of attentive daughterhood:

[If a girl] never learns how to be a daughter, she can't never know how to be a woman. . . . You don't need your own natural mother to be a daughter. All you need is to feel a certain . . . careful way about people older than you are. . . . A daughter is a woman that cares about where she came from and takes care of them that took care of her.[14]

Learning how to be daughters includes learning to expect and respect maternal thinking. And this means really listening when mothers speak. Obviously, listening respectfully to maternal thinking cannot mean accepting the conditions in which mothers have been disdained and their work devalued. Indeed, given the contempt that mothers suffer, listening could be considered an act of resistance. Nor does respectful listening mean accepting, let alone celebrating, maternal voices as they are. Daughters are not likely to give up a hard-won, hard-held critical stance.

More important, speaking changes a speaker. Most mothers are women; hence maternal thinking is dominated by women's voices trying to say what they know. In their study of women's epistemological development, the authors of *Women's Ways of Knowing* reported about the subjects they interviewed:

In describing their lives, women commonly talked about voice and silence: "speaking up," "speaking out," "being silenced," "not being heard," "really listening," "really talking," "words as weapons," "feeling deaf and dumb," "having no words," "saying what you mean," "listening to be heard."[15]

To borrow the words of Audre Lorde and Alicia Ostriker, women want to "name the nameless so that it can be thought," "to seize the language," "to make female speech prevail, to penetrate male discourse, to make the ear of man listen."[16]

Maternal voices have been drowned by professional theory, ideologies of motherhood, sexist arrogance, and childhood fantasy. Voices that have been distorted and censored can only be *developing* voices. Alternately silenced and edging toward speech, mothers' voices are not voices of mothers as they are, but as they are becoming. As mothers struggle toward responsible thinking, they will transform the thought they are beginning to articulate and the knowledge they are determined to share.

Mothers, Fathers, and Caretakers

To describe mothering as a work out of which a distinctive thinking arises, I develop a somewhat eccentric way of identifying "mothers." Briefly, a mother is a person who takes on responsibility for children's lives and for whom providing child care is a significant part of her or his working life. I *mean* "her or his." Although most mothers have been and are women, mothering is potentially work for men and women. This is not to deny, in advance of future data, that there may be biologically based differences in styles of mothering. "Biology" is not fixed; we have no idea of the potentialities and limitations of male and female bodies in a society free of gender stereotypes and respectful of female humans. I am suggesting that, whatever difference might exist between female and male mothers, there is no reason to believe that one sex rather than the other is more capable of doing maternal work. A woman is no more, a man no less "naturally" a mother, no more or less obligated to maternal work, than a man or woman is "naturally" a scientist or firefighter or is obligated to become one. All these kinds of work should be open to capable and interested women and men.

Although maternal work can, in principal, be performed by any responsible adult, throughout the world women not only have borne but have also disproportionately cared for children. Since most of the people who have taken up the work of mothering have had female bodies, mothers, taken as a class, have experienced the vulnerabilities and exploitation as well as the pleasures of being female in the ways of their cultures. Although some individual mothers may be men, the practices and cultural representations of mothering are strongly affected by, and often taken to epitomize, prevailing norms of feminity.

We cannot at will transcend a gender division of labor that has shaped our minds and lives. Although men can be mothers, and although many women now refuse maternal work and many more would do so if they could without penalty, in most cultures the womanly and the maternal are conceptually and politically linked. This means that to elucidate maternal thinking is also to elucidate a "woman's way of knowing." This would be true so long as mothers were women, no matter how many women were mothers. But the other side of that coin is that in most cultures many more women than men who have not actually become mothers nevertheless expected or still expect to engage in maternal work or identify with those who do. This identification with maternal work, in mental anticipation and sympathy if not in present reality, suggests that when critics, psychologists, artists, and others speak of women's minds they may be speaking also — though of course not only — of maternal thinking. I myself adopt this methodological hypothesis when I look at studies of women's ways of knowing for an illumination of maternal thinking.

To say that mothering is inseparable from the condition of being female means only that understanding mothers involves understanding what it means to be a woman and that we learn something about women, their fears, desires, expectations, and ways of knowing when we learn about the work and thinking of mothers. I have put this point cautiously because, obvious as it may seem, it raises three questions: Where are the fathers? Where are the caretaking women who are not mothers? Where is the female body? These questions lead in conflicting directions.

Where Are the Fathers?

Although men can be mothers, in most of the cultures I consider most male parents are Fathers and most Fathers are men. Whether men or women, Fathers are not, in my terms, simply the male counterpart to mothers. Fathers, historically, are meant to provide material support for child care and to defend mothers and their children from external threat. They are supposed to represent the "world" — its language, culture, work, and rule — and to be the arbiters of the child's acceptability in the world they represent. In many cultures, Fathers have legal control over important aspects of their children's lives and moral authority to judge their choices, though they have neither developed the gifts nor borne the burdens of maternal work. This does not mean that Fathers are bad people; like mothers, Fathers are not predictably good or bad. Some are wise, generous, restrained, and loving; others are mean and abusive. The point about — or against — Fathers is that their authority is not earned by care and indeed undermines the maternal authority that is so earned.

I follow linguistic practice in treating "mother" and "Father" as correlative terms, but I capitalize "Father" to challenge the correlation. Fatherhood is more a role determined by cultural demands than a kind of work determined by children's needs. Many women do maternal work without a Father in sight. Many men would like to be Fathers, but they have neither the resources nor the power to fulfill the role. For women without connection to providers or defenders or for men impoverished and powerless, Fatherhood is an elusive condition, not a real choice. The point against Fatherhood is that it offers unrealistic hopes and burdens to women and men who take up the caring labor of maternity.[17]

Although the myth of Fatherhood may be cruel to women and men, I look forward to the day when anyone who actually takes pleasure and pride in her or his children or has authority over their lives also shares in the work of *caring* for them. It is not just or healthy for women, men, or children if men, as a group, are denied or deny themselves the work and pleasures of mothering. This does not mean that women should not undertake mothering without men. Single mothers, lesbian mothers, and women mothering in communes are contributing courageously to our collective invention of new forms of "family" life. It does mean that male (or female) parents who have enjoyed or been burdened by the ideology of Fatherhood can and should take up the work of mothering instead.

Almost every time I make these points about Fatherhood and men as mothers, I am asked why I don't speak of "parenting." Bell Hooks's remarks are typical:

Because the word "maternal" is associated with the behavior of women, men will not identify with it even though they may be behaving in ways that have traditionally been seen as "feminine." . . . Telling a boy acting out the role of caring parent with his dolls that he is being maternal will not change the idea that women are better suited to parenting; it will reinforce it. . . . Seeing men who do effective parenting as "maternal" reinforces the stereotypical sexist notion that women are inherently better suited to parent, that men who parent in the same way as women are imitating the real thing rather than acting as a parent should act.[18]

When I imagine telling my once adolescent son that he would be a "good mother," I see the psychological point behind Bell Hooks's remarks. It is essential, as Hooks argues, that mothering be re-visioned as an activity "naturally" undertaken by men, that boys *and* girls see men mothering, that children with male parents are mothered by them. Indeed, if I believed that boys and young men were at all likely to be influenced by my choice of words, I would make an effort to speak evenhandedly of mothers and fathers and keep quiet about Fatherhood. Given, however, that I am writing for adults, I retain the vocabulary of the maternal, for several reasons.

At the simplest level, I want to recognize and honor the fact that even now, and certainly through most of history, women have been the mothers. To speak of "parenting" obscures that historical fact, while to speak evenhandedly of mothers and fathers suggests that women's history has no importance. Moreover, I want to protest the myth and practice of Fatherhood and at the same time underline the importance of men undertaking maternal work. The linguistically startling premise that men can be mothers makes these points while the plethora of literature celebrating fathers only obscures them.

Although many men do and many more could take up maternal work, in our present, sexually divided world, there is an ever-present danger that male parents will continue to become Fathers. It is of the first importance, epistemologically and politically, that a work which has historically been feminine can transcend gender. But "transcendence" has not yet been achieved. Despite affection and egalitarian commitment, individual women and men may find it difficult to resist entrenched romantic fantasies and habits of domination and sacrifice. For example, in some middle-class cultures in the United States women are — or feel they are — rewarded for their subordination and consequent self-limitation with social praise, sexual desirability, economic benefits, and some measure of domestic authority. The men are similarly rewarded for a control that verges on domination and exploitation of the services of others, including the mothers of their children. In these circumstances, "shared parenting" can mean bringing the authoritarian Father and compliant and dependent mother straight into the nursery. A man who wishes to share mothering can then seem to usurp, and frequently to override, a woman's already limited authority.[19] It is necessary for women and men to insist to themselves and each other that male parents can be and are no better than *mothers* and that mothers, whether they are women or men, should be respected and self-respecting in the presence of their children or when speaking about them, whether at home or in public places and gatherings.

Entrenched personal habits and fantasies are also augmented by social and economic policies that tend to restrict mothering to women and then restrict mothers to limited lives. The best-intentioned individuals can do little to transcend gender until communities support the work of mothering and the well-being of children with free and effective medical services, day-care centers, flexible working hours, and pervasive respect for maternal work. Restructuring the work life requires acknowledging that women are still held responsible for mothering and that this genderization offers overwhelming economic and professional advantages to men. Men may be as able as women to challenge the economic realities of gender, but not without appreciating the social consequences of holding women responsible for maternal work. Evenhanded talk of mothers and fathers or abstractions about parenting only delay this necessary, troubling acknowledgment of difference and injustice.

Finally, what Hooks calls the "real thing" really has been "feminine." Since the maternal and the womanly are politically and conceptually connected, a man who engages in mothering to some extent takes on the female condition and risks identification with the feminine. The fear of becoming "feminine" — more common in men but also evident in many women — is a motivating force behind the drive to master women and whatever is "womanly." Although I am not recommending that young boys be told they will be mothers, grown men should confront the political meaning of "femininity" and their own fear of the feminine. A man does not, by becoming a mother, give up his male body or any part of it. To be sure, by becoming a mother he will, in many social groups, challenge the ideology of masculinity. To a man taunted for "being a woman," talk of parenting may be temporarily comforting. But if he is undertaking maternal work, he is identifying with what has been, historically, womanly. What is so terrible — or so wonderful — about that? This is a question women and men might well sit with rather than evade.

Where Are the Caretakers?

While some people have urged me to replace the maternal with the parental, others have suggested that I include maternal work under the more general category of "caring labor."[20] "Care" is a general designation covering many activities — maintaining a shelter in which children, among others, are safe (housework); sustaining a circle of connections — of kin and friends — on whom children, among others, depend (kin work);[21] securing, preparing, and serving food to a household or community, including its children; attending to the needs of the vulnerable, children as well as the elderly; and teaching the very young or the previously untaught. The work of mothering is a central instance and symbol of care. Although caring practices differ, certain elements of caring work seem sufficiently common and central to identify it as a practice just as, despite the varieties of science or religion we still speak of scientific or religious practices. Caring labor gives rise to a "rationality of care," exemplifying many of the alternative ideals of reason recently formulated by feminists.[22] Maternal thinking is one central expression of this rationality.

There are several advantages to speaking generally of care. Although in many cultures most kinds of caring labor are performed by women, care is not tied in any way to particular activities of female bodies, as mothering is often mistakenly taken to be. Moreover, many more women engage in caring labor than in the mothering of small children. Women (and men) who feel excluded by the vocabulary of maternity but nonetheless recognize that they think maternally can more easily include themselves in the historically female work of care. Moreover, when it is conceptualized as exploited work, the notion of "caring labor" lends itself to feminist labor politics. Since women provide most caring services, it is a feminist demand to secure for caretakers the autonomy, economic benefits, and political powers they need for themselves and their work. The demand is also immediately applicable to any man who engages in caring labor.

Despite the advantages to speaking of care, I once again, at least for the moment, retain the maternal idiom. My reasons are in part intellectual. Different kinds of caring cannot be simply combined. For example, caretaking always involves teaching the subjects of care, and teaching itself can be understood as a kind of caring labor. But the teaching of healthy children differs from the teaching of the ill or elderly, while a description of teaching itself goes beyond the language of care. Similarly, mothering may be inseparable from, but it is not the same as, homemaking, feeding, teaching, and nursing. If we don't distinguish these kinds of work we will not be able to see their differences or specify their connections. For example, caretaking requires patience, whether a mother waits for a six-year-old to finish her sentence, a teacher helps the child to write one, or a nurse tends a dying patient and his distraught family. But patience takes on distinctive meanings for mothers, nurses, teachers, and adult children who engage in these tasks. I believe that distinctive kinds of thinking arise from these different activities and I also suspect that these kinds of thinking can be interestingly connected to maternal thinking. But it is disrespectful to each kind of thinking and to the rationality of care as a whole to combine the varieties of thinking without attempting to describe them individually and mark their connections and differences.

My reasons for not speaking generally of "care" are also practical. To confuse the care of healthy children with nursing, or tending the elderly with caring for children, is harmful to children, patients, the elderly, and the caretaker herself. Moreover, because mothering is for many women and men the symbol and formative experience of caring labor, people who speak generally of care often slide into talk of maternal work. This elision then insults many caretakers who are not, and do not choose to be, mothers. Mothering is a central human work whose struggles and thinking merit close study. But the maternal is not the whole of care and cannot be made to stand for it.

Where Is the Female Body?

While I have consciously retained the vocabulary of the "maternal" rather than adopting the inclusive abstractions of "parenting" and "caretaking," I have only slowly realized that "maternal work" is itself an inclusive abstraction. The reality that it evades is the biological fact that a small but significant fraction of maternal work is ineluctably female. Only females give birth; when babies are breastfed, only women feed them.

Although birthing labor is an undeniably female activity, it is possible to minimize its importance to mothering as a whole. Adoptive or stepmothers are no less qualified maternal workers because they have not given birth. Nor is giving birth sufficient grounds for undertaking maternal work or doing it effectively. Pregnancy, birth, and lactation are different in kind from other maternal work and, measured by the life of one child, are brief episodes in years of mothering. A scrambling, temperamental toddler in reach of poisons under the sink, a schoolchild left out of a birthday party, a college student unable to write her papers — these children are more emblematic of the demands on a mother than is a feeding infant, let alone a silent fetus.

It is understandable that men and women would want to minimize (as I have done) the one aspect of child care (and of life) that men cannot share — the bodily potentiality, vulnerability, and power that is woman's alone. This hitherto ineradicable division in the ability to give life evokes guilt, envy, and resentment. It is understandable that male parents appropriate birthing labors — "we are giving birth in June," "we are still nursing" — and that both men and women refuse to acknowledge such a disturbing difference in the origins of their relationship to an infant they may fervently desire.

However generous it may be, I find this vision of shared, genderless birth unfounded and dangerous. It is increasingly clear that the envy that lies behind the minimalization of birth fuels a technocratic and legal apparatus able to intrude on and exploit *women's* bodies in unprecedented ways. To be sure, a few utopian researchers hope that male bodies can be altered so that embryos can gestate in and proceed forth from them. Moreover, fantasies of "test tube" babies flourish among feminists and scientists alike. However, even if it becomes technologically possible to produce children without women's bodies, women's ova will be intrusively and not painlessly extracted for extrauterine reproduction. Whatever the state of technology, a man engages in no activity that can match, in labor, a woman's pregnancy, with its anxieties, discomfort, intrusive testing, painful delivery, and unique excitements and pleasures. We have learned from confronting racism and sexual bigotry that we cannot make our differences disappear. To deny the different relations of women and men to human birth founds the entire egalitarian project on an illusion.

More deeply, so long as we fear and deny the distinctly female character of birth, we risk losing the symbolic, emotional, and ultimately political significance of birth itself. There is a philosophical tradition that honors mind over body, idea over matter, the word over the bloody, shitty, mortal flesh — a tradition that feeds off fear and contempt for female procreative bodies. Technologists redescribe birth as a controlled production rather than a physically innovative act. It is commonplace to talk of women's *r*eproductive rights and powers and the *r*eproductive technologies that affect them. To be sure, birth replenishes the species and reproduces, though never exactly, a social or kin group. But the vocabulary of reproduction, with its heavy emphasis on repetition and its indebtedness to the material production of inanimate goods, misses altogether the originality of birth. An infant is born into a social context and therefore into a past. Yet an infant is also a beginning. To give birth is to create a new life. Mothering is a sustained response to the promise embedded in that creation.

How can a conception of mothering as work that transcends gender be reconciled with respect for female procreativity? How can mothers and other people who respect women respond to new technologies in ways that empower birthing women while not detracting from the work of adoptive mothers? How can we celebrate the creative act of birth without reromanticizing an instinctive bonding, thereby denying the ambivalent responses of many birthgivers to their infants and the richly various arrangements in which lesbian, gay, and heterosexual women and men take up maternal work? I begin to address these questions by conceptually separating birthing labor from mothering. My aim is to honor both kinds of work and at the same time to provide the conceptual and emotional space to raise questions about the relations between them.

By "birthing labor" I mean everything a woman does to protect and sustain her fetus. The culminating moment and defining hope of the work is the act of giving birth. Neither pregnancy nor birth is much like mothering. Mothering is an ongoing, organized set of activities that require discipline and active attention. It is best divided among several people who, in an egalitarian society, would be as likely to be male as female. Birthing labor, by contrast, is essentially female, performed by one woman (aided in many ways by others). Pregnant women — especially if they look forward to mothering — often take a maternal attitude toward the fetus, becoming deeply attached to an infant they have yet to meet. These eager mothers usually engage projectively in maternal tasks — making clothes or buying a crib, for example. But these tasks relate directly not to the fetus but to the baby it will become. A mother takes care of her *fetus* by taking care of herself.

Cultures differ in their prescriptions for birthgiving women; and within a culture there are radical differences in women's abilities to procure the care they need. For a North American woman who has access to medical services, the work of birthing labor is more like an athlete's training or a patient's cooperative participation in her own care than like a mother's care for a child. Even very small infants could not survive two days if they got from their mothers as little direct attention as fetuses get from most birthgivers. Birthgivers who eagerly await their infants and are delighted with the sensations of fetal activity nonetheless actively care for their *own* bodies in the hope and for the good of a child to come.

The culmination of birthing labor is the act of giving birth. It is not hard to see that this dramatic, physically encompassing activity is also unlike mothering. But, given the suspicion and silence that surrounds birth, it is not at all easy to describe the physical realities and social relations of birthgiving. In Chapter 8, I develop a maternal conception of the body and of giving birth that is opposed to Western philosophical and militarist conceptions.

A corollary to the distinction between birthing labor and mothering, is that all mothers are "adoptive." To adopt is to commit oneself to protecting, nurturing, and training particular children. Even the most passionately loving birthgiver engages in a social, adoptive act when she commits herself to sustain an infant in the world. It is not possible to limit a priori the forms of respectful relations between birthgivers and adoptive mothers. Generally, since no life can survive without mothering, the defining hope of birth is to create a life-to-be-mothered. A particular birthing woman articulates that hope by arranging the conditions of adoption that suit her. The work of a birthgiver is not compromised if she carefully transfers to others the responsibility for the infant she has birthed. Similarly, there are many ways in which adoptive mothers who have not given birth can respect the autonomy and intentions of birthgivers and the work of birth on which all mothering depends. What respect for birth and birthgivers does always require is practically effective respect for the birthgiver so that she has the resources to determine and to satisfy the desires she has for herself and her infant.[23]

Commonality, Difference, and Oppression

In setting out the idea of maternal thinking, I made certain claims about what all children demand and then defined a "mother" as, essentially, someone who responds to the three main demands of preservation, growth, and social acceptability. Despite the variations among children and those who care for them, these demands, I claimed, define, essentially, a kind of work.

This assumption of commonality runs counter to the philosophical and feminist mood of the last decade. It is now widely agreed that becoming a "woman" or a "man" is a social and multiply determined ongoing activity. The opening sentence of the second part of *The Second Sex* has become classic: "One is not born, but rather becomes, a woman."[24] Anatomical and chromosomal differences — which are not nearly so sharp as we are usually taught — mark biological females and males, not the social creatures they become. Cultures are markedly inventive in the ways they use biological difference to create men and women. One does not become a "woman" in some general sense but, for example, a French or Mexican or Japanese woman, living in a particular decade as a member of a particular class.

As it is with women so it is with mothers. Neither a woman nor a man is born a mother; people become mothers in particular historical and social circumstances. Even if pregnancy and birth are taken as part of mothering, the biological fact of birthgiving is, both medically and symbolically, culturally various. Once a child is born, maternal work can assume radical differences. Although all children need protection, some need protection from snakes, others from cars, some from poisons under the sink, others from open wells or drug dealers on the street. Some are protected by the police, others from the police.

Any mother speaking in or about a maternal voice is a particular person of a particular temperament, social location, and politics. A mother may get some grasp of the peculiarities of her experience by traveling, reading, and listening. But however widely she looks about to extend her experiences, she will be one person looking, from a particular vantage that is hers. I might take some distance from my experience when I set out conceptual frameworks or engage in political debates about my project. But once I begin to write, I must feel and remember mothering as clearly as possible. The closer I come to what I have known, the more confidently I speak, and, simultaneously, the more limited is my vision. In fact, I know nothing about protecting children from wells or about the life in which that kind of protection plays a part. I vividly remember a time in the kitchen over forty years ago when we listened endlessly to the radio and talked of a child who had fallen into a well and of her mother who would not leave the spot until rescuers, after four and a half days — much too late — raised her daughter. The identification in protective work that I still feel and claim with that farm woman cannot depend on my being *like* her. Nor do I aspire to replace a description of her work and thinking with a generalized version of my own.

Conceptions of "maternal thinking" are as various as the practices of mothering from which they derive. There were three children in my original family, and I have mothered two of my own. My mother took primary care of us; I have shared the primary care of two children with my husband. It is not surprising that when I think of mothering, I imagine one or two mothers taking primary responsibility for a fairly small number of children. My account of maternal thinking would probably seem eccentric to a mother raising eleven children alone, to a group of women of different generations raising several children together, or to a society where children are raised collectively as in the guardian class of Plato's *Republic* or Charlotte Perkins Gilman's utopian *Herland*. Although I can predict that these mothers would not recognize the awesome responsibility that mothers I know (and am) feel for a particular child, I cannot predict the thinking that will arise from their different circumstances of mothering. But I do expect sufficient commonality in the demands made by our children to enable us to compare, which also means to contrast, the requirements of our work.

Throughout my years of mothering, I have lived a heterosexual life with one man who is the biological father of our children and who also is, after some conscious efforts on our part, their egalitarian co-mother. My family arrangements, although statistically atypical, reflect two wishes that appear dominant in the contemporary United States. Many mothers, heterosexual, gay, and lesbian, men and women, desire to share with a sexual partner the duties and complicated feelings of caring for children. A narrower desire for specifically heterosexual continuity among generations is apparently shared by most ethnic groups.

My particular sexual domestic history has consequences. In my abstract rendition of maternal thinking, I extract the work of mothering from its context, treating it as figure to the ground of sexual and domestic life. This is possible only because my sexual arrangements elicit public approval and, moreover, have served me well. If, like the heroine of Sue Miller's *The Good Mother,* I felt punished for my passion and deprived of maternal love, or if I were a lesbian, I would most likely write a different book.[25] For example, I probably could not speak of children's demands while placing to one side the sexual life of the mother who meets them.

As it is, I run the danger of underestimating the conflicts between a maternal life and an adult sexual life and distorting (both minimizing and exaggerating) the difficulties of caring for children alone or in less socially acceptable and therefore more visible sexual domestic arrangements. Although I try to correct for these biases, I cannot speak for any other mother — nor is there any need to "include" those who are speaking more knowingly and more eloquently for themselves. Many kinds of maternal stories need to be told: by heterosexual, gay, and lesbian mothers; by mothers who are coupled, single, or live in groups; by mothers separated from their children's female or male biological parent; by mothers who are celibate or monogamous or who have many sexual partners. It is only by collecting our many stories that we can address the urgent task of rethinking the connection between sexual and mothering lives.

The peculiarities of my experience affect my fundamental conceptions of maternal thinking and work. For example, I devised a way of speaking that honors women who give birth as well as adoptive mothers who may be grandmothers, aunts, fathers, or persons biologically unrelated to their children. I write out of a middle-class, technocentric, property-oriented culture ambivalently obsessed with the bonds of biology. But even in my own country, many communities of Native Americans would find my efforts strangely belabored since such a double honoring of birthgiving and adoptive mothering is already richly inscribed in their culture. By contrast, the Abuelas (Grandmothers) of Argentina's "disappeared" children fervently seek out genetic linkages that will reconnect them to their grandchildren who were "adopted" by their children's captors. These women engage in an act of biological reclamation that is both political and deeply personal. As Rayna Green, a Native American scholar, generously but firmly insists, other North American women cannot adopt as their own the maternal imagery and concepts of Native Americans, no matter how comforting and liberating they may seem.[26] Nor can I think as an Argentinian Abuela, although in Chapter 9 I celebrate the resistance in which the Abuelas participated.

I make claims about *all* children and I believe them. But I make those claims out of a particular intellectual training and Protestant heritage that taught me to look for human needs and desires underlying the divisions between women and men and between cultures. This particular social history is reflected in my conceptual choice to let the demands of human children essentially define a human maternal work.[27]

It is not only philosophy and ecumenical protestantism that lie at the root of my universalizing vocabulary. I live in a society where children are at risk yet can be, from a medico-technological perspective, rather effectively protected. I have two healthy children, ages twenty-two and twenty-five. I *expected* them to survive; that is, although I can barely write these words without "knocking on wood" and had many scares over time, their serious illness or death would have been unexpected and emotionally devastating. To be able to have by choice only two children, both of whom are expected to survive, distinguishes me from most of the world's mothers past or present. I live in a nation and in a city where I have been able to turn to experts trained to deal with children's illnesses. In the same city and nation, however, many poor and "minority" women, if they have any access to medical services, are often treated carelessly and contemptuously by the experts they consult.

I know that many of my fellow citizens and many more mothers around the world could speak only with anguish of a child's "demand" that her life be protected. I am under no illusion that my response to my children's demand for protection is *like* theirs. Nonetheless, I continue to identify a "maternal" work. I take a child's demand that her life be protected as a demand *children* make upon the world — a demand intrinsic to the promise of birth that mothers in many cultures around the world can and, so far as I can tell, do organize to meet. I hope to endorse the universal demand of children for protection while recognizing that many mothers try to preserve their children's lives and to comfort them in circumstances more terrible than I can imaginatively apprehend.

I root my project — including its claims for universality — in a particular sexual and social history; I neither expect agreement nor attempt to predict which of my concepts are offensive to another mother or inapplicable to her experience. Nonetheless, I also repeatedly and provocatively hint at a "maternal identity" and in the end explicitly invoke and expand that identity for the sake of peace politics. To claim a maternal identity is not to make an empirical generalization but to engage in a political act. At least in my social class, mothers themselves frequently describe fundamental moral commitments in "maternal" terms. In Gloria Naylor's *Women of Brewster Place,* an affluent, middle-class Black woman provides a clear example of the kind of maternal identification with which I am familiar:

When I brought my babies home from the hospital, my ebony son and my golden daughter, I swore before whatever gods would listen — those of my mother's people or those of my father's people — that I would use everything I had and could ever get to see that my children were prepared to meet the world on its terms, so that no one could sell them short and make them ashamed of what they were or how they looked. And Melanie, that's not being white or red or black — that's being a mother.[28]

The speaker, Mrs. Browne, is not denying difference — she speaks in the midst of a bitter argument with an admirable daughter who has rejected even the name her mother gave her, her maternal grandmother's name — in favor of an African name of her own. Mrs. Browne neither reports nor seeks agreement. She declares "maternity," identifies herself, and takes pride in the identification.

For any mother, declaring maternity is a particular act that, at least in our troubled world, is almost always located in a social nexus of violence and oppression. As a small child, I learned that "good" mothers in Germany and elsewhere cruelly persecuted other mothers and children or stood by while their governments, including men whom they loved and lived with, did so. Later I identified the faces of white American women jeering at Black school children with the faces of the German mothers I scrutinized as a child. As a white and gentile woman, I also include among "my people" the white American and gentile German mothers who in small or dramatic ways, sometimes with considerable courage, resisted the racial violence that their governments planned and their neighbors applauded. But it was the sometimes contorted, often smiling faces of racial violence that haunted me. Even now, it is the mothers who are "good enough" at home but participate in the violence outside their door, that I most often find myself addressing.

In the following pages I speak of the parochialism of maternity, of passionate loyalties to one's own children, kin, and people. Mothering offers distinctive occasions for tribalism and for racism. Yet with my own heritage of oppression in mind, I nonetheless argue that mothering itself can be a training in attending to unsettling differences and that maternal identification can be transformed into a commitment to protect the lives of "other" children, to resist on behalf of *children* assaults on body or spirit that violate the promise of birth. "That's being a mother."

Bernice Reagon, a Black civil rights activist, feminist, and musician, envisions a universal maternal work in the world:

Mothering/nurturing is a vital force and process establishing relationships throughout the universe. Exploring and analyzing the nature of all components involved in a nurturing activity puts one in touch with life extending itself. . . . We can choose to be mothers, nurturing and transforming a new space for a new people in a new time.[29]

These words express exactly what I believe and hope. I cannot share Reagon's confidence, however inspired I am by her vision. I see mothering, at its best, as a *struggle* toward nonviolence, a *struggle* not to hurt what is strange, not to let other children be abused out of fear or loyalty to one's own. Yet it is Reagon's vision to which I aspire. After all the caveats and qualifications are in, it is the promising political consequences of maternal identification that underly my language of commonality and justify the loyalty to mothers that fuels it.

PART II

Protection, Nurturance, and Training

Making It Up

IN THE NEXT three chapters, I identify some of the specific metaphysical attitudes, cognitive capacities, and conceptions of virtue that arise from mothering. I treat separately the thinking that arises from the three demands of preservation, growth, and acceptability, partly with the aim of highlighting the conflict that arises between them. While this abstract, tripartite division is true to maternal experience of conflict, it belies the jumbled unity of mothers' lives. It is maternal work as a whole that gives rise to a distinctive kind of thinking called forth by the demands of children.

"Gives rise to," "called forth by" — these are provocatively vague phrases in search of a method. Several years ago, a social psychologist Michelle Fine asked me how I knew what mothers think. "I make it up," I said, at a loss for a more respectable response. In fact, I was formulating the beginnings of an answer. I began, as I did in Chapter 1, by speaking about the epistemological connection of practice and thought, action and knowing. Appealing to an intuitive sense of mothering as a kind of work and drawing the consequences from the epistemological claim that labor or practice forms consciousness, I suggested that there must be distinctive kinds of maternal thinking that arise from and are appropriate to the demands of maternal work. How, I asked, would a person repeatedly responding to these demands come to think? How indeed? As I admitted to this particular social psychologist, whose evident intellectual generosity puts defensiveness at rest, I made it up.

Sometime later, I was considerably relieved when another sympathetic listener, this time a political scientist, Jean Bethke Elshtain, compared my approach to a cultural anthropologist's. I was, she said, a participant-observer of mothering. Seizing her suggestion, I began to think of myself as having been a participant-observer of maternal practice since I was old enough to realize that my mother was a woman with distinctive responsibilities, doing a particular kind of work. For many years, starting in 1963, I actively participated in maternal work and, with my friends, especially my husband, in maternal thinking. For a long time my young children's demands, as well as my desperate desire for an intellectual life utterly apart from them, inhibited "anthropological" reflection on the kinds of thinking in which I engaged. Now, however, missing my children and their demands, I have become an interested observer of maternal practices and thinking. As an "anthropologist," I begin by remembering as honestly and deeply as I can my own experience as a mother and daughter and that of my closest friends. I then extend my memory as responsibly as I am able, by reading, by eavesdropping, by looking at films, and, most of all, by mother-watching. I can no longer identify the particular sources of my inventions, but they include the insights about mothers in the works of Julie Olsen Edwards, Jane Lazarre, Audre Lorde, Tillie Olsen, Grace Paley, and Ann Petry. These are the writers I explicitly draw on in the next three chapters; I am indebted to countless others. But finally, as mother, reader, and observer, once again I make it up. When I say "Mothers know . . . ," "Mothers acquire . . . ," "Mothers learn . . . ," I mean that this is how *I* now remember, hear, and then invent maternal thinking.

While I have been making it up, philosophers, psychologists, and literary critics have engaged in a lively feminist inquiry into women's experiences and expressions. Some have listened to women speak and have looked at photographs, paintings, music, films, philosophies, dances, poetry, sculptures, quilts, scientific theories, ideals of education, and other works that women have produced. Others have looked through the lens of theory — Marxist, psychoanalytic, structuralist, post-structuralist — at the increasingly abundant knowledge of women's lives in various historical and social locations. These theorists set out to redefine and revalue "femininity," asking whether certain themes recur in the stories that very different women tell of their lives and, if so, what their social, political, and psychological determinants are. Together, empirical investigation and a priori philosophical reflection have combined to produce both the idea that different and suppressed voices are associated with women and an account of what those voices might be saying.

To my delight, I have discovered that what I have made up finds its place in and is often confirmed by the work of feminist investigators. It would now be impossible for me to separate what *I* think about mothers from what feminist psychologists think about women.[1] My retrospective understanding of the concept of maternal thinking as well as the content and cognitive style I ascribe to maternal thinkers is decisively shaped by these feminists' work. Nor can I sort out just where I differ from or am indebted to the work of other philosophers and critics who are now articulating women's or mother's distinctive perspectives. I know that my understanding of maternal thinking has been enriched by the published writings, manuscripts, public talks, and conversations with numerous feminist inquirers now identifying and reevaluating women's different voices.[2] Those whose names appear in my acknowledgments and footnotes only selectively represent the community of lively, contentious feminists whose work directly informs mine.

It is gratifying to find that what so many feminists hear from women and ask for them is remarkably congruent with what I hear from and ask for mothers. It is also invigorating to respond to writers who take intelligent and serious exception to the concepts I have invented and the use to which I have put them. My writing has been immeasurably strengthened by the work of all these inquirers, whether they challenge, confirm, or amplify my inventions. Finally, however, I am one reader, observer, mother. When I speak of what "mothers" do, say, or think, I am still making it up.

CHAPTER THREE

Preservative Love

I BEGIN WITH a story of preservative love told by one young woman, Julie Olsen Edwards, about her first baby.[1] This mother is not Everywoman. She lives on the West Coast of the United States in a subculture that offers her doctors, visiting nurses, allergy tests, and inhalators. As the protagonist of her story, she is young and new to mothering, unlike the politically active writer-narrator who is remembering an earlier time that was too confusing and painful for speech.

The plot is simple: A young mother, Julie, lived with her first child in the third-floor flat on the back side of a tall, dark building. Julie had not always wanted children. Twice she had aborted the "nonlove" fetuses she had conceived. It was *this* child she wanted.

You were such a wanted baby. I would rub my belly in awe of your growing. Sit motionless waiting for your kicks and stretches. Think of you, wonder about you, wait for you — totally caught in the miracle of your coming to life. First child, child of hope, child of commitment.

65

Once born, this baby — fervently desired, blessed with the names of ancestors — would not sleep. She was awake every other hour around the clock, day and night, for four long months and slept only two hours at a time for the next six. Although the trouble wasn't immediately clear, it turned out to be croup and bronchitis, caused by allergies, that kept the baby awake.

Like many mothers in our society, Julie spent hours alone with her baby. Day and night she set up the steamer and helplessly paced the floor as the baby gasped for air. She later said:

Sleep deprivation drove me mad. . . . I moved with constant aching bones, could stand no closed doors or shut-in spaces, lost track of days or weeks and wrote long lists of things to do — which turned out to be, on later reading, totally unintelligible.

Julie's baby had a Father who spent much of his time away studying and working, thereby providing for his child. What Julie says about her husband, as well as the tact with which she says it, attests to the value she placed on their love and the efforts she made to sustain it. Though the Father's physical absence plays a larger part in the story than his presence, he hovers emotionally between and over its lines.

He, who fathered you, is kind and pleased. . . . He is a silent man, who lives within himself. . . . You pulled your Daddy's beard and said, "papa pretty," and his face crumpled as I have never seen it do before.

After school and work the baby's Father sometimes came home. Predictably it was he who, free from guilt and cumulative stress, could quiet the baby, enabling the mother to sleep but also making her feel "consumed with failure." It is not surprising that a frightening episode occurred on a night when the Father couldn't come home.

On that night Julie, alone with the baby, slept lightly. Though the baby seemed well and was quiet, in her dreams Julie heard the familiar cries. Dream soon revealed reality: the baby was wailing as usual. Or, rather, screaming. How difficult it is to remember what it is like when a baby *screams*.

I stumble towards your room and switch on the low lamp so the light will not startle you. You toss your body back and forth, arch your back and wail and call. Trembling, I walk to your bed and check your diaper. I try to speak, to soothe, to give voice to my presence, but my throat constricts in silent screaming and I find I cannot touch your tangled blankets. I force myself to turn and walk away, leaning against the door jam. My knees buckle beneath me and I find myself huddled on the floor. "Please do not cry. Oh child I love, please do not cry. Tonight you can breathe, so let me breathe." And I realize my chest is locked and I am gasping for breath. I picture myself walking towards you, lifting your tininess in both my hands and flinging you at the window. Mixed with my choking I can almost hear the glass as it would smash and I see your body, your perfect body, swirl through the air and land three stories below on the pavement.

Sickened by her vision, Julie vomited and then felt calmer. After changing the baby's diaper and propping a warm bottle so that she could drink, Julie shut the door to the baby's room, barricading it against herself with a large armchair. Later that night, she carefully wrapped her daughter in blankets, carried her downstairs and rode a bus from one end of the city to another, "thinking you would be safe with me if we were not alone."

The child overcame her allergies and grew as children do. Yet for many years this mother carried a shameful secret: she had wanted to murder her child. Finally she gathered the courage to tell a friend of her mother's the story of that night. Trying to see beneath the feelings of guilt, the friend asked: But what did you *do?* And together the two women could realize what the grown-up mother was able to retell. The young woman did all she could to keep her child safe; what she did was enough.

Thought and Feeling

If we take this story as emblematic of maternal work, what can we learn of protective thinking? We see that mothering can be imbued with such passionate feelings that onlookers, accustomed to distinguishing thought from feeling and work from love, can barely recognize amid the passion either the thinking or the work. In this short story we hear of anger so strong that it is literally sickening, of guilt so severe that it was kept secret for years, of a sense of failure, fear, frustration, and emotional exhaustion. There was also love, joy, hope, and appreciation of the "natural" facts of growing.

Child, I weep when you are born. In joy and disbelief . . . I am overwhelmed with love and fear. How will I care for you? How will I keep you safe? . . . You explored the world with intense concentration, and each discovery startled me as well . . . . I watched . . . delighted . . . fascinated.

What we are pleased to call "mother-love" is intermixed with hate, sorrow, impatience, resentment, and despair; thought-provoking ambivalence is a hallmark of mothering. If Julie's emotions seem extreme (though I have witnessed the resonance of her story for mothers who have heard it), quieter, exemplary stories and memoirs attest to the intensity of mothers' feelings about their children and about the alternately exhilarating and exhausting demands of their work. From across the continent another young mother, from Jane Lazarre's *The Mother Knot,* speaks:

While we [the narrator and her friend] watched the children together, or at night after they had gone to sleep, we talked about them.
"I love them and everything, but I hate them," she would say.
"I would die for him," I emphasized. "All those movies about mothers running in front of trucks and bullets to save their children are true. I would much prefer to die than lose him. I guess that's love" — I winced and we both laughed — "but he has destroyed my life and I live only to find a way of getting it back again." I finished slowly, for without the second part of the sentence, the first part was a treacherous lie — a lie we had sworn to be done with.
"I can't wait until tomorrow when it is your day to keep the children," she would say, "but I dread leaving them in the morning." We learned always to expect sentences to have two parts, the second seeming to contradict the first, the unity lying only in our growing ability to tolerate ambivalence — for that is what motherly love is.[2]

Thinkers, generally, are not affectless. They have feelings about the subjects they think about and emotional, often erotic, responses to their own thinking processes. But some kinds of thinking are more separable from feeling than others. A computer expert may be deeply attached to her machine, resent her dependence on it, and fear any threat to its life. She may get an erotic high from working with it. Nonetheless, she can understand computer science more or less independently of the feelings provoked by her computer and their work together. It is not possible to understand preservative love "purely" intellectually, nor can protective mothers understand themselves and their children without calling on and understanding feelings.

In protecting her child, a mother is besieged by feeling, her own and her children's. She is dependent on these feelings to interpret the world. The world that mothers and children see and name, separately and together, is constructed by feeling. Objects, events, people, and feelings themselves are selected and given meaning in terms of emotional stories: watch out for "this," "this" is what or who I hate; "this" is the fearful place/person; "this" can be approached, should be hugged close. A mother's angry, fearful, or solicitous responses to her children are often her best clue to the meaning of the actions that evoked the emotions. Even more clearly, a child's emotional expressions, however difficult they may be for a mother to witness, are essential to the understanding that makes protection possible. To be sure, mothers often seek relief from their own and their children's feelings. But "freedom" from these feelings, in the unlikely case it became habitual, would inhibit the intellectual capacities mothers require of themselves.

When viewed in the light of the commitment to protect, the "test" of a feeling is the safety it makes possible. Does this worry protect a child or needlessly confine her? Should this fear be acted on or soothed away? As feelings are tested in terms of protection, the effectiveness of protection is tested in part by the feelings it allows: the mother's "now I can rest without worry" is matched by the child's "I feel safe." Because they work amid intense, ambivalent feelings and because these feelings must be tested in terms of safety, mothers find themselves talking about feelings with each other and with their children. Feelings do not bear their meaning on their faces or in their voices. Exasperation is not hate, anger may threaten but does not always lead to injury. Fear is a signal of danger that can be neither ignored nor trusted. Contentment is not the same as safety, nor is tender solicitude a substitute for effective protection. Feelings cry out for thought; hence, reflective assessment of feeling is a defining rational activity of mothers.

In maternal thinking, feelings are at best complex but sturdy instruments of work quite unlike the simple and separate hates, fears, and loves that are usually put aside and put down in philosophical analyses. They are certainly quite unlike the simple fears and hates on which military endeavors depend. Rather than separating reason from feeling, mothering makes reflective feeling one of the most difficult attainments of reason. In protective work, feeling, thinking, and action are conceptually linked; feelings demand reflection, which is in turn tested by action, which is in turn tested by the feelings it provokes. Thoughtful feeling, passionate thought, and protective acts together test, even as they reveal, the effectiveness of preservative love.

Few deny that mothering is imbued with feeling, although the conjunction of feeling with thought may go unnoticed. Indeed, at times a mother seems, to herself as well as observers, utterly defined by the feelings that overpower her. But the activity of preservative love, although intensely emotional, can never be reduced to the sum of its feelings. Although feeling and action are conceptually connected, to feel is not tantamount to acting. The question for Julie, the mother — as her own mother's friend reminded her — is not "What did you feel?" but "What did you do?" Mothers' feelings toward their children vary from hour to hour, year to year. A single, typical day can encompass fury, infatuation, boredom, and simple dislike. Protective care itself can vary only within a narrow range. Preservative love cannot alternate evenly with violence or negligence without ceasing to be itself. Although imbued with intense, ambivalent, thought-provoking feelings, mothering is an activity governed by a *commitment* that perseveres through feeling and structures the activity. Many mothers, like Julie, remember a specific appreciation of the overwhelming obligation that preservative love presumes.

I remember saying "Pregnancy takes away one's right to suicide. You must take care of a life you birth."

Cognitive Capacities and Virtues of Protective Control

Although maternal caring may be emotionally laden, the protection that it produces is, in a sense "natural." Julie's baby often screamed in pain — she couldn't breathe — and sometimes screamed for "no reason." She didn't die. With adequate care, and barring disasters, children do not die. Even the tiniest infant is a living creature whose mere survival is not the miracle it may seem to be. To be sure, many mothers suffer from poverty and violence; caring requires of them superordinate efforts against great odds. But in a politically decent and minimally prosperous society, children become cooperative partners in their own well-being.

Yet even in prosperous and just societies, no mother counts on normal times. Children are prey to major and minor disturbances that make watching over them mandatory. Somebody must be alert for things that go wrong and be ready to set them right and get help. In Julie's story, doctors, allergy tests, and inhalators became part of the infant's life. Soon the stairs have to be barricaded. The lethal tools of household work, from needles to cleansers to glue, will be locked away. Mild medicines can turn poisonous if a child mistakes them for candy. A mother has to childproof her home, but she cannot childproof her city or farm. A child has to be taught general strategies of safety so that she can protect herself from dangers when she is outside her mother's domain where it sometimes seems that there is no limit to the risks the world offers. Yet barring extreme poverty, violent racism, physical battering, and war, children do, on the whole, survive.

Children are not so fragile as goldfish seemed to me; nor will they flourish if they are perpetually watched and guarded. On the other hand, they are not like roaches and weeds, hardy survivors regardless of what is done to them. A mother can never stop looking, but she must not look too much. Attentiveness to a creature who perseveres in its own being and at the same time is perpetually at risk is peculiarly demanding. In the service of protection, mothers develop a mental habit or cognitive style which

I call "scrutinizing."[3] In city streets or at the beach, traveling or at home, mothers are on the lookout for dangers before they appear. Their alert, action-ready glances are often furtive, so that children don't feel observed, and apparently intermittent, so that the mother has enough energy for a chat or a chore.

The scrutinizing gaze, the watchful eye of preservative love, can become obsessive or intrusive. For her own sake and her child's a mother learns when to intervene and when to look away. To give birth is to create a life that cannot be kept safe, whose unfolding cannot be controlled and whose eventual death is certain. Scrutinizing is an appropriate habit for mothers of children who are at risk yet persevere in their own being, who must be watched but not watched too closely. But scrutiny must be tempered by a metaphysical attitude which, following Iris Murdoch, I call "humility." In a world beyond one's control, to be humble is to have a profound sense of the limits of one's actions and of the unpredictability of the consequences of one's work. In Murdoch's words, "Every 'natural' thing, including one's own mind [including one's own children], is subject to chance. . . . One might say that chance is a subdivision of death. . . . We cannot dominate the world."[4]

Mothers identify humility as a virtue when they recognize in themselves the delusive, compulsive efforts to see everywhere and control everything so that a child will be safe. With "humility," a mother respects the limits of her will and the independent, uncontrollable, and increasingly separate existences she seeks to preserve. A mother without humility would become frantic in her efforts to protect. But she cannot, out of degenerative humility or passivity, relinquish efforts to control. The idea of control has received bad press among feminists. Ideals of reason are controlling and, within Western scientific thinking at least, the capacity to control is made a test of reason. Both the experience of being controlled by alien ideals of reason and the value put on control by these ideals make it tempting to disparage control altogether. But this thinking is misguided. No one who has watched over a small toddler, counseled an adolescent, nursed an ill child, or supervised a birthday party abandons control to spontaneity. Protection without control would be a horror.

Mothers do not relinquish control. Rather, because control is a preoccupying maternal issue, mothers come to think about control in distinctive ways. Although mothers know that children are not objects but subjects, they must work to perceive children as purposive agents, especially when they appear recalcitrant or self-destructive. Then too, mothers are liable to depend emotionally on their children's dependence on them. Often they have to learn to relish reciprocity, to identify as a maternal virtue respect for the independent, uncontrollable will of the other. If her care is successful, a mother will ensure the safety of someone whose will she cannot control. The mother of even a tiny child can respect his ability to formulate and act on desires of his own. But none of this is tantamount to relinquishing control.

While some mothers and feminist thinkers romantically reject the idea of control, most mothers are more easily tempted by fantasies of perfect control. These mothers have to remind themselves that, although protecting work is never finished, there are no perfectly protected children and that the best control provides for the limits of that control. Mothers are also tempted to give up the patient work of control and resort to domination. Children's recalcitrance or a mother's fatigue and preoccupation can turn protectiveness into impatient abuse. "If you don't get off that windowsill I'll shake you till your bones fly apart" — a type of threat that, in the usual case, wards off rather than leads to actual violence.

Mothers are also beset by the multiple temptations of passivity. Advice from experts can lead women, who frequently have never been encouraged to trust their judgment, to relinquish control to others. Often a mother feels paralyzed by her children's rash behavior or the indifference of her community to their safety. When mothers are despairing or powerless, silenced and silent, their humility may well degenerate into passivity, "a peculiar habit of self-effacement, rather like having an inaudible voice."[5] At its best, however, humility is "a selfless respect for reality and one of the most difficult and central of virtues,"[6] a way of persevering and controlling in an exhausting, uncontrollable world.

Mothers protect where protection cannot be assured, where failure usually means disappointing someone they passionately love, where chance and unpredictable behavior limit their efforts, and where their best efforts are flawed by their own impatience, anxiety, fatigue, and self-preoccupation. Recognizing how close protectiveness comes to giving up on itself and recognizing as well the costs of that surrender, mothers identify cheerfulness as a virtue.

To be cheerful means to respect chance, limit, and imperfection and still act as if it is possible to keep children safe. Cheerfulness is a matter-of-fact willingness to accept having given birth, to start and start over again, to welcome a future despite conditions of one's self, one's children, one's society, and nature that may be reasons for despair. To be cheerful is to ride the bus up and down the nighttime city streets, keeping yourself and your baby safe even though you've imagined murdering her. The mother overcome with fury is cheerful when she learns to forgive herself — to ask herself "What did you do?" as well as "What murderous fantasies filled your mind?" The abusive mother is also cheerful when, despite her shame and confusion, she attends a counseling center and demands of the women who help her, "Teach me something so that I will never do that again." Unlike the good humor valued in friends, colleagues, and, for that matter, in mothers, cheerfulness is compatible with many temperaments and moods.

In circumstances of personal or social disaster that warrant despair, maternal cheerfulness is an extraordinary feat. Many mothers, with resourcefulness and restraint, help their children die well; others sustain seriously damaged children in hopefulness. Still others fight daily for their children's survival amidst racist bigotry and terror. In happier circumstances, clear-sighted cheerfulness is not an extraordinary virtue but a common strength. Ordinary mothers school themselves to look realistically at their children and the dangers that confront them, cheerfully controlling as best they can what is never fully controlled, creating around them beautiful artifacts, rituals of play, and small ceremonies of loving so that the day's disasters can give way to the next morning's new beginnings.

Cheerfulness serves mothers well; in Spinoza's words, it "increases and assists the power of action."[7] For children, too, their mothers' cheerfulness is a necessity. To be cheerful is to see a child hopefully and to welcome her hopes; for children, hope is as important as breathing, certainly more important than sleep. According to Spinoza, "cheerfulness is always a good thing and never excessive."[8] So long as cheerfulness includes resilient clear-sightedness, there is no reason to doubt him.

But for mothers, cheerfulness threatens to break down into cheery denial, its degenerative form. Mothers are tempted to deny their own perceptions of harsher realities because they so wish the world were safer for their children. In the interests of protection, they are tempted to assume a false cheerfulness in front of their children, whose sharp eyes must ferret out and interpret, often fantastically, the troubles hidden from them. In the worst case, mothers may demand cheerfulness from the children themselves, in an effort to make their children's apparent happiness into a confirmation of their work and a mind-easing satisfaction of their love. Cheerfulness that encourages children to deny their sadness and anger or that protects them from truths they will have to acknowledge only confuses and inhibits them; cheerfulness that allows a mother herself to mystify reality drains her intellectual energy and befuddles her will.

When mothers recognize resilient cheerfulness as a virtue, they are not celebrating an achievement. To identify a virtue is not to possess it; often one sees most clearly a need for the virtues one lacks. To value maternal cheerfulness is to acknowledge a *struggle* typical of maternal work. Those mothers who speak often of their efforts to sustain a clear-sighted and resilient cheerfulness most likely are especially tempted by the destructive cheery denial, passivity, or despair to which the identification of a virtue is a response.

"Nature" as Constructed by Protection

As mothers engage in the work of protection with cheerfulness and humility, they may come to acquire a distinctive concept of the "nature" that they engage. When I speak of a maternal conception of "nature," I am not suggesting that mothers themselves are more "natural" than other women and men.[9] My question is not about the alleged naturalness of either women or mothers but about the conception of "nature"* that people acquire by engaging in the work of protection.

In protective love, the natural is, before any moral judgment of it, what is given. The bodies of children are, in this sense, given. They come in different shapes and colors, have distinctive chemistries, respond in distinctive ways to pains and pleasures, and are susceptible to particular diseases. In myriad ways, they assert themselves: this physical being is here; whoever deals with me deals with my body. If a child suffers from a heart defect, scoliosis, or dyslexia, these are givens that a mother and those who help her and her child work with as well as against. Many of the body's diseases and many of the accidents that befall it are natural, though mothers (perhaps especially middle-class mothers in the United States) may come to believe that if only they are good and careful enough their children won't get sick. Children's strongest emotions appear to be given. The fury of a child is a powerful force. You can hit and terrify a child and perhaps drive her fury beneath the surface. But it exists. So do high-spirited, manic giddiness and physical restlessness that seem intrinsically unsuited to domestic life. To respect that fury or those giddy high spirits or a body that seems perpetually mobile is respecting nature, much as one respects the strength of a hurricane, the rush of a waterfall, or the onset of age.

To identify the natural with the given does not mean that protecting mothers accept whatever is natural. Mothers fight their babies' diseases and soothe their emotions. Nature with its unpredictable varieties of poisons, diseases, germs, fires, tornadoes,

---

*I use the quotation marks as a reminder that the idea of "nature" I discuss is constructed within maternal practice. Indeed, the "nature" constructed by preservative love is only one of four maternal constructions of "nature" that I will discuss. To speak of a social, or more specifically maternal, construction of "nature" is not, of course, to say that "nature" doesn't really exist. To use the language I developed in Chapter 1, protective love and, more generally, maternal practice as a whole give rise to conceptions of "nature" appropriate to maternal experience, conceptions different from, though connected to, religious or scientific conceptions of "nature." Having made this general epistemological point, I will now drop the quote marks for ease of reading.

floods, and "accidents" is often an antagonist whose effects are countered with various strategies from vaccinations and caps on poisons to tornado shelters and fire drills. Yet mothers cannot deny what is natural. Their children are nothing before they are natural, and their growing is itself a working of nature. When children thrive, it is nature that thrives — always, to be sure, within a particular sociohistorical, culturally interpreted context, but nature nonetheless.

Mothers might be said to negotiate with nature on behalf of love. Nature can be thought of as a respected opponent with whom they are watchfully and sometimes antagonistically engaged. Like the "ordered" nature Evelyn Fox Keller envisions for genderless science, the nature protective mothers confront is

Generative and resourceful . . . an active partner in a . . . reciprocal relation to an observer [and protector] equally active but neither omniscient nor omnipotent.[10]

In quiet moments, a mother appreciates the workings of nature around and within herself and those she loves. Even when she battles, she is like the Gandhian nonviolent activist, refusing to separate herself from an opponent she will live and work with when the fighting stops.

This respectful, appreciative, yet at times confrontational engagement is less romantic and more secular than many mothers might suggest. In particular, many religious mothers believe that a divine order is manifested in nature and that nature is therefore a proper object of love. A similar quasi-mystical construction of nature holds sway among many maternal ecologists and poets. Even for those less religiously inclined, some elements of mothering might in themselves inspire a sense of nature as ordered. The birth of an infant often seems the miracle it is said to be. A baby's vitality or young children's responses to the world around them often reawaken or evoke in mothers a sense of nature's enchantment. Even in cities, numerous events — from heat waves to sudden thunderstorms to the birth of pets to small signs and rituals of changing seasons — seem wondrous to children. Certainly many mothers do not respond to their children's wonder or to the natural phenomena that provoke it. Preoccupation or harassment turns the most glorious sunset invisible. But for some mothers, giving birth to and living with children inspires something akin to a religious respect for nature.

All of these religious, mystical, and secular attitudes are compatible with mothering. However, there is nothing in maternal practice itself that demands a religious or mystical response to nature and, whatever the solace and inspiration of faith, most mothers cannot will themselves to believe. Mothers respond variously to the religions of their cultures and to the evidence of supernatural order that different religions present.

Whatever a mother's religious predilections, the work of protective love is likely to encourage in her a cognitive capacity for double focus, an ability to think about last as well as first things. Mothers have to take the near and banal quite seriously. A tooth has to be filled, a meal prepared, homework finished, a fight stopped. Everyday events are immediately and ineluctably demanding. Time is short, tasks are specific, deadlines fixed, time for musing nonexistent. But deadlines pass. A child's day is filled with time in which nothing needs to be done, a child's life is bounded by a birth and a death that place teeth, schoolwork, childhood battles, and thousands of dinners *sub specie aeternitatis*. Birthdays, serious illnesses, first and last days of school, births and deaths of pets, first loves, first jobs, and many other unscheduled events of childhood prompt larger questions of meaning: Why? For whom? To what end? Many mothers answer: To no higher purpose, for no reason; the point of childhood is expressed within the child's life, not outside it. Even for these mothers, this simultaneous, or at least rapidly shifting, double focus on small and great, near and eternal, characteristically marks their maternal vision.

Holding

Negotiating with nature on behalf of love, harassed by daily demands, yet glimpsing larger questions, mothers acquire a fundamental attitude toward the vulnerable, a characterological protectiveness that I call "holding." To hold means to minimize risk and to reconcile differences rather than to sharply accentuate them. Holding is a way of seeing with an eye toward maintaining the minimal harmony, material resources, and skills necessary for sustaining a child in safety. It is the attitude elicited by the work of "world-protection, world-preservation, world-repair . . . the invisible weaving of a frayed and threadbare family life."[11] Scrutiny, humility, and cheerfulness mark the minds of those who protect because the holding that these virtues make possible is as sturdy and sane for both protector and protected as nature (human and otherwise) allows.

Holding, the fundamental attitude of protectiveness, is, like the virtues that enable it, liable to lapse into degenerative forms: holding too close, too timidly, too materially, collecting and accumulating possessions in which to embed lives that are slipping away. There is no doubt that holding can drive adolescent children crazy. Protectiveness characterized by holding is no one's idea of "adventure" — a quintessentially mother-free notion. Mothers themselves can feel the victim of their own habits of protectiveness that stand in the way of children's need to grow their own way.

Protective mothers often take on themselves the task of holding together relationships — with Father, lover, grandparents, teacher — on which their children depend. Such holding and harmonizing has its risks. Some mothers, out of concern for their children, are inappropriately courteous to rude doctors or teachers, flatter their bosses, and stay in marriages that harm them. Moreover, the cognitive gifts and virtues of preservative love — scrutiny, cheerfulness, and humility — are, like protective holding itself, not only convenient in subordinates but also associated with and perhaps more highly developed in powerless peoples. To celebrate them can seem tantamount to celebrating oppression itself. On the other hand, these same capacities may prove more effective in political struggle than their detractors suspect.

Preservative Love in the World

The domain of maternal protectiveness is continually expanding. It is children themselves who first extend their mothers' protective efforts. For the first few months, it may seem that only biological life needs preserving, although even in infancy the distinction between physical and other needs is spurious. The tiniest babies seem lonely, excited, angry, frustrated, or friendly. And soon complexities multiply. As a child grows, so does the work of protection. It sometimes seems as if a mother helps create the very fragilities — the moral, mental, and psychological capacities —she then needs to protect. She helps a child learn to climb stairs and then has to keep him from falling down; she encourages the child to walk to school alone but then must warn her against strangers and cars; she urges him to travel farther and make new friends and then worries about potentially harmful playmates. As her task enlarges, it also remains constant: to keep safe whatever is vulnerable and valuable in a child — not only her body, but her mind, spirit, and developing conscience.

Mothers extend their care to the homes they maintain, purchasing, borrowing, maintaining tools, cleaning and harmonizing a space. The nurse may have recommended an inhalator for Julie's baby, but it was probably Julie who bought it and almost certainly Julie who kept it clean and working. Shelter and kinship, the physical home and the social household, are usually part of a larger social-physical community. There is nothing romantic about the extension of mothers' activity from keeping a safe home to making their neighborhoods safe. No one is surprised when mothers petition for traffic cops at school crossings or drive drug dealers off the block. If children are threatened, mothers join together, in all varieties of causes, to protect the neighborhoods they have made.

Maternal care may extend as widely as the community on which growing children depend for their projects and affections. Often, for example, mothers come to feel that their children's well-being depends on the military or economic strength of their nation and its allies. Even mothers who claim that their "country is the whole world" may want for their country or community first and a little more fervently the safety they ask for everyone.[12] Few mothers take the world as an object of extended maternal care; fewer still believe that they can keep the entire world safe. No one can, and mothers, considered collectively, have less power than many. Yet if the world itself seems under siege, and if that siege holds any community and all children hostage, the effort of world protection may come to seem a "natural" extension of maternal work.

Keeping the world safe is human work and in no way the special responsibility of mothers. Yet I am not surprised when a mother testifies that her love requires a commitment to world protection nearly as demanding as the feeding, holding, and nursing of her infant. Julie Olsen Edwards ends her story explaining just such a commitment, taking on herself a responsibility that she understands as an extension of the discipline of preservative love:

There came a night (he was away — at study work in a far-off place) when an early storm came across the Pacific. . . . I woke from a deep sleep to the sound of a siren, the air-raid alert. . . . It was a short circuit, a meaningless accident. But that night I did not know. And I believed. . . . We stand there you and I, body to body. And wait. I believe it is the end. I know this holocaust will take not only you and me, but all the world, all children, all trees and songs, all promises. The sirens have sounded and I believe. . . . I hold you and can do nothing. Nothing to give you tomorrow, nothing to save you, nothing to protect what might be. There is no gesture of defiance, no gallant last battle. Just you and I in this room with the wind and rain against the window. . . . I hold your pulsing wrist to my lips, feel again your struggle to be born, and know I must promise you the only thing I have left. If we live through this night, dear child of my body, if we survive these moments of ultimate madness, I will do what I can to shift the balance. . . . And if, in the end, we lose, I will look at you, straight at you, and say I tried.

CHAPTER FOUR

Fostering Growth

TO FOSTER GROWTH is to nurture a child's developing spirit — whatever in a child is lively, purposive, and responsive. To my ears, the word "development" has acquired an ugly sound. I think of "women in development," of "developmental aid," in which technocratic and imperialist experts usually impose on others inappropriate plans intended to serve the planner economically or ideologically. Closer to home, I associate "development" with particular schools of psychologists who order hierarchically people's cognitive and moral capacities.

I mean by "development" something closer to the dictionary meaning: to develop is to "unfold more completely," "to unfold gradually, as a flower from a bud," "to free from that which enfolds or envelops," "to form or expand by a process of growth," "to evolve the possibilities or power," "to make active (something latent)," to "perfect, advance, further." It is my hope that these standard meanings of "development," which are suitable to describe a child's spirit, could infuse our understandings of developing countries and psychological theories of development.[1]

The term "spirit" may also be misleading. To speak paradoxically, from a maternal perspective the spirit is material. A child's body, from its birth, is enspirited. A primary experience of preservative love is an admiring wonder at what a new body does. An enspirited body is, in turn, a source and focus of mental life. From children's perspective, "bodies," both their own and others', provide some of the most poignant fantasies and puzzles of mental life. As children name, desire, avoid, or touch bodies, the bodies become resonant with "spiritual" significance.

To foster growth, then, is to sponsor or nurture a child's unfolding, expanding material spirit. Children demand this nurturance because their development is complex, gradual, and subject to distinctive kinds of distortion or inhibition. The belief that children's development is complex in these ways is culturally variable and individually contested. Many mothers who engage in preservative love and training do not recognize a distinctive task of fostering growth although outsiders watching them may interpret their behavior as doing so. I do not want to enter into controversies about the complexities of children's development, still less to contest other mothers' descriptions of their work. In my view, children's emotional, cognitive, sexual, and social development is sufficiently complex to demand nurturance; this demand is an aspect of maternal work as I have known it, and it structures maternal thinking.

The mind of a mother fostering growth is marked by a sense of children's complexity and of the difficulties of responding confidently to them. For those mothers who recognize the demands of fostering growth, meeting them is as arduous as any task of maternal work. As Mrs. Ramsay laments in *To the Lighthouse,* what one does and what one says becomes "so important":

No, she thought to herself, putting together some of the pictures he had cut out — a refrigerator, a mowing machine, a gentleman in evening dress — children never forget. For this reason, it was so important what one said, and what one did, and it was a relief when they went to bed.[2]

"Nature," Normality, and Nurturance

As a child is naturally meant to survive, so too her spirit is natural and naturally developing. In speaking of a child's natural development, I appeal to a concept of nature more benign than that of the engaged ally-antagonist of preservative love. When mothers excuse their children's behavior on the ground that it is "natural" to their age, they also implicitly appeal to a beneficent nature. Although the current manifestation of a child's nature may be unpleasant, it is assumed that nature itself will take care of the unpleasantness. Nature offers a promise of healing; natural processes move toward health and integrity, despite their moments of undeniable ugliness and fear.

Nature is a mother's ally, so long as she actively cooperates in its purposes. In "normal" times, the only task of a nurturing mother may be to provide a safe setting where a child can be herself. To be sure, in adverse conditions natural development seems miraculous and for some mothers nurturing consists of all-consuming efforts to provide minimal protection. How is it that some children develop even though they are hungry, chronically ill, threatened by random violence, or assaulted by their neighbors' bigotry? If even in the midst of social and personal disaster children develop, their wondrous resistance suggests that spirited development is in a child's nature.

The beneficence of nature does not preclude the necessity for maternal judgment. A mother must identify a child's feelings and behavior as "natural" — appropriate to the child's age and circumstances, however unpleasant. Nor does their being natural mean that mothers can ignore them. Nightmares, phobias, and shame may be natural, but a child who suffers from them without sympathetic attention may not benefit from the natural processes in which a mother trusts. When children are left to cope on their own with crises, abuse, and intense emotions, they sometimes do as well as adults could do for them, but sometimes they don't. Neglected children, trying to control intense fears and passions that they barely understand, damage themselves intellectually and aid may misunderstand, intrude unwisely, and magnify the troubles. A mother has to judge whether intervention is called for and, if so, whether she should attempt to change her child or the forces upsetting him or both. Sometimes a mother needs to act, to control, as best she can. And many times she schools herself to wait, to listen, and to trust. This abstraction becomes real enough when a mother is faced with a child who is, for example, terrified by a nightmare, obsessively committed to war games, angered by a parent's illness, or experimenting with drugs.

For a mother who sees her children as demanding not only protection but nurturance of the spirit, the troubling questions begin early: When and how should a child be fed? Where and how long should she sleep? What do her cries mean and what should one do about them? Typically the questions of nurturance crystallize retrospectively as a mother tries to understand a particular instance of her child's unhappiness. In Tillie Olsen's "I Stand Here Ironing" a mother reruns the past in search of the meaning of her actions, unable to be reassured by a friend's question "But what did you do?"

I nursed her. They feel that's important nowadays. I nursed all the children, but with her, with all the fierce rigidity of first motherhood, I did like the books then said. Though her cries battered me to trembling and my breasts ached with swollenness, I waited till the clock decreed.

Why do I put that first? I do not even know if it matters, or if it explains anything.[3]

Once an infant moves into childhood, a mother is confronted with daily questions, either from the child herself or from helpers — Father, experts, grandparents, friends — who counsel her. Should a child be allowed to stay indoors all weekend when all the other children are out playing? Should children be forced for their own good where they fear to go — into classrooms or to birthday parties, for example? Does a boy's identity require that he play with guns, a girl's liberation that she be denied the dollhouse she wants? How much should a mother tell her children about adult sexual life, her own past and current moral failures, or the bigotry of their neighbors? When is allowing a child to grow "naturally" a cover for impotence in the face of her will? In some households, these questions and countless others like them make up the staple of maternal worry.

General formulations of children's needs have a child-guidance (and economically prosperous) ring to them. Children should not be left alone too often or kept so constantly in company that they cannot develop inner resources; they should be stimulated, but not overexcited, with objects, tools, books, pictures, and sounds. No amount of generalizing is sufficient to identify specific needs on a particular day, let alone to meet them with the resources available. City and country mothers, mothers who work mainly at home and those who work long hours outside, establish conditions of growth in different ways. Harassed, financially strapped, and pressured mothers find time and energy for tending their children's spirit, keeping their world in order. At the very least, under impossible pressures their worries indicate an acknowledgment of spiritual complexity, revealing an attentiveness that might in less trying circumstances characterize their maternal lives. In Ann Petry's *The Street,* Lutie Johnson, exploited, impoverished, and desperate, feeling "the way a fighter feels after he's been knocked down twice in succession . . . except that she had received, not two blows, but a whole series of them," worries about her son Bub:

> Then she saw with surprise that there was a light under her door and she stopped thinking about how she felt? "Why isn't he asleep?" she said, aloud. . . . He is afraid here alone, she thought, looking down at him. . . . The lamp on the table was shining directly in his face. . . . Every time she had come home from the Casino, he had been sleeping with the light on. Yes, he was definitely afraid.[4]

I have seen mothers watching over their children in hot, crowded subways, poor villages, pleasant beaches, and playgrounds some would think dangerous. They listen, talk, console, and entertain in ways that go far beyond the requirements of physical safety. Often both children and mothers forget these small efforts of maternity invisibly woven into a child's life. But not always, as Toni Cade Bambera testifies: "The manuscript . . . is dedicated to my first friend, teacher, map maker, landscape aide,

Mama, Helen Brent Henderson Cade Brehon, who in 1948, having come upon me daydreaming in the middle of the kitchen floor, mopped around me."[5]

Central tasks of fostering growth are administrative. In communities that support mothers and their children, mothers organize places and times in which infants and toddlers can socialize and mothers can have time to find themselves. Later, in classrooms, playing fields, blocked-off streets, and meeting houses, mothers arrange for or provide safe occasions for learning and friendship. At the heart of a mother's arrangements is a "home." A home may consist of several families, of all the women and children of a community, of one mother in one room with several children, of a male and female parent and their children, of two or more men or women together, who may or may not be lovers. Whatever its particular structure, a home is the headquarters for a mother's organizing and a child's growing. Home is where children are supposed to return when their world turns heartless, where they center themselves in the world they are discovering.

A mother's hope is that she, along with responsible people in her community, can make a home happy and stable enough to allow a child to grow naturally. Since nature itself promises to heal and make whole, preservative love would then be sufficient for growth. Unfortunately, even in "happy" homes and responsible communities, a child's world is continually destabilizing. Minor and major illnesses, adult projects and passions, disappearing pets, failed exams, horror shows on TV, harmful friends, and cruel teachers disrupt children's lives and the best maternal plans for them. And, moreover, homes are not, predictably, happy. There is nothing in the mere presence of children to immunize adults from vicious and harmful behavior. Mothers and other adults at home can turn violent and abusive, sicken and die, or become addicted to drugs, enthralled with jealousy and ambition, or embittered by failure. Even when homes are good enough, children sabotage the best arrangements made in their interests. Although children are delightfully, wildly different from each other, any child can be furious, depressed, inhibited, lonely, terrified, nasty, or withdrawn despite a mother's best efforts. Children do not simply receive the world that is offered. They interpret, welcome or reject, cooperate or withdraw. The happiest home is replete with the passionate rivalries, fears, disillusions, and angers characteristic of childhood life.

Sometimes a mother simply becomes exhausted, finding herself unable to attend to a "difficult" child. Anger or a sense of helplessness and failure can join with fatigue to create a temporary paralysis of will. All mothers sometimes fail to identify children's needs and to respond to needs that they recognize. Sometimes a mother must make herself look away; like the scrutinizing gaze of protection, the attentive eye of nurturance can be intrusive. Whether she acts out of self-restraint or is paralyzed by overwhelming circumstances, a mother may turn away, only later to believe or be told, like the narrator of "I Stand Here Ironing," that her attending presence was necessary.

She did not get well. She stayed skeleton thin, not wanting to eat, and night after night she had nightmares. She would call for me, and I would rouse from exhaustion to sleepily call back: "you're all right, darling, go to sleep, it's just a dream," and if she still called, in a sterner voice, "now go to sleep, Emily, there's nothing to hurt you." Twice, only twice, when I had to get up for Susan anyhow, I went in to sit with her.

Now when it is too late (as if she would let me hold and comfort her like I do the others) I get up and go to her at once at her moan or restless stirring. "Are you awake, Emily? Can I get you something?" And the answer is always the same: "No, I'm all right, go back to sleep Mother."[6]

The work of fostering growth is not essentially unhappy. Children themselves, with support from the playground, woods, or classroom, come to a mother's aid with a high-spirited resilience. They reward their mothers efforts by learning, making friends, and sleeping through the night. Some children seem born to flourish. But no one should take lightly or lightly undertake the work of fostering growth. Like the narrator of "I Stand Here Ironing," the person who assumes responsibility for identifying and responding to children's needs, who attempts to nurture their developing spirit, risks guilt, self-doubt, and tormenting, "engulfing" questions: What could have been done differently? What could not be helped? What now can make it right?

I stand here ironing, and what you asked me moves tormented back and forth with the iron.

"I wish you could manage the time to come in and talk with me about your daughter. I'm sure you can help me understand her. She's a youngster who needs help and whom I'm deeply interested in helping."

"Who needs help." Even if I came, what good would it do? You think because I am her mother I have a key, or that in some way you could use me as a key? She has lived for nineteen years. There is all that life that has happened outside of me, beyond me.

And when is there time to remember, to sift, to weigh, to estimate, to total? I will start and there will be an interruption and I will have to gather it all together again. Or I will become engulfed with all I did or did not do, with what should have been and what cannot be helped.[7]

A Metaphysical Attitude: Welcoming Change

Whatever mix of happiness and sorrow it brings, a commitment to fostering growth expands a mother's intellectual life. Routines of responsibility, exhausting work, and, for some, the narrowing perspectives of a particular profession or academic discipline conspire to undermine most mothers' — and most adults' — active mental life. But children are fascinating. Even as caring for children may reawaken a mother's childhood conflicts, in favorable circumstances her children's lively intellects rekindle her own. The work of fostering growth provokes or requires a welcoming response to change.

If the child who is kept safe sometimes seems to be endangered and slipping away, it is the same child who, as she grows, seems to be purposively moving away. A nurturing mother must at the same time hold close and welcome change. This welcoming attitude, comparable to the humility of preservative love, is the most exigent intellectual demand on those who foster growth. Children are expected to change; rapid conversions, shifts of interests, new loves and sudden hates are part of childhood life, however unsettling they may be for a mother who may wish to count on yesterday's friendship or passionate ambition. Mothers also change. Contrary to myth, a mother is not a fixed buoy around which her children circle. Most mothers are young. Any mother has a developing, changing nonmaternal life of her own — however much she may fear it is buried by the demands of mothering. Children reawaken in their mothers earlier childhood conflicts that can be resolved only through psychological change. Even the most stable mother has to change her strategies of mothering in response to her children's changes. In the words of psychologist Jean Baker Miller, a woman who is welcoming learns "to live for change":

People who are most attuned to psychological growth are those most closely in touch with it, those who are literally forced to keep changing if they are to continue to respond to the altering demands of those under their care. For an infant and then a child to grow there must be someone who can respond to the child. As the child grows, one's responses must change accordingly. What sufficed today will not suffice tomorrow. The child has come to a different place, and the caretaker must move to another place too. If you are the caretaker you keep trying to do so. Thus in a very immediate and day-to-day way women *live* for change.[8]

As Miller points out, those who change with change and welcome its challenges acquire a special kind of learning. What one learns on one day or in one phase of a child's life cannot be applied exactly, often not even by analogy, to a new situation. If science agrees to take as real the reliable results of repeatable experiments, its learning is quite different in kind from maternal learning. Miller herself believes that maternal experience with change and the kind of learning it provokes will help us to understand the changing natures of all peoples and communities. It is not only children who change, grow, and need help in growing. We all might grow — as opposed to simply growing older — if we could learn how. For everyone's benefit, "women must now face the task of putting their vast unrecognized experience with change into a new and broader level of operation."[9]

Some mothers — probably all mothers sometimes — resent changes that they perceive as threatening to their arrangements and to the children themselves. As children change and live more privately and separately, most mothers feel a sense of loss, whatever their pleasure may be in the adult child that is emerging. In middle classes of the United States, clichés of popular therapy about "overdependent mothers" "wrapped up" in their children often shame a mother into denying her feelings of loss. In this way, the dominant culture obscures even the existence, and certainly the difficulty, of the maternal task of letting a child grow into her life — which also means growing away.

Despite such psychological conflicts and social pressures, many mothers may recognize the difficulty of changing with their own and their children's changes. Recognizing the ability to welcome change as a governing maternal ideal, they strive to look anew at their children and at themselves. Both the ideal and a successful effort to fulfill it are exemplified in Audre Lorde's account of her changing relation to her son's fear and to her pride in her own hard-won toughness in the face of bullying and bigotry.

And no, Jonathon didn't have to fight if he didn't want to, but somehow he did have to feel better about not fighting. The old horror rolled over me of being the fat kid who ran away, terrified of getting her glasses broken.

About that time a very wise woman said to me, "Have you ever told Jonathon that once you used to be afraid, too?"

The idea seemed far-out to me at the time, but the next time he came in crying and sweaty from having run away again, I could see that in some way he felt shamed at having failed me, or some image he and I had created in his head of mother/woman. This image of being able to handle it all was bolstered by the fact that he lived in a household with three strong women, his lesbian parents and his forthright older sister. At home, for Jonathon, power was clearly female. . . .

I sat down on the hallway steps and took Jonathon on my lap and wiped his tears. "Did I ever tell you about how I used to be afraid when I was your age?"

I will never forget the look of that little boy's face as I told him the tale of my glasses and my after-school fights. It was a look of relief and total disbelief, all rolled into one.[10]

The capacity to change with and through a child's changes requires an attitude that is, in traditional terms, a philosophical position. To understand her child, a mother needs to assume the existence of a partly conscious, continuous mind. This mind is not a substance separate from the body and interacting with it. The mental expresses itself physically; the physical is mentally interpreted. Nor is the "mind" separate from feeling. Children's thoughts and perceptions are infused with feeling, and their world is revealed to them through their own and others' fears and desires.

It is not the usual dualisms — mind/body, mind/feeling — that I allude to when I attribute to a mother a belief in her child's continuous mental life. Rather, I mean to contrast her view with one that would take a child's *behavior* as sufficient for understanding and responding to him. And I suggest that a mother striving to understand a child cannot assume that his experience is irreducibly episodic, disconnected, and fragmented. On the contrary, as a mother tries to make sense of her child's actions, she assumes that he is moved by interdependent perceptions, feelings, and fantasies and by multiple, potentially unifying acts of responding and interpreting. A child hears in fear, defends himself against what he heard, denies what he has seen or runs from it, is ashamed or relieved or thrilled. Such scenarios structure a child's behavior, and a mother assumes their existence in positing for her child a coherent experience.

To attribute a coherent mental life to a child is not to assume that she possesses a unified self, "a little God who inhabits [her]" waiting to come out.[11] As children try on shifting identities, their ability to create a self is inextricably and often painfully mixed with others' ability to recognize the self they are creating. A "self," however fixed and personal it may seem, is always in the process of being socially constituted. Mothers themselves often suffer from a sense of fragmentation as they experience, within and between their homes and more public places, rapid shifts of power and powerlessness, recognition and invisibility, nearly awesome love and routine contempt. They are unlikely to attribute to their children a metaphysically coherent self established in advance. What they do recognize and presume in their nurturing is a child's efforts to create coherence and the shame and confusion he feels when he and the world together cannot find a satisfactory identity.

In assuming their continuous mentality, mothers construe their children as constructive agents of their world and their life in it. A child's natural intellect is not passive, but, again like the "nature" Evelyn Fox Keller envisions for a genderless science, "generative and resourceful . . . complex and abundant . . . an active partner in a reciprocal relation" to the people fostering that nature's development.[12] From the first screaming fit, through inexplicable sullenness, to manic ambition (1,000,000 baseball cards) through adolescent despair, mothers ask: Just what *is* that child thinking up? Often mothers are looking less for quick answers to these questions than for a chance to talk. Indeed, the too quickly helpful friend turns off conversation rather than satisfying the need for it. Moreover, it is often a mother's task to let a child keep her mind to herself. No child (or, for that matter, no mother or other adult) should be deprived of the rich and secretive mystery and, more prosaically, the self-respect that comes with having a private life.

Yet a mother cannot simply leave a child alone with her constructions, to "stew in her own juices," as one kindly teacher once put it to me. She needs to know what her children are up to if she is to protect them effectively, ward off distortions and inhibitions that beset their developing spirits, and seek counsel and consolation when they are troubled and neither she nor the best of her arrangements seems sufficient to help. Although "privacy" is part of mental life, a developing spirit, in connection with others, has to participate in forms of life that are shared. As much as a child needs his "secrets" and the pleasure of silence, he also needs to speak and confide. There are many ways in which a mother makes herself into a trustworthy listener. One of the most important is that she lets her child know she wants to understand.

Abstract and Concrete Thinking

As she practices her understanding of a child's mind, a mother comes to develop a cognitive capacity for "concrete" thinking, which is called forth by and enables the work of fostering growth. Concreteness is opposed to "abstraction" — a cluster of interrelated dispositions to simplify, generalize, and sharply define. To look and then speak concretely is to relish complexity, to tolerate ambiguity, to multiply options rather than accepting the terms of a problem. Because feminists (including me) often speak, albeit abstractly, against abstraction and because researchers reveal that many women are almost repelled by abstraction, it is worth dwelling a moment on this point.

A well-known dilemma used by Lawrence Kohlberg[13] in constructing his theory of moral development and later criticized by the feminist psychologist Carol Gilligan can be used to draw the contrast between concreteness and abstraction. A man, Heinz, has a wife who is dying. The only pharmacist in town has a costly drug that will help her. The man cannot afford the druggist's price (which in some versions represents a considerable markup), and the druggist refuses to sell it cheaply or to donate the drug. Should the man steal the drug? If so, what are the general principles that justify his choice? The first step in taking this problem abstractly is to accept its terms. Alternatives are sharply defined: to steal or not to steal. This sharpness also characterizes some answers that are standardly proposed by the people presented with the dilemma. For example, respondents typically cite the principle that a life is worth more than property.

When a dilemma is abstractly defined and its abstractions accepted, the listener is not meant to consider alternatives that fall outside the stated terms. It is as if no social or personal options exist — the husband can't talk to the druggist, the wife doesn't consider going to a public hospital where drugs are available. (Oddly, the wife in this dilemma has nothing at all to say about her husband's decision on her behalf.) Nor is there any mention of consequences. Respondents aren't meant to ask what will happen to Heinz, what legal or psychological or moral trials he will undergo if he steals or lets his wife die. Nor may anyone ask what it means to the druggist to hold a monopoly on medicines that people need. Stealing or not stealing is abstracted from the context in which it arises, a socioeconomic system that sanctions a druggist's greed, a medical establishment that makes exaggerated claims for a drug's effectiveness, a family system in which one individual husband is finally responsible for his spouse's health.

Most people who deal with the dilemma recognize it as "unreal." Under what circumstances would an individual be stealing a single dose of a miracle drug to cure an advanced state of cancer outside of a hospital? As I have often repeated in exasperation to students who raised this kind of objection, these are *meant* to be hypothetical, artificial dilemmas. Psychologists use them to rate their subjects' development. I repeat them to elicit principles of moral reasoning. In both cases, the first step for the listener is to accept the terms. In one of Carol Gilligan's studies of moral development, eleven-year-old Amy, asked whether Heinz should steal, refuses to play the game:

Well, I don't think so. I think there might be other ways beside stealing it. Like if he could borrow the money or make a loan or something.[14]

Amy doesn't get it. She doesn't realize that the dilemma is meant to foreclose options, so that no "extraneous" considerations blur the picture.

If we keep in mind Kohlberg's dilemma and the kinds of thinking it requires, the capacity to abstract becomes clearer. To abstract is to simplify complexity, in particular to reduce the manifold issues of moral life into dichotomous choices — to steal or not to steal — which can then elicit general principles — such as life over property. Concreteness requires inventing alternatives even when there seem to be none, looking closely at what is happening, talking to the druggist or to the wife, asking hard questions: will the drug really help? why in this town or country would these choices ever have to be made? To think concretely is to refuse to "get it," to accept abstraction's terms. Given the value that is placed on abstraction in academic life, concreteness can become a combative insistence on looking, talking, and asking troublesome questions.

It is widely believed that women have a cognitive style distinctly more concrete than men's. Women have been said to value open over closed structures, to eschew the clear-cut and unambiguous, to refuse sharp divisions between self and other or outer world and inner experience. To use familiar terms, women's thinking has been called "holistic," "field-dependent," "open-ended." Recently, Carol Gilligan and her co-workers, especially Kay Johnston, and the *Women's Ways of Knowing* collective have made these claims more precise by eliciting women's responses to moral dilemmas, especially those made up by women themselves.[15] Although women are able to reason abstractly, they tend to reject the demands of abstraction and instead look closely, invent options, refuse closure. They learn to value "connected" ways of conversing and to ask about the circumstances in which a person comes to believe and the consequences of that belief in her life. This way of knowing requires a patient, sympathetic listening to the complexities and uncertainties of another's experience quite unlike the acceptance of the given terms required for abstraction.

If concrete cognition does indeed make up one strand of the suppressed and developing different voices attributed to women, we might look to women's maternal work as a partial explanation of this epistemological predilection. It seems a plausible working hypothesis that children's minds would call forth an open-ended, reflective cognitive style in those who try to understand them. A child's acts are irregular, unpredictable, often mysterious. A child herself might be thought of as an "open structure," changing, growing, reinterpreting what has come before. Neither a child nor, therefore, the mother understanding her can sharply distinguish reality from fantasy, body from mind, self from other. The categories through which a child understands the world are modified as the changing world is creatively apprehended in ways that make sense to the child. If there are comfortably sharp definitions, they are emphemeral. A mother who took one day's conclusions to be permanent or invented sharp distinctions to describe her child's choices would be left floundering.

Although I am not qualified to assess psychological data, as a young mother I experienced a disconcerting gulf between the kinds of thinking required of me at home and those I engaged in "outside." Philosophical discussion is of course abstract and is meant to be. More striking is the way in which people govern their allegedly "personal" relations abstractly, letting disconnected, rule-dominated "fairness" override care and sympathy. During those early years as a mother, it never occurred to me that mothering might offer distinctive epistemological perspectives. Some years later I wrote that the richness of my maternal life made "the clever academic world, with its exhibitionism, defensiveness, and self-preoccupation, seem like a heightened version of elementary school."[16] At the time, however, I accepted as "adult" and "professional" the mindless procedures that did not serve teachers, students, or the life of the mind. I accepted the terms, I "got it," or, to the extent I didn't, I blamed myself for my alienation.

Whatever their other benefits, psychological tests themselves abstract from the daily course of intellectual life. Abstract and concrete moments of thought cannot be sharply distinguished, even though one or other mode may be dominant in some people's thinking. To accept as a working hypothesis that mothering tends to elicit, and women tend to reveal, a markedly concrete cognitive style is not to say that either mothers or women are unable to think abstractly. Although extensive concrete cognition may induce a certain distaste for abstraction, women, and among them mothers, have shown themselves fully capable of abstract thinking. The virtues of abstraction and concrete cognition vary with the contexts of thinking. Abstract hypothetical dilemmas can clarify urgent moral issues. In our family, they certainly make for lively mealtime conversations.

I feel it necessary to make these points because of claims that are frequently made, and that I have endorsed, about women's ways of knowing on the one hand and the deleterious uses to which abstraction can be put on the other. I believe that abstract rules of fairness badly serve the institutions that rely on them to structure personal relations or to resolve moral issues. In practice, abstract "fairness" is often a cover for manipulations and aggrandizements that even minimally honest concrete attentiveness would reveal. Several philosophers have claimed, as I will later, that abstraction is central to militarist thinking. Indeed, strategic plans and worst-case scenarios of defense intellectuals can make the Heinz dilemma seem like a maternal rumination. But however suspicious I am of relying on abstraction, there is no doubt that abstract thinking is often useful for mothers, is of some value in any disciplined thinking, and is central to scientific, mathematical, and philosophical writing.

Maternal Stories

Partly because it is believed that women think concretely, concrete cognitions sometimes appear as defective thought or thoughtlessness. Actually, the reflectiveness of concreteness must be developed through disciplined attentiveness and then expanded and tested through critical conversational challenge. In gossip and focused conversations, mothers refine their capacity for concrete ways of knowing, practicing together attentive noticing and disciplined reflectiveness about what they notice. Maternal conversations are important instruments of self-confidence. In their storytelling, mothers share and elaborate their observations, making a coherent, often amusing, dramatic, or poignant story of their children's particularities. Individually and collectively, they rehearse their judgments and establish continuities in their ongoing nurturing activities. Ideally, a mother's stories are as beneficial to her children as they are to her. As she pieces her children's days together, a mother creates for herself and her children the confidence that the children have a life, very much their own and inextricably connected with others.

Children love to hear stories that tell of their astonishing changes and remind them of reassuring continuities. Well into their twenties they ask about who they were, before they can remember, before they could write or play basketball or fell in love. Through good stories, mothers and children connect their understandings of a shared experience. They come to know and, to a degree, accept each other through stories of the fear, love, anxiety, pride, and shame they shared or provoked. Children are shaped by — some would say imprisoned in — the stories they are first told. But it is also true that storytelling at its best enables children to adapt, edit, and invent life stories of their own.

The principal virtues of maternal stories are *realism, compassion,* and *delight.* Like politicians, mothers and children, through editing and inventing, tell stories they can live with. Ideally they are creative historians who learn what politicians often forget: overediting destroys a story's usefulness. Children themselves insist that adults stop prettying up: they heard the fight, saw the embrace, watched the whiskey disappear. It would in any case be unwise of a mother to deny or seriously distort the less flattering episodes of a child's life or of adult personalities. When falsely cheerful, overedited stories, are taken to heart, they make for false selves. Moreover, a child can make use of maternal narratives only if she believes her mother is a trustworthy narrator.

Although they identify realism as a virtue of stories, mothers also find it necessary to edit in the interests of a truth that is caring. Children cannot rely on stories if, because of secretiveness or denial, they are riddled with inconsistencies and silly cheeriness. Yet many of the details of adults' emotional lives — sexual liaisons, economic reverses, serious illnesses — may be beyond a child's emotional or intellectual grasp. It requires judgment to know what and how much to tell. Even without deliberate concealment, given the mysteriousness of adult life to children's eyes, it is impossible to avoid the appearance of secrecy and privileged information. Tantalized by what they don't know, inventively constructing their world, children easily arrive at distorted stories. If children are to share and correct their stories, they will need to trust the good will as well as the truthfulness of the maternal narrator.

For a child to be able to trust them, maternal stories should include mothers' and children's anger, their mutual or separate failure, their regret, loss, and shame. *All* people are moved by fear, lust, anger, cruelty, and the desire to dominate, by what Simone Weil called "natural movements of the soul" and likened to laws of physical gravity.[17] This is not to deny that the soul is also blessed by "grace" or that children have what Weil called an erotic hungering for goodness. But mothers can ill afford to deny the myriad self-aggrandizing, self-deceiving, self-consoling operations of childhood — or for that matter maternal — life. They have to teach their children to remember and to forgive if their stories are to be of use.

However realistic they are, maternal stories should also be compassionate.[18] The compassionate narrator sympathizes with her characters' difficulties, including moral ones. While she sees imperfection or bad luck as human, rather than a peculiarity of her child, she is not a fatalistic bystander. Compassion implies the willingness to act — to search for ways to come to a person's aid, devising strategies for reversing failures while forgiving or including those who fail. Compassionate narrators need not conceal their own or their subjects' anger. Many maternal stories are witty and sharp. Indeed, maternal narrators may be tempted to indulge in a sarcasm inappropriate for children. But whatever anger a compassionate narrator includes in the plot or the telling, she also reveals that she is on her child's side — even when he seems his own enemy — and that she judges generously and would, if she could, make his world happier. Children who learn about themselves through compassionate stories may develop a maternal generosity toward their lives, learning from their mothers the capacity to appreciate the complex humanness of their plight, to forgive themselves as they have been forgiven.

Although trustworthy narrators must be realistic, and realism often requires compassion, the primary mood and virtue of a maternal narrator is delighted admiration for a child's accomplishments and shared pleasure in her pleasures. It might seem that delight in their children would come too easily to mothers to count as virtue. To be sure, we admire mothers' capacity to delight in children who are "failing" or "disabled" by conventional standards. It is less obvious that mothers need to school themselves to delight in "normally" thriving children. Yet delight is often a disciplined response.

When children are very young, it often takes patient curiosity even to identify the accomplishment of which they are proud. Later, it requires imaginative generosity — not to mention "time out" in the midst of other duties and pleasures — to appreciate what children present: one-act plays, rock collections, magic tricks, surprise parties. With older children, aesthetic incomprehension of "strange" tastes and appearances may pervasively inhibit delight. Moral difference can paralyze a mother's efforts to delight in her late adolescent children's sexual, political, social, or intellectual life. With children of any age, perfectionism can crush a mother's capacity to appreciate herself or her child. Mothers are not free from competitiveness with their children or from resentment, fear of high spirits, and a host of other emotions that could stand in the way of delight. Mothers often know this, I believe. Repeated stories, scrapbooks, and pictures inscribe publicly a mother's delight so that it can become part of a child's sense of herself, surviving the daily preoccupations, resentment, narrowness, anger, and competitiveness of the mother herself.

I believe that many mothers more or less consciously recognize the importance of good maternal narratives and identify realism, compassion, and delight as among their stories' virtues. As I said earlier, to identify a virtue is not to possess it but to identify a struggle. As they talk to and about their children, mothers often fail to resist many temptations: they deny their own confusion and children's failure, punish or pity rather than sympathize, manipulate or prematurely console rather than speak truthfully, delight too halfheartedly and too late out of self-preoccupation or perfectionism. If mothers count realism, compassion, and delight as virtues of the stories they tell, then they recognize and set themselves to resist such temptations. By listening to mothers assess and correct themselves, onlookers can get a sense of what mothers are trying to do and therefore of the many ways they fail as well as succeed.

I believe that mothers can be heard telling and revising their stories in the light of the virtues I've identified. I also believe that many mothers only partially and slowly identify realism, compassion, and delight as maternal virtues. Even if they have identified these virtues, a habit of good maternal storytelling is, for many mothers, a rare and fragile achievement. Often, a mother finds that the story she would tell of her own and her children's lives is overwhelmed by what she perceives as others' greater knowledge or "expertise." Freudian psychoanalytic theory, with its clear phases, stages, dramas, and "interpretations," can cause a mother to question how well she knows herself and her child and understands their shared history. Heroic national or political sagas stir grand feelings in a child while leaving unarticulated the smaller, intense emotions of his own life. These and many other public stories illuminate and inspire. But no public story can substitute for the story of a child in her world. It is this story that no expert or patriot should drive underground.

Learning to make up, share, and revise good maternal stories is a social project. Many mothers are cut off from other mothers, because they do their mothering work in isolation or because they are driven by competition or inhibited by self-doubt or simply because they are exhausted. They do not have the company in which shared stories can be collectively judged and improved. To be sure, mothers spend long, often sleepless, nights wondering about their stories and the effect they have on their children. It is striking, however, that three of the women whose writings I quote in this and the last chapter — Julie Olsen Edwards, Jane Lazarre, and Audre Lorde — speak of friends responding to what we assume are their narratives. Tillie Olsen's heroine, by contrast, speaks of a counselor whose questions seem as unsettling as they are helpful, while Ann Petry's Lutie Johnson is starkly alone. Each of the women, I believe, speaks at least indirectly of the pain of maternal isolation and the need for maternal conversations.

Maternal conversations, whether with children, other mothers, or sympathetic adults, take the time that only enlightened employment policies, free and effective health services, and flexible work schedules can provide. Shared, undefensive maternal reflections assume a collectivity of mothers, engaged together in the separate or joint project of raising children. In a misogynist society that routinely misdescribes or silences the suppressed and developing voices of women, in a competitive society that adores Motherhood but barely notices maternal thinking, it is not surprising that such maternal conversations are as difficult as they are rare.

CHAPTER FIVE

Training: A Work
of Conscience?

ALTHOUGH THE VIEW that children require training seems nearly universal, there are marked disagreements among individuals and cultures about human nature, moral values, and the extent to which mothers, rather than teachers, priests, Fathers or even government officials are responsible for training. Because people hold such various views about its fundamental structure, anyone who speaks about training knows that her account is only one among many.

Underlying my discussion of training are two ideas: first, children's natures are hospitable to goodness; and second, maternal work is potentially a work of conscience. Within maternal practice, as I know it, certain views of nature and training are detrimental to mothers and children. To elicit the opposition between my own and alternative views of nature and training, I identify two struggles within maternal practice: between inauthenticity and conscience and between domination and educative control. In diagnosing what I consider seriously flawed aspects of maternal thinking, I ascribe to mothers not only a humanly ordinary failure to fulfill appropriate ideals but also, and more seriously, the articulation of ideals that dangerously misidentify what counts as "success" or "failure" in the first place. In this chapter, where I sound harshest in speaking of mothers, it is especially important to repeat that there is no failure I mention that isn't my own.

Challenges

Many mothers find that the central challenge of mothering lies in training a child to be the kind of person whom others accept and whom the mothers themselves can actively appreciate. Grace Paley's heroine Faith explains that work is a requirement for happiness and that "work" includes training children:

By work to do she included the important work of raising children righteously up. By righteously she meant that along with being useful and speaking truth to the community, they must do no harm. By harm she meant not only personal injury to the friend the lover the coworker the parent (the city the nation) but also the stranger; she meant particularly the stranger in all her or his difference, who, because we were strangers in Egypt, deserves special goodness for life or at least until the end of strangeness.[1]

Training can be invigorating and happy work. Yet for most mothers, the work of training is also confusing and fraught with self-doubt. As one young mother, Shirley Grubka, laments:

Suddenly, for example, I was to pass on values to a malleable young soul. "Pass on" was, in my case, quite a euphemism. My own ethical stance and value system were still in the process of being reconstructed after the blitz of the late sixties. I felt absolutely inadequate to the task of building a strong structure for a preschool child. I struggled painfully with every situation that called for a decision about values: Should I teach him nonviolence or the art or self-defense? Should I encourage him to question my commands or respect my need to have things done in certain ways? Should I demand that he maintain order in his room or allow him a measure of chaos? Every decision seemed to matter immensely — and to present unresolvable difficulties.[2]

The rewards of training are deeply felt, and the failures are wrenching. Yet rapidly changing and mobile societies leave a mother without guide or firm ground to walk on, surrounded by a cacophony of conflicting advice.

Attending to a child's spirit would be challenging even in the absence of demands to shape the spirit in acceptable ways. Unfortunately, the pressures to train a child to behave acceptably are coextensive with parenthood itself. Even before a baby is born, a mother is likely to daydream about the kind of person her child will become, seeing in her imagination's eye someone virtuous and accomplished. Once a child is born, the dialectic of pride, pleasure, blame, and doubt begins. Some parents read moral significance into the youngest infant's behavior — into a "friendly" smile, "fussiness," or energetic kicking. Particular behaviors are applauded or discouraged; the "good" baby is exhibited on visits and dotingly appreciated at home; the troubles of the worrisome baby are gnawed over, and the drive for moral improvement begins.

However good the baby, matters soon become more complicated. Children rarely take easily to the training mothers offer; moreover, too easy acceptance of maternal demands is, we are told, itself a cause for worry. For their part, mothers also find the demands of training personally unsettling. A mother may be prompted to self-doubt even by her daydreams about her children's future lives. For example, mothers who pride themselves on their maturity, egalitarian sympathies, or unworldly aspirations may recognize in their fantasies for their children atavistic desires to impress their parents or other charmed authorities as well as competitiveness and desires for worldly achievement they thought they had outgrown. Whatever she learns from her daydreams, inevitable conflicts with her children as well as competing demands for time of her own and "peace in the home" soon lead a mother to question her own values: What is really wrong with messy rooms? Why is it important to say thank you? Why does the ability to catch a ball or solve a math problem matter so much?

Often the dilemmas of a child's life provoke a mother to reflect on her own moral principles. Helping her child decide between lying and paying the penalty or between lying and hurting a friend, a mother reconsiders the place of truth-telling in her life. Observing children in their gangs, parties and clubs, as they rank themselves, exclude others, and create "enemies," she wonders about the hurtful hierarchies she accepts, the injuries she perpetrates. Working against her child's phobic, contemptuous, or ignorant responses to people of a different race or class or style, she confronts her own prejudice. Watching her child fail to achieve the particular excellences dear to her or her social milieu, she attempts to include new varieties of success, to reduce the cost of failure, and to place achievement in a human context. Comforting a child who has run from a fight rather than lashing out at him for his "cowardice," she asks herself what bravery and courage mean for a son, for any child? Audre Lorde speaks directly to the point:

This is the way we allow the destruction of our sons to begin, in the name of protection, and to ease our own pain. *My* son get beaten up? I was about to demand that he buy that first lesson in the corruption of power, that might makes right. I could hear myself beginning the age-old distortion and misinformation about what strength and bravery really were.[3]

Self-questioning can be invigorating for a mother, especially when her children seem to thrive under her beneficent rule. On the better days, in the better years, mothers take intense pleasure in their children's virtues and accomplishments. But even the most fortunate mothers cannot count on the comforts of maternal pride. Not all days can be terrific. All children sometimes find it hard to be happy or good, and some children seem angrily or hopelessly out of step with the world a mother offers, despite her best efforts. While many mothers sometimes thrive on the challenges children present, most of them are also sometimes plagued with shame and powerlessness. The more personally invested a mother is in her children's acceptable behavior, and therefore the more rewards she expects from her maternal work, the more angry and ashamed she will be when her influence does not have the desirable effects.

In many kinds of work — teaching, operating a complicated machine, or writing about peace — actually beginning a task relieves doubts about one's capacity or the worth of the activity. This is not the case with the work of training, where the actual experience of disciplining a child is typically fraught with divided consciousness. Some mothers are tender to their children, quick to salve their hurt feelings and to defend them against others' criticism. Training their children often means working against deep inclinations to rescue and comfort. Their self-control is as apt to fail because they are paralyzed by sympathy as because they are overtaken with anger. Other mothers hear in their own voice a self-righteousness or tyrannical impatience which, in the first cooler hour, they will regret. They, like other adults, remember from their childhood instances of unjustly coercive, obtuse, hurtful maternal power. They would like to be generously permissive where their mothers were anxious and controlling. Still other mothers, or these same mothers at other moments, are demoralized by their children's "refusal" to respond to training. Faced with behavior they can neither alter nor accept, the best they can do, short of abusively striking out, is to walk away. Like mothers paralyzed by sympathy or fear of their own anger, they wait for their children to become "naturally" good.

Unfortunately, children are not "good." They make noise, throw food, and run out of their beds at night; they torment their siblings, refuse to kiss their grandmother, and have to be forced to go to school; they seem obstinately unable to ride a bicycle, do a sum, carry a tune, be decently sociable; they can't or won't do their homework, be kind to the neighbor's child, remember their chores, and come home on time. Most children display each of these faults at some time, and many children display some of them often. To make matters worse, at least in the middle classes of the United States, mothers tend to confuse the symptoms of psychological pain and moral failure — not surprisingly, since they are blamed for both. Children who stand shyly in the background, fear their teachers, stutter and squint — children who will not be *happy* — are also not considered "good."

The passions evoked by children's undesirable behavior, especially when it seems willful, are tumultuous. Disobedience can be infuriating; infuriated mothers may shout and hit and hate; a shouting, hitting, hating mother may become bad in her own eyes. Worse still, the recalcitrance of beautiful, adored children and the infuriating yet vulnerable beloved body can be powerful stimuli to sadism. The desire to cause a child pain takes many forms, of which the desire to cause physical pain may be the least common. Nor is the desire typically accompanied by conscious erotic pleasure in the act. But even the hint of her sadistic pleasure can unnerve a mother.

If training young children is trying, living with the children one has trained has its own challenges. To be responsible for children's moral well-being means helping them to become people who will be reliably moral when they are alone or among peers. This means turning over moral initiative to the children themselves. At least in late-twentieth-century North American societies, ideas of acceptability vary from generation to generation. Whatever their parents' wishes, older children are apt to develop principles and ideals that differ from those of their parents. At some point, a mother will almost certainly hear from her children moral disagreements that she would find discomfiting even in a distantly friendly colleague. She may well have to take pleasure in achievements that to her are no achievements at all. She cannot resort to "cultural relativity" within her home to account for radical differences. Nor can she simply give up her values or keep them quiet. Her children's differences require the most demanding of a mother's many balancing acts: alongside her own strong convictions of virtues and excellence she is to place her children's human need to ask and answer for themselves questions central to moral life. This means that she has to require of herself an appreciation of alternative excellences and virtues within her own family circle and within her own heart. Struggling against her tendency to take a child's disagreement as a repudiation of her, resisting the temptation to withdraw or fight back, she may still hear the plea of even the most grown-up children: "Judge tenderly of me."[4]

To judge tenderly yet with confidence is, from the earliest years, a primary maternal task. Inevitably, a judging mother inflicts on her children varieties of psychic pain — frustration, shame, guilt, remorse, rage — and usually some physical pain as well. Even as she hurts she sets herself to enable her children to protect themselves from the hurt she causes. Conscientiousness — the ability to identify, reflect on, and respect the demands of conscience — is slow to develop and unpredictable in its growth. The capacity for guilt and shame seems necessary to developing conscientiousness. Yet these moral emotions easily take on a destructive power beyond their use. It is dangerous to let children be seen or see themselves as "bad." Moral bullying or harsh-mindedness, and the shame and guilt they produce, lead easily to anger, indifference, or uncontrollable inhibition. It becomes a maternal task to teach children ways of overcoming even the shame and regret that is maternally induced. Only if children and mothers alike know how to make amends and start again will children become both moral and able to take pleasure in themselves and their friends.

Inauthenticity and Domination

It is especially in training their children that mothers become aware of the contradictions of maternal power. Training is a matter of intervention and control: a mother decides what behavior to allow, insist on, or ignore and then tries to shift her child's behavior in the direction she desires. When she adopts particular techniques for getting her children to do what she has decided they must do, the effects of her power are visible. A slap, harsh word, even a look can cow or enrage; demands can shape a child's day; rewards and punishments can shape their emotions. Making decisions, manipulating behavior, palpably affecting children's moods — these are all exercises of power. This real power should be distinguished from the nearly magical omnipotence that children and some critics ascribe to mothers to shape their children's and even their nation's lives.

For it is abundantly clear that mothers' real power is severely circumscribed. A mother's feelings often limit her ability to act. A disciplining mother in the grip of impatience, disgust, or despairing passivity can find the whole of her energies used up in the self-restraint necessary for *not* acting or *not* leaving the scene. Children's complicated psyches and recalcitrant wills time and again make nonsense of a mother's best-conceived strategies. Moreover, a mother's daily power to make or to implement decisions is brooked by the world — by the people, policies, institutions, or natural happenings that contradict her values and disciplinary strategies. A Father who can't stand noise, a store manager who temptingly displays candy at the checkout, a teacher who insists on a particular pace of learning checked by competitive tests, a government that will not or cannot fight youth unemployment, a defense department that decides whether, when, and where her children will be forced to kill — these and other outsiders deny mothers a world in which maternal training can effectively yield the excellences and virtues for which it strives. Children's unpredictable, independent wills, mothers' feelings, and the world's obstacles always limit mothers' effectiveness. The limit cuts more sharply in training because disciplining mothers appear to be exercising power and are extravagantly blamed or praised for the apparent results of their efforts.

To complicate matters still further, mothers are often expected to relinquish the power they do have and are blamed if they do not. To free themselves from "infantile" dependency and "excessive" intimacy with their mothers, children must submit to and later internalize the Law of the Father. Hence, separation of children from mothers means separation from maternal authority. To be sure, mothers are meant to train children in the conventional behavior acceptable to their social and cultural group. If a child doesn't know how to dress, act politely, play happily, and pass to the next grade in school, her mother will probably be blamed. But when morality turns "serious," it is the Father's will that must be placated, the public Law of the Fathers that holds sway. Indeed, mothers often school themselves to trust Fathers and their emissaries, believing that they are *meant* to determine not only the fundamental discipline of a child's life but also the larger public issues for which it is a preparation. Children's lives will be profoundly affected by policies about what freedoms ordinary folk are allowed, when and whom they are required to kill, or what conditions of work and what dispensation of its products are just. But these are not maternal matters, except perhaps for a mother who, in her professional guise, has herself become an emissary of the Fathers. In short, ultimate authority belongs to Fathers; whenever they conflict, maternal power is meant to submit to paternal authority.[5]

Beset by the difficulties of her work, the recalcitrance of her children, much inappropriate praise and blame, and the real limitations of her power, a mother is apt to become fearfully susceptible to the "gaze" of others.[6] Teachers, grandparents, mates, friends, employers, even anonymous passersby can judge a mother by her child's behavior and find her wanting. Often I have heard mothers ward off the gaze of others — correcting their child loudly for small infractions, for instance, so that observers know she is really trying. Under the gaze of others, mothers punish behavior they would otherwise gently correct and accept blame for "failures" that, in private, they would not recognize as such. Relinquishing authority to others, they lose confidence in their own values and in their perception of their children's needs.

This loss of confidence and integrity should not be surprising. Most mothers are young women. They may never have been encouraged to reflect on the values of the group that they are now to pass on to their children. Advice from experts, widely varying moral perspectives of other mothers, teachers' disapproval, and the complexity of her children's responses conspire to undermine the confidence she may have developed. Whatever the causes of self-disrespect, its price is high. Children are betrayed by mothers whose judgment and loyalty they have learned to trust; mothers accept policies detrimental to their own and their children's interests; both mother and child are confused by the discrepancy between the private and the public mother, the powerful, confident mother rendered confused and powerless by the gaze of others.

I call this particular kind of self-loss the "abdication" of maternal authority. This abdication should not be confused with that in another situation, in which a mother is rendered powerless in her children's eyes because she is treated with contempt. Fathers, landlords, welfare workers, teachers, therapists, playground supervisors, and numerous other authorities can and do insult mothers, even in front of their children. The abdication I speak of exists when a mother hides from her child her real feelings and the realities of the power situation as she sees them. The abdicating mother talks as if the authorities are legitimate, as if their will should be obeyed. Abdication can take many forms. Sometimes mothers invoke external authority in the hope of buttressing their own: wait til Daddy comes home; I'll tell your teacher; the police will get you. At other times mothers convey their loss of self-respect through a fearful tone of voice or a posture of timidity in the presence of authority. At the worst, mothers take the authority's side against their children, abjuring maternal understanding or requiring their children to suppress a lively sense of injustice done to them or their friends.

The influence of the gaze of others can be difficult to determine; the same remark can be heard in many ways. "Don't put that in your essay, the teacher will be angry" can be an uncoercive prediction of consequences that leaves a child free to act on his own interpretations. Or it may be a timid mother's manipulative attempt to ensure that the child pleases the teacher. "After what she did, the principal had to kick Ann out of class" may express a mother's honest assessment. Or she may be taking the principal's side so that her own daughter will not be tempted to rebel. Turning her authority over to someone else, thereby masking her anger and impotence, leaves a mother free to comfort and protect. A mother herself may not know when she is relinquishing her authority to another, using outside authority to buttress her own, or sacrificing her own and her children's sense of justice to expediency.

Fear of the gaze of others can be expressed intellectually as "inauthenticity," a repudiation of one's own perceptions and values. Inauthentic mothers construct, before the eyes of their children, a world in which maternal values do not count. Although they teach appropriate behavior, the purposes of that behavior is not theirs to determine. Abdicating their authority, they replace for themselves and their children the idea of conscience with that of submission. They identify unquestioning obedience as a virtue and dominant people as the authorities to be obeyed. They accept the injunction "travaillez pour l'armée"[7] ("work for the army"), allowing others — Fathers, experts, managers, "leaders" — to determine the uses to which children will be put.

Inauthenticity is an attitude that admits of degrees. Mothers experience typical progressions from occasional submission to the habit of submitting to a principled defense of submission that has become habitual. Occasions for a mother's submission are many. A mother may refuse to let her child watch a particular TV program but simply walk away when the Father gives permission. She may sympathize with her son's desire to study ballet but submit to "expert" advice about his "masculinity." She may see that competitive testing corrupts and inhibits students whether they score high or low yet tell herself that the school knows best. She may believe an employer exploits and humiliates her child yet insist that he is only demanding his due. She may hate wars in general or despise a particular war policy yet urge her son to register because "the law" requires that he do so.

In each case, a mother may believe that she is bowing to reality in the interests of her child. She may regret the necessity to comply or may chastise herself for her own timidity in the face of authority. Mothers are no more — and no less — blessed with stamina and gifted in courage than other women and men. It is not when they submit or are prudent or timid that mothers are inauthentic. It is when they lose sight of the cost of prudence, deny their timidity, and tell their children that unquestioning obedience is actually right. Inauthenticity is a matter of form, not content. "Fathers know best," whether they are pacifists or militarists; "Psychologists say," whether what they say is sexist, egalitarian or actively feminist. When she thinks inauthentically a mother valorizes the judgment of dominant authorities, letting them identify virtues and appropriate her children for tasks of their devising. It is these authorities — some good, some evil, most ordinarily flawed — who determine the limits of moral reflection, deciding when questioning must come to an end and acceptance begin. They say what harms are necessary, what lying is permissible, which excellences are praiseworthy and for whom. It becomes the task of a mother to train her children in the ways and desires of unquestioning obedience to "them."

As I write these words, I feel their cruelty. Mothers cannot let their children continually get into trouble with people who have the power to hurt them and to withhold what they need. Moreover, most mothers have pitifully little power to fight the interests of armies that they as well as their children serve. Most mothers are women, and most women live in societies in which they are relatively powerless with respect to men and to public officials and experts of both sexes. Self-contempt and self-loss are understandable, predictable responses to demoralizing, frightening social and psychological violences perpetrated against women and, for many women, against people of their race or culture. It is a struggle for women to make their own viewpoint heard, even to each other and to themselves. Some women acknowledge the effort of making maternal thinking audible. Others give up the struggle but in recognizing defeat avoid inauthenticity. It is when the struggle is denied and rendered invisible that thinking becomes inauthentic.

Although she cannot make training her children a work of conscience, a mother who submits to the gaze of others and thinks inauthentically can still be effective and kindly in the service of others' causes. In a virulent deformation of the work of training, a mother takes her children's and her own nature as an enemy. The most welcoming mothers will sometimes train themselves and their children to act against "natural" impulses. However, when nature is consistently taken as an enemy, it becomes hostile matter, subject to domination. Wills must be broken, desires subdued. What is natural, in a mother as well as her children, becomes dirty, aggressive, lustful, frightening. Maternal narratives become punitive and threatening instruments of control. Ancestral, "genetic" traits and fates shadow a child's life, imbuing ordinary peccadilloes with portentous meaning. The marvel — look what this human body can do — is replaced by fear — can this human body be controlled? The complexly developing mental life of a child is reduced to Reason and Reason to an instrument for controlling weakness and desire. Spontaneous play, sensual delights, surprising tastes and pleasures — whatever challenges a mother's control of herself or her child — are fearsome. What is natural, unruly, spontaneous, must be brought to heel. This is the fascist moment of maternal life.

The settled antagonism of treating "nature" as an enemy is at odds with the engaged, sometimes adversarial, but fundamentally respectful relation to "nature" characteristic of preservative love, and even more with the "natural" beneficence underlying growth. To make unquestioning obedience a good in itself contradicts maternal identifications of rigid or excessive control as dangerous and flouts maternal efforts to measure the limits of control in terms of the development as well as the safety of a child. Hence, when she treats "nature" as an enemy, a mother thinks against her own best thought. How is this transvaluation of values possible? How can a mother who delights in the wondrous body she protects, who nurtures a spirit she delights in, then take her child's nature as enemy?

Though more benign, a mother is similarly inconsistent when she first asserts the authority that training requires and then later relinquishes it to authoritative others. Does she *see* that gender stereotyping, humiliating conditions of work, and many other "legitimate" policies actually *hurt*? Does she suffer the pain of self-contradiction when she denies her own values and perspectives in front of her children?

The strain of consciously denying her own authority, combined with the much greater strain of knowing that she is hurting or betraying her children, would seem insupportable for a reflective mother. To be sure, some domineering mothers are incapable of nurturance and benign protectiveness; others, threatened by "unruly" desires, lose touch, at least temporarily, with their earlier welcoming attitudes. Occasionally mothers advocate openly a kind of self-blinding: "When evils are unchangeable, it is best not to look at them closely." More often, mothers exhibit telltale signs of the strains of self-deception, the edgy defensiveness of self-doubt, as they justify their tyrannies or defend their own and their children's submission to people too powerful to be challenged. But many reflective mothers, realizing that their inauthenticity and domination are at odds with their nurturance and preservative love, must suffer the kind of disharmony that Socrates found so painful:

Yet, I think, my good sir, that it would be better for me to have a musical instrument or a chorus which I was directing in discord and out of tune, better that the mass of mankind should disagree with me, and contradict me, than that I, being one, should be out of harmony with myself and contradict myself.[8]

Conscientiousness and Educative Control

Fortunately mothers need not choose between the pain of contradiction and the requirements of training. Alternative conceptions of acceptability are sometimes present and almost always latent in maternal practice. Inauthentic moments and domineering tendencies may be aspects of most mothers' experience. Often, however, mothers display a sturdy independence of mind and the courage to stand up for their children even when this means standing against Fathers they love or fear. And while domineering maternal tendencies do not disappear, they are often reliably assimilated into a work of training that views children's natures as hospitable to the virtues a mother hopes her children will attain.

Mothers may prize order and develop a sharper than ordinary sense of the value of social conventions, since they depend on stable continuities to establish conditions conducive to protection and growth. Ideally, however, they are not governed by a rage for order that unpredictable desires disrupt. Training presumes the trainer's ability to judge "natural" tastes, desires, and behavior. But judgment need not lead to battle. In hard moments, children's natures may appear as evils to be combated; then mothers will be tempted to dominate rather than to appreciatively shape them. But children's natures, like a mother's own, can be seen as capable of desiring the good. Such natures are educated, that is, they are "led out of" temptation into the virtues "naturally" awaiting them.

When acceptability is taken to demand the education of a responsive nature rather than the domination of a hostile one, then the work of training can become, in a double sense, a work of conscience: a mother aims to foster and then protect her child's conscientiousness — her ability to identify, reflect on, and respect the demands of conscience. The making of her child's conscientiousness is an exercise and discipline of her own. As a conscientious person, a mother is capable of judging against, as well as in accord with, dominant values. She does not relinquish authority to elders or urge unquestioning obedience even in good causes. Her training is not aimed only or primarily at producing pleasing behavior, important as this is for family and community life. If her children are to become conscientious people, she must help them learn that they cannot count on her own or any other person's authority. Or rather, since adults and children seek and trust the authority of others, conscientiousness requires taking responsibility for judgments of trust while maintaining a respectful independence from the authority judged trustworthy. To be sure, conscientiousness is a slowly acquired capacity. For young children, simple directions matched by willing obedience have their place. But even then, the aim of training and the authority of the trainer distinguishes the work of conscience. A mother's conscientiousness becomes a model for the child's own.

Whether she undertakes a work of conscience or trains her children in unquestioning obedience, a mother will be challenged by serious moral and aesthetic differences from her children. She can neither relinquish her own values and tastes nor take a distant stance toward her children's values, which, however alien, she believes to be in part her creation and responsibility. Nor can she deal with difference by separation — though separateness and literal distance are a help — since children and mothers cannot effectively exit from a shared, binding life. When unquestioning obedience is the primary virtue of a trained child and when pleasing behavior is the principal sign of a training's success, moral and aesthetic differences become signs of rebellion and failure. As a mother attempts to convert, tame, or dominate a child's rebellious will, it becomes almost impossible for "difference" to find a voice. When, in contrast, training is a work of conscience and a child's conscientiousness is a criterion of a training's success, mothers aim to maintain in themselves and develop in their children responsibility for reflective judgment. In aid of reflectiveness, they will likely develop conversational habits that are valuable when, despite their disappointment and incomprehension, they speak with, not at, their children. Reflective conversations allow for reinterpretation as well as revision of choices that may be disturbing to mothers. Despite temptations to mutual disavowal, mothers and children, in conversation, can experimentally and tentatively envision current options and future life prospects that are attractive to a child and acceptable to a mother, though she might never have imagined, let alone chosen, them.[9]

Developing habits of conversational reflection depends on ongoing mutual trust. When training is a work of conscience, proper trust[10] is a virtue of which unquestioning obedience or blind trust are degenerative forms. Proper trust is a relation between mothers and children for which, in the first instance, a mother is responsible. A child cannot trust a mother who is capricious, manipulative, or mean. Mothers are, of course, each of these some of the time. A trustworthy mother acknowledges these tendencies in herself and, by working against them, manages to achieve a fairly reliable, goodwilled respect for her child. This, however, is not sufficient for trustworthiness. In her children's eyes, a mother's trustworthiness is shown not only in her relation to them but in her relation to others. To be trustworthy in the world, a mother must be trusted to stand by her children reliably, not caving in to teacher, Father, or community. If she is to stand by her children she cannot put too much trust in anyone's promise to act on their behalf but rather must maintain a wary ability to judge policies and people in terms of her children's needs.

A trustworthy mother instills trustworthiness in her children. Although children may hold on to their often legitimate anger despite their mother's best efforts to reconcile and atone, trustworthy children also typically display the minimal truthfulness and goodwill that make a work of conscience possible. Their truthfulness and goodwill are in part a consequence of their mother's trust in them. If mothers forever suspect their children of mean-spirited, deceptive, manipulative behavior, their work of conscience will give way to coercive training, which is more like battle than love. On the other hand, mothers too trusting of their children do not identify their manipulative moments and cannot respond to them with the anger and hurt appropriate to trust betrayed. In that situation, children do not learn the consequences of breaking trust or what it means to be trustworthy.

If she is lucky, a trustworthy mother earns from her children a trust that in turn reinforces her ability to be trustworthy. Yet even in the best situations children should not trust their mothers absolutely. If, when their mothers fail them, as they inevitably do, children deny their hurt and rage so that they can continue "trusting," they are in effect giving up on their mothers. By contrast, when they recognize and protest betrayal, they reaffirm their expectation that their mother has been and can again become worthy of their trust. Children are vulnerable, often frightened small people. They will be capable of protesting maternal failure only if they trust their mother not to turn on them or — surrendering to guilt — on themselves. They will most likely know how to protest if they have watched their mothers struggle against their own excessive trust both of dominant people and of themselves.

Proper trust is one of the most difficult maternal virtues. It requires of a mother clear judgment that does not give way to obedience or denial. It depends on her being reliably goodwilled and independent yet able to express and to accept from her children righteous indignation at trust betrayed. Ideally, proper trust is prepared by maternal protectiveness and nurturance. It survives a mother's inauthentic moments, domineering tendencies, and evident failures to be reliable. In proper trust the separable strands of attitudes toward nature and authority come together. To see children's natures as hospitable to goodness is an act of trust; to see them or dominant persons as only good is excessive trust, blind obedience, or denial. Clearly, to identify proper trust as a virtue is not to identify an achievement but an ongoing and difficult struggle.

Attentive Love

The concept "attentive love," which knits together maternal thinking, designates a cognitive capacity — attention — and a virtue — love. It implies and rewards a faith that love will not be destroyed by knowledge, that to the loving eye the lovable will be revealed. Attentive love is prey to the self-loss that can afflict maternal thinking; indifference, passivity, and self-denial are among its degenerative forms. Attentive love is also a corrective to many defects of maternal thinking, including an anxious or inquisitorial scrutiny, domination, intrusiveness, caprice, and self-protective cheeriness.

The idea of attentive love was central to the philosophy of Simone Weil and was later developed by Iris Murdoch. I will use their words in trying to make this complex concept clear. Attention is at once an act of knowing and an act of love. In Weil's words, "The name of this intense, pure, disinterested, gratuitous, generous attention is love."[11] Attentive love, or loving attention, represents a kind of knowing that takes truthfulness as its aim but makes truth serve lovingly the person known. In Murdoch's words, it constructs "in relation to the progressive life of a person [a child]" an "objective reality," a real child but one whose reality is "revealed [only] to the patient eye of love."[12]

For both Weil and Murdoch, the enemy of attention is "fantasy." As we ordinarily use the word, "fantasy" refers to many kinds of activity conducive to mothers' and children's well-being. Nothing about daydreaming, rich imaginative play, or art goes against attentive love. By fantasy, Weil and Murdoch mean the "proliferation of blinding self-centered aims and images."[13] The word "blinding" is important. Mothers indulge in active daydreaming that they know to be vengeful, grandiose, self-pitying, or at least impossible to execute. As one friend put it:

Knowing a fantasy is unreal, and if real, forbidden, I can then indulge in it and derive strength and endurance for attention. The fantasy acts like a medicine which allows me to breathe deeper though artificially.[14]

According to Weil's and Murdoch's pejorative conception, "fantasy" is intellectual and imaginative activity that has blindly put itself in the service of consolation, domination, and aggrandizement. Fantasy is reverie designed to protect the psyche from pain, self-induced blindness designed to protect it from insight. It is the dreams one invents or is driven by to assuage pain and achieve desires, irrespective of the intentions and projects of others. Fantasy creates children to meet a mother's desires; creates an abstract plan for their lives that will fulfill a family's or nation's aims; creates a mind for the child that embraces a mother's world and a will that satisfies her desire. A mother whose vision of herself or her children was primarily a fantasy would manipulate realities in the service of that fantasy, would act capriciously, and would strike out at herself or her children when fantasy failed.

For Weil, the capacity for attention is integral to a religious quest for blessedness:

In the first legend of the Grail, it is said that the Grail . . . belongs to the first comer who asks the guardian of the vessel, a king three quarter paralyzed by the most painful wound, "What are you going through?"[15]

The ordinary secular mother also learns to ask "What are you going through?" and to wait to hear the answer rather than giving it. She learns to ask again and keep listening even if she cannot make sense of what she hears or can barely tolerate the child she has understood. Attention is akin to the capacity for empathy, the ability to suffer or celebrate with another as if in the other's experience you know and find yourself. However, the idea of empathy, as it is popularly understood, underestimates the importance of knowing another *without* finding yourself in her. A mother really looks at her child, tries to see him accurately rather than herself in him. "The difficulty is to keep the attention fixed on the real situation" — or on the real children. Attention to real children, children seen by the "patient eye of love," "teaches us how real things [real children] can be looked at and loved without being seized and used, without being appropriated into the greedy organism of the self."[16]

Weil and Murdoch explicitly recognize the lure of masochistic fantasy. Nonetheless, Murdoch occasionally and Weil repeatedly emphasize the capacity to attend to another's suffering over the equally important ability to share in the other's pleasures. A king paralyzed by a painful wound makes a poor emblem of childhood, (nor did Weil intend him to serve as one). Important as it is to acknowledge a child's pain, it is equally important and sometimes as difficult to really look at her excitements, ambitions, and triumphs, to see her quirky, delighted, determined independent being and let it be. Attention lets difference emerge without searching for comforting commonalities, dwells upon the *other,* and lets otherness be. Acts of attention strengthen a love that does not clutch at or cling to the beloved but lets her grow. To love a child without seizing or using him, to see the *child's* reality with the patient loving eye of attention — such loving and attention might well describe the separation of mother and child from the mother's point of view.

On repeated occasions, attention calls for a kind of radical self-renunciation. "The soul empties itself of all its contents in order to receive into itself the being it is looking at, just as he is, in all of his truth."[17] But such renunciation, necessary at moments, is not identical with attentive love. To court self-denial for its own sake perverts rather than expresses attentive love. Mothers are especially prone to this perversion, since they are rewarded for self-sacrifice. They are familiar with the danger of denying their own needs only to find they have projected them onto their children. A person who counts herself as nothing lacks the confidence needed to suspend her own being to receive another's. Since her emptiness is involuntary and often frightening, she searches in her child to find the self she has sacrificed. The soul that can empty itself is a soul that already has a known, respected, albeit ever-developing self to return to when the moment of attention has passed.

Weil and sometimes Murdoch come close to identifying the human spirit with a fantasy-driven mechanism, "a greedy organism." This seems wrong. Self-protective, self-consoling self-aggrandizing fantasizing is a temptation rather than the essential character of psychic life. Nor is fantasy an enemy to be crushed. The "cure" for fantasy is gentle — turning outward, welcoming what is seen, trusting the attachments that inspire as well as reward a "knowledge of the individual."[18] Attentive love is a discipline but not, as Weil would have it, a miracle. Like Murdoch, I take attention to be a familiar triumph over the allure of fantasy. "The task of attention goes on all the time and at apparently empty and everyday moments we are 'looking,' making those little peering efforts of imagination which have such important cumulative results."[19] All mothers are prey to manipulative and projective fantasy and some of the time act primarily under its sway. It is also true that mothers train themselves in the task of attention, learning to bracket their own desires, to look, imagine, and then to accept what is different. They can be heard doing so in any playground or coffee klatch.

Maternal thinking is a discipline in attentive love. Clear-sighted attachment, loving clear-sightedness, is the aim, guiding principle, and corrective of maternal thinking. However, neither attentive love nor any other cognitive capacity or virtue sufficiently epitomizes maternal work. Mothers learn to wait, but maternal waiting occurs in the context of action. The love of a child, in all its fullness, could not consist solely of being able to ask, say, or hear. To love a child is to *do* whatever is required to keep her safe and help her grow. Maternal attention is prompted by the responsibility to act and, when it is most successful, gives way to the action it informs.

Mothers could not give, nor do children need, constant attentive love. What children and mothers require of each other is proper trust. Through the discipline of attentive love, a mother tries to make herself trustworthy. By training herself to "really look," she learns to trust a child she loves and to love a real, and therefore trustworthy, child. Trusting herself and her child, she can express and hear the pain of betrayal. Children and mothers fail each other in trust, fail in attentive love, are driven by fantasy, succumb to the gaze of others, and generally reveal themselves to be the imperfect creatures they are. When they identify proper trust as a virtue and attempt the discipline of attentive love, all that they can assure is that the work of training will not become a battlefield but a hard, uncertain, exhausting, and also often exhilarating work of conscience.

PART III

Maternal Thinking and Peace Politics

Maternal Thinking as a
Feminist Standpoint

I HAVE WRITTEN of maternal thinking as if it were only one discipline among others — no ax to grind, no particular story to impose upon the many stories people tell, no meta-message in the quilt that different artists make together. To be sure, women's and mothers' voices have been silenced, their thinking distorted and sentimentalized. Hence it will take sustained political and intellectual effort before maternal thinking is truly heard. Well-intentioned generosity and space and time to speak are not enough. Nonetheless, I have envisioned a future in which maternal thinkers are respected and self-respecting without making for them/us any claims of moral and political advantage.

Temperamentally I am a pluralist. From grade school, I welcomed the idea that there were many perspectives and hence many truths. In my childhood, it was Nazis, white supremacists, and later McCarthyites who claimed to speak from a privileged standpoint. Not surprisingly, when I studied philosophy I was drawn to traditions that rejected the ambition, pervasive among philosophers, of ordering ways of knowing from the least to the most adequate. I learned that to imagine a language — or a discipline — was to imagine what Wittgenstein called a "form of life."[1] If there was no God, then there was also no philosopher who stood outside or at the beginning, giving grounds, justifying evidence, making a place for epistemological and moral certainty. Reasons begin in and ultimately end in action. To quote Wittgenstein again:

Giving grounds, however, justifying the evidence, comes to an end; but the end is not certain propositions striking us immediately as true, i.e., it is not a kind of seeing on our part; it is our *acting,* which lies at the bottom of the language game.[2]

If the statement "A child's life must be protected" strikes us as immediately true, this is because we daily act protectively and our true statement expresses as it reveals our commitment. What the sentence expresses and the commitment reveals is not only the truth that children are deserving of protection but also the form of life in which that truth is indubitable. Preservative love is a "form of life": "What has to be accepted, the given, is — so one could say — *Forms of Life.*"[3]

In feminism too I have applauded those who reject the large picture for multiple perspectives. Catherine MacKinnon, for example, expresses my epistemological stance:

Feminism not only challenges masculine partiality but questions the universality imperative itself. Aperspectivity is revealed as a strategy of male hegemony. . . . Nor is feminism objective, abstract, or universal. . . . Feminism does not begin with the premise that it is unpremised. It does not desire to persuade an unpremised audience because there is no such audience.[4]

I continue to share the epistemological prejudices of the *Women's Ways of Knowing* collective, whose members celebrate women for recognizing "that all knowledge is constructed . . . that answers to all questions vary depending on the context in which they are asked and on the frame of reference of the person doing the asking."[5]

Nonetheless, only a few years after I began writing about maternal thinking, my pluralism began to give way to angry and insistent claims of superiority. My son was reaching draft age in a country whose government was prone to invade the islands, gulfs, and governments of peoples and resources it wished to control. If conscripted, my son would serve a "defense" establishment that deliberately "targets" millions of strangers with weapons no one could survive and devises war plans that no one could live long enough to execute. I became preoccupied with the immorality — and the madness — of organized, deliberate violence. I read the works of pacifists, just-war theorists, and military historians, began teaching seminars on the choice between violence and nonviolence, joined a women's peace group, and took part in a working conference of philosophers, defense department analysts, and defense sociologists who were charged with studying conscription but often spent their time planning and remembering war. Soon I had frightened myself thoroughly. For a time I felt as if I were pathologically obsessed and hopelessly sentimental.

> I didn't raise my son to be a soldier
> I brought him up to be my pride and joy
> Who dares to put a musket on his shoulder
> To kill some other mother's darling boy?[6]

It was in this mood that I received a copy of an article by Nancy Hartsock that both developed and transformed the Marxian notion of a privileged political and epistemological "standpoint."[7] A standpoint is an engaged vision of the world opposed and superior to dominant ways of thinking. As a proletarian standpoint is a superior vision produced by the experience and oppressive conditions of labor, a feminist standpoint is a superior vision produced by the political conditions and distinctive work of women. Although the epistemological and moral values of any standpoint are obscured by dominant ideals of reason and despised by dominant peoples, subordination can be overturned through political and intellectual struggle. Even now, the vision offered by a feminist standpoint reveals that dominant ways of knowing are, in Hartsock's words, "partial and perverse."

By "women's work" — the basis for a feminist standpoint — Hartsock has in mind "caring labor": birthing labor and lactation; production and preparation of food; mothering; kin work; housework; nursing; many kinds of teaching; and care of the frail elderly— all work that is characteristically performed in exploitative and oppressive circumstances. I believe, as I argued in Chapter 2, that it is at least premature to assimilate these different kinds of work as maternal work. Nonetheless, it is certainly the case that maternal practices make up a central part of caring labor, and hence maternal thinking in its many variations could be considered a constituent element of the standpoint that Hartsock envisions. Or, to put the point romantically—adapting Foucault—maternal thinking is a "subjugated knowledge," "lost in an all-encompassing theoretical framework or erased in a triumphal history of ideas"—"regarded with disdain by intellectuals as being either primitive or woefully incomplete" yet likely to become "insurrectionary."[8]

This invigorating language is more than rhetoric. Hartsock not only proclaimed the worth of caring labor; she substantiated her claim by detailing characteristics of caring labor that were responsible for the standpoint's superiority. Caretakers are immersed in the materials of the physical world. The physical phenomena of human and other bodies must be interpreted in relation to the demands of caretaking. It is not useful to abstract to "air, earth, fire, and water," let alone to electrons. Whether care workers are cleaning toilet bowls, attending to the incontinence of dying patients, or toilet training children; whether they nurse a baby, invent a sauce, or mash potatoes thin enough to allow a toothless, elderly person to feed herself, care workers depend on a practical knowledge of the qualities of the material world, including the human bodily world, in which they deal.

This means that the material world, seen under the aspect of caring labor, is organized in terms of people's needs and pleasures and, by extension, of the needs and pleasures of any animal or plant that is instrumental in human caring or is tended for its own sake. The value of objects and accomplishments turns on their usefulness in satisfying needs and giving pleasures rather than on the money to be made by selling them or the prestige by owning them or the attention by displaying them. Finally, caretakers work with subjects; they give birth to and tend self-generating, autonomously willing lives. A defining task of their work is to maintain mutually helpful connections with another person — or animal — whose separateness they create and respect. Hence they are continuously involved with issues of connection, separation, development, change, and the limits of control.

If this characterization of caring labor sounds like the maternal practices and thinking I have described, this is not coincidental. Reading Hartsock from a perspective influenced by my own concerns, I felt as if "maternal thinking" were given both an epistemological and political base; moreover, from the time I first read "The Feminist Standpoint," my understanding of maternal practice has been deepened by Hartsock's account of the characteristics of caring labor. Even more heartening, by looking and acting from a feminist standpoint, dominant ways of thinking — and I had in mind primarily militarist thinking — were revealed to be as abstract and destructive as I suspected. This gave maternal thinking, as part of the feminist standpoint, a critical power I had not imagined.

To diagnose and account for the destructiveness of dominant modes of thought that the standpoint reveals, Hartsock constructed an account of the "abstract masculinity" that characterizes dominant views, adapting a well-known story to her purposes.[9] According to this now familiar story, in societies where young children are tended almost entirely by women, where authority and power are ascribed to men, and where independence is valued over the capacity to sustain relations of mutual interdependence,[10] young children associate with women the dependence and care they both fear and desire and the achievement of independence with masculinity. In these societies, boys and girls value masculinity, both because of its association with independence and because of its distance from fearsome, desirable female bodies and care. But boys, who are meant to become "masculine," are more apt than girls to define themselves as not-maternal-female. To a degree that girls do not, boys fortify themselves against the needs and pleasures of care that they depended on as infants and will rely on more or less intensely throughout their lives. Their incipiently misogynist fear of women and repudiation of "feminine" care is exacerbated if, as men, they are able to exploit the caring labor of others rather than undertaking it themselves.

According to this story, especially "masculine" men (and sometimes women), fearful of the physicality and needs of care, develop a fantasy of transcendence based on a "tradition of freeing the thinking brain from the depths of the most pressing situations and sending it off to some (fictive) summit for a panoramic overview."[11] From this perch they promulgate views that are inimical to the values of caring labor. They imagine a truth abstracted from bodies and a self detached from feelings. When faced with concrete sensuousness, they measure and quantify. Only partially protected by veils of ignorance that never quite hide frightening differences and dependencies, they forge agreements of reason and regiment dissent by rules and fair fights. Fearful of the dependencies in which connection begins, they become attached to detachment, developing ideals of objectivity that turn on separation and distance. Beset by needs they are ill equipped to name or satisfy and faced with an anarchically lively, caring world on which they fearfully depend, they misdescribe in abstractly sentimental or demeaning ways what they insist on labeling "women's work." At worst, from their fictive summit they deliver abstract understandings that systematically invert "the proper valuation of human experience."[12] They might, for example, accord superiority not "to the sex that brings forth but to that which kills," considering the "sacrifice" of a child in an abstract cause to be the vindication of caring labor.[13] Or, as in violent pornography and rape, they might transform "the force of life in sexuality" into fearful relations of dominance and submission.[14]

Feminist standpoint philosophers — among them philosophically minded and feminist maternal thinkers — directly oppose this "masculine" fantasy of transcendence. Their task is to redefine reason and restructure its priorities so that thoughtful people will be able to "generalize the potentiality made available by the activity of women" — i.e., caring labor — to society as a whole.[15] Since they actively participate in caring labor and therefore know firsthand the temptations, failures, and subtle intellectual challenges of their work, they will not idealize caretakers. What they have been taught by Hartsock, they will recognize daily: "[masculine] men's power to structure social relations in their own image means that women [and other caring laborers] too must participate in social relations which manifest and express abstract masculinity."[16] However alienated they are by the discrepancy between their experiences and the sentimental and abstract conceptual schemes that distort them, maternal thinkers know that they have learned to speak in the dominant languages, as do all members of a culture. To articulate maternal thinking they have had to cling to realities that they were in danger of forgetting and at the same time forge a way of thinking that is new. They will bring this heritage to the philosophical task of articulating standpoint theory, setting themselves to resist the lure of abstraction and the social rewards that "transcendence" brings. Together with other standpoint theorists, they work to articulate an engaged vision that must be "struggled for and represents an achievement."[17]

These standpoint theorists are feminists. The work that they believe should be the basis of an alternative moral and epistemological vision has been performed by women and has created "women" as they are. As feminists, standpoint theorists fight against the exploitation and abuse of women caretakers while valuing the particular knowledge that women acquire from their suffering of and resistance to oppression. But their focus is not in the first place on gender but on the work itself and the political conditions in which it is undertaken. Their attention to exploitative and unequal power does not stop artificially with men's abuse of women; many women, and not only those advantaged by attachments to privileged men, exploit the caring labor of others, usually, but not always, of other women. Men as well as women caretakers are besieged by violences and abstractions that overwhelm their vision and mock their efforts to provide and protect.

Standpoint theorists are also feminists in virtue of their political ambition to generalize the values of caring labor that are, for reasons of history, inextricably bound up with the lives and values of women. But their aim is not to create a future that is female.

In the "fully human community"[18] they envision, institutionalized gender differences of power and property disappear, replaced by inclusive playful, inventive variations on sexual identities.

Although standpoint theorists ground themselves in the values of caring labor, they reject a division of all human activities into caring labor and everything else, a division that has been so debilitating to caretakers and women. Most of what goes on in our minds and lives eludes the conceptual division between care and abstract masculinity. Standpoint theorists, like anyone else, enjoy singing, computing, storytelling, and argument and heartily commit themselves to philosophy, farming, business administration, ballet, and all other disciplines, contesting only the dominance in any discipline of abstractly masculine values. They do not, for example, give up science but limit its domain so that detachment and abstraction take their rightful place; better still, they imbue science itself with the values of care. Certainly the maternal thinkers among them have no patience with the idea that a person's identity is wholly formed by her principal work or, still more confining, by the gender identity a particular society expects. If nothing else, on the basis of their knowledge of adolescent children they assert that a rigid insistence on being either a caretaker *or* scientist, either philosopher *or* poet, either man *or* woman, is a sign of personal anxiety and social coercion. Their task, as they have learned from the work of training children, is to articulate conditions of respect for unpredictable and as yet unimagined difference and variety among and within people.

Despite their rejection of dualisms and their respect for difference, these standpoint philosophers seem very different from the Wittgensteinian pluralist who imagined maternal thinking as one discipline among others. Standpoint thinkers are ready, as the Wittgensteinian pluralist would never be, to declare that dominant values are destructive and perverse and that the feminist standpoint represents the "real" appropriately human order of life. One might say that standpoint theorists, including the maternal thinkers among them, have seen the Truth — and, indeed, many of the standpoint theorists whose invigorating work I have found indispensable seem to say just that.

Although I count myself among standpoint theorists, I do not take the final step that some appear to take of claiming for one standpoint a Truth that is exhaustive and absolute. Epistemologically, I continue to believe that all reasons are tested by the practices from which they arise; hence justifications end in the commitments with which they begin. Although I envision a world organized by the values of caring labor, I cannot identify the grounds, reason, or god that would legitimate that vision. There is, for example, nothing above or below preservative love, only the ongoing intellectual-practical acts of seeing children as vulnerable and responding to that vulnerability with a determination to protect rather than to abandon or assault.

I am also suspicious of any dualistic ordering of appearance and reality, perversion and utopia. The values of care do not stand to dominant values of abstract masculinity as the one reality stands to appearance; standpoint theorists know this, of course, but any dualistic formulations tend to reduce the richness and unpredictability both of the world and of the ways in which we think about it. I also fear that despite their stated convictions, standpoint theorists or their followers will lose sight of the failures and temptations of the caretakers they celebrate. It would then be easy to slip into a formulation of a feminine/feminist standpoint as an achievement rather than a place from which to create a sturdy, sane vision of the natural and social world. Perhaps most worrisome, being on the side of good can foster a repressive self-righteousness that legitimates killing or, alternatively, condemns violence without attending to the despair and abuse from which it arises. Directly to the point of my project, dualistic righteousness encourages a mythical division between women's peacefulness and men's wars that is belied by history and obscures the flawed, complex peacefulness that is latent in maternal practice and thinking.

In the last few years I have consciously assessed moral and political decisions in the light of the values of care and then in turn reassessed those values. I am confident that persistent efforts to see and act from the standpoint of care will reveal the greater safety, pleasure, and justice of a world where the values of care

are dominant. But I realize that for those who are not already committed to the values of caring labor, a case must be made for the moral and epistemological superiority of the kind of thinking to which it gives rise. This requires specific oppositional comparisons between particular concepts and values of caring labor and their counterparts in dominant, abstractly masculine ways of knowing — for example, comparisons of maternal and military concepts of the body and of control. These specific comparisons will reveal incrementally the superiority of the rationality of care to the abstract masculine ways of knowing that dominate our lives.

In the remainder of this book, I bring maternal thinking to bear on military thinking. As part of a feminist standpoint, I take maternal thinking to be an engaged critical and visionary perspective that illuminates both the destructiveness of war and the requirements of peace. Yet one of my principal points is that maternal thinking itself is often militarist. Like the standpoint of which it is a part, an antimilitarist maternal perspective is an engaged vision that must be achieved through struggle and change.

Accordingly, in Chapter 6, I reassess the mythical division between men's wars and women's peace. Although distinctly maternal desires and capacities for peacemaking exist, it is through maternal *efforts* to be peaceful rather than an achieved peacefulness that I find resources for creating a less violent world. In Chapters 7 and 8 I discuss ideals of nonviolence that govern some maternal practices and propose a maternal conception of birth and bodily life that symbolizes nonviolent connection. In these chapters, I repeatedly contrast maternal concepts with their military analogues. At the same time, I identify characteristics of distinctly maternal militarism and underline the limitations of maternal nonviolence. In the last chapter, I look for ways to re-create maternal practice as a sturdier, more reliable instrument of peace. I celebrate two transformative social movements, women's politics of resistance and feminism. Each movement transforms the practice of mothers who engage in it. Together, they work on the maternal imagination, inspiring new powers to know, care, and act.

I do not think maternal thinking, any more than the standpoint of which it is a part, represents a True or Total discourse. Nor

are mothers, any more than other women, the quintessential revolutionary subjects. It is enough to say that there is a peacefulness
latent in maternal practice and that a transformed maternal thinking could make a distinctive contribution to peace politics. Given
the violence we live in and the disasters that threaten us, enough
seems a feast.

A Preliminary Note About Peace

Peace, like mothering, is sentimentally honored and often secretly
despised. Like mothers, peacemakers are scorned as powerless
appeasers who are innocent of the real world. Just because mothering and peace have been so long and so sentimentally married,
a critical understanding of mothering and maternal nonviolence
will itself contribute to the reconception of "peace." Peace activists
themselves often speak of the need to create more active, robust
images of peace. One of my aims in the next four chapters is to
contribute to this task. It is not, however, only from mothering
that I gain a sense of what peace might look like. On the contrary,
as I attempt to articulate maternal struggles to become peaceful,
I implicitly assume an understanding of peacefulness derived from
reading, listening to, and observing nonviolent activists. It is the
peacefulness of nonviolent activism to which I hope mothers,
along with other women and men, can contribute and that I believe
is latent in maternal practice. The idea of peacefulness implicit in
nonviolent action is different from what is usually called pacifism.
To forestall misunderstandings, I want to clarify this difference.

Peace is not sharply distinguished from war. Wars are prepared
for in a time of "peace" that includes many violences and is often
secured by violence. One of the central tasks of peacemaking is
to identify violences wherever they occur — in boardrooms, bed-
rooms, factories, classrooms, and battlefields. Peacemakers do not
turn away from violence but ferret it out, asking in detail who is
hurt and how. Indeed, the light of imagined peace reveals to
peacemakers violations of body and spirit that are mystified,
disguised, and invisible to the realist eye. A defining characteristic

of peacemakers is their commitment to resist the violences that a lively appreciation of peacefulness reveals.

Peace requires a sturdy suspicion of violence even in the best of causes. The effectiveness of violence is repeatedly exaggerated, while its moral, social, political, economic, psychological, and physical costs are minimized or ignored. Peacemakers set themselves to reveal and count the costs while questioning, at every turn, the benefits. But — and here is the primary difference with pacifists — a sturdy suspicion of violence does not betoken absolute renunciation. Although pacifists perform an essential service among peace activists by requiring every act of violence to be critically appraised, it is unnecessary and divisive to require of all peacemakers an absolute commitment not to kill. Nor does a sturdy suspicion of violence require self-righteous condemnation of others' violent acts or a prizing of violence from historical situations such as in Nazi Germany or South Africa today. Peacemakers can remain sturdily suspicious of violence and able to count its costs in the best of causes yet refuse to judge from a distance the violent response of others to violent assault on them. Although she will never celebrate violence, a peacemaker may herself act violently in careful, conscientious knowledge of the hurt she inflicts and of its cost to her as well as her victim. Alice Walker and Jane Lazarre speak about this kind of conscientious knowledge. Alice Walker's heroine Meridean speaks from the civil rights movement:

And certainly to boast about this new capacity to kill — which she did not, after all, admire — would be to destroy the understanding she had acquired with it. Namely, this: that even the contemplation of murder required incredible delicacy as it required incredible spiritual work and the historical background and present setting must be right. Only in a church surrounded by the righteous guardians of the people's memories could she even approach the concept of retaliatory murder. Only among the pious could this idea both comfort and uplift.[19]

Jane Lazarre describes the "full knowledge" that should be part of every violent act:

The denial of ambivalence — whatever *action* one takes — is the beginning of tyranny. The soldier who said that it had been easy for him to kill was saying something not only about himself, but about the nature of war. My father fought in the Spanish Civil War — a just war if there is any just war. He said exactly the same thing to me about killing in Spain. If I were ever in a situation in which I had to kill that man who found it easy to kill Vietnamese, or the man who said he would drop a nuclear bomb tomorrow if so ordered, I would rather kill him in full knowledge of his humanity, thinking about the son he loves, the father he lost as a little boy, than to kill under the illusion that I was doing nothing more than extinguishing a butcher or a pig. It's an illusion which would accelerate my trigger finger, but stop my heart.[20]

The sturdiest suspicion of violence is of no avail to threatened peoples who do not have alternative nonviolent ways of protecting what they love and getting what they need. Thus peacemakers must invent myriad nonviolent actions and then name, describe, and support them. Whenever a collective decides to invest in the weapons and the training that organized violence requires, it is also choosing against the nonviolent alternatives. Only a people sturdily suspicious of violence will be able to hold the choice between violence and nonviolence in mind. Of these people, only those who have multiplied and strengthened strategies of nonviolent resistance and change will be able to invent the myriad actions and connections of "peace."

Although peace can be hinted at in a general vocabulary, peacemaking is always specific. Social and military violence are rooted in particular technological, economic, and military conditions, and so is resistance to them. In the United States, the plans and rhetoric of war are permeated with a distinctive blend of abstract fanaticism, professionalized bureaucracy, and complicated high technology that leaves many citizens helpless. I grope for images of peace and strategies of peacemaking responsive to this incarnation of militarism — for ways to make manifest in the United States now a maternal resource for peace.

CHAPTER SIX

Mothers and Men's Wars

THE RHETORIC THAT pervades dominant understandings of war and peace is dichotomous and split along gender lines — a perfect illustration of standpoint theory. Within militarist thinking, as well as within larger militarist cultures, a warrior's death — and murder — is set against a child's birth; male violence against feminine connection; military destruction against preservative love.

The soldier* male wears a double face. He is a victim:

> From my mother's sleep I fell into the State
> And I hunched in its belly till my wet fur froze.
> Six miles from earth, loosed from its dream of life,
> I woke to black flak and the nightmare fighters.
> When I died they washed me out of the turret with a hose.[1]

---

*To avoid clumsy repetition, I use the term "soldier" to stand for anyone in the military. I mean no insult to the air force, navy, marine corps, coast guard, or any other branch of the service.

He is a monster killer:

With loud sobs, she rushes up to the child who is lying next to the dead soldier, drops to her knees, and draws the limp little body to herself. The soldiers' guns are lowered again. . . . She raises her skinny fist to the sky, trembling with impotent rage. . . . Zing, zing, zing. A whole pack of bullets zips past. The woman is hit.[2]

Often he is both:

> In bombers named for girls, we burned
> The cities we had learned about in school —
> Till our lives wore out; our bodies lay among
> The people we had killed and never seen.[3]

Whether victim or killer, War is his. A woman's name is on his weapon, her body is riddled by his bullets; it is her life, sleep, and care from which he has "fallen." But she cannot share the war he makes and which makes him. And although he counts on her to preserve a place that survives his madness, he also has contempt for what he sees as her innocence and safety:

We soldiers are in the habit of respecting only those who have stood their ground under fire. That is why so many of us inwardly turn away from women, even when outwardly we can't do without them.[4]

The representative heroine of maternal peacefulness is the *mater dolorosa* ("mother of sorrows"), familiar from the lithographs of Käthe Kollwitz. Scrounging for food to keep her children alive, weeping over the body of her son, nursing survivors, sadly rebuilding her home, reweaving the connections that war has destroyed — as she grieves over her particular loss, she mourns war itself. Where she gives birth and sustains life, his war only hurts and destroys.

Faced with the division between men's wars and the life that the *mater dolorosa* sustains, women, mothers, and feminists cast their lot:

> My heart is moved by all I cannot save:
> so much has been destroyed
>
> I have to cast my lot with those
> who age after age, perversely

with no extraordinary power
reconstitute the world.[5]
— *Adrienne Rich*

The Myth: The Masculinity of War and Women's Peacefulness

Even from the soberest perspective, there is much to be said for
dividing the world between men's wars and the women's world
which they threaten. War certainly seems to be men's business.
It is mostly men who make civil and foreign battle plans, who invent weapons and supervise their construction. Men predominate
among the spies, police chiefs, judges, and governors who construct a peacetime order guaranteed by the threat of violence. The
world's generals and negotiators, bombardiers and captains, chiefs
of staff, and defense secretaries have been and still are mostly men.
More men than women shoot the pistol and work the missiles;
certainly more men than women command them.

Traditionally, in most cultures, it has been men's lot to fight
while women watch, suffer, applaud, ameliorate, and forgive. In
war men become "warriors." If they are killed, they are killed in
action. Their deaths represent a sacrifice that is in part chosen and
thus is a testament to courage. A man makes war partly for the
woman whom he protects, who is his audience. "She loved me
for the dangers I had passed, / And I loved her that she did pity
them."[6] Her admiring tears make his fighting possible; her danger
from his enemy makes his fighting necessary. Raped or killed, her
possessions plundered, "his" woman is the last prize and the sweet-
est revenge his enemy exacts from him.

Militarists use the myth of war's manliness to define soldierly
behavior and to reward soldiers. Boot camp recruits are "ladies"
until, trained in obedient killing, they become men. Misogyny is
a useful element in the making of a soldier, as boys are goaded
into turning on and grinding down whatever in themselves is
"womanly." "Women are dinks. Women are villains."[7] Sexist
language for women and — almost the same — their bodies is
common in military discipline, as many battle chants reveal. Even
where misogyny and lust are absent, the warrior embodies a pe-

culiarly masculine ideal of camaraderie and lonely heroism:

The idea is manliness, crudely idealized. You liken dead friends to the pure vision of the eternal dead soldier. You liken living friends to the mass of dusty troops who have swarmed the world forever. And you try to find a hero.[8]

Rarely does anyone, man or woman, deny the manliness of war. The views of David Marlowe, chief of the department of psychiatry at the Walter Reed Army Research Institute, are representative. According to Marlowe, men's strength and physical endurance qualifies them to fight. Physical characteristics shade into others that are first biochemical and then social or sociochemical. Men's famous propensity for aggression is an example:

[Men and women] are indeed better and worse at doing certain kinds of things. One of these things is fighting, certainly in the forms required in land combat. The male's greater vital capacity, speed, muscle mass, aiming and throwing skills, his greater propensity for aggression and his more rapid rises in adrenaline make him more fitted for physically intense combat.[9]

Social-biochemical properties become frankly social and sexual:

Not only is the capacity to carry out aggression — i.e., to fight — related to the nature of the male bond, but a greater part of the bond's sustaining power lies in the language of male sexual identity. . . . The soldier's world is characterized by a stereotypical masculinity. His language is profane, his professed sexuality crude and direct; his maleness is his armor, the measure of his competence, capability and confidence of himself.[10]

Erotic male friendship is actually feared in most militaries, while erotic "male bonding" is celebrated. This bonding becomes a condition of fighting, as men's love for each other is wound into their capacity to kill:

Combat in all human groups is and has been an almost exclusively male preserve, and organized warfare has been, in a sense, the expression of male-bonded groups that constitute armies and their analogues. As Lionel Tiger put it, "males are prone to bond, male bonds are prone to aggress, and therefore aggression is a predictable feature of human groups of males."[11]

Even ostensibly antiwar movies, such as *Platoon* and *Full Metal Jacket,* manage to celebrate the manliness and men-lovingness of war.

Virtually no one denies that military thinking is imbued with masculine values. Yet a boy is not born, but rather becomes, a soldier. Becoming a soldier means learning to control fears and domestic longings that are explicitly labeled "feminine." The soldier earns the right to violence and sex; to fail is to remain "womanly" while losing the right to women. This much has long been familiar. What is increasingly clear is that becoming a militarist means acquiring a distinctive way of thinking that has also been associated with masculinity. As feminist critics have noticed, philosophers often honor, even as they construct, conceptual connections between reason, war, and masculinity. As Plato warned, the struggle to become reasonable "mustn't be useless to warlike men"; on the contrary, philosophers see to it that those men and (sometimes) women who are called "reasonable" have "proved best [both] in philosophy and with respect to war."[12] Both philosophy and war require transcending the particular affections and concrete complexities of "womanly" material and domestic life that I have outlined in Parts 1 and 2.

As the tendency to define reason in opposition to the feminine takes different historical and philosophical forms, so too the masculinity and abstractness of military thinking change with the changing economic and technological contexts of war. In nuclear defense establishments, a "language of warriors," a "technostrategic rationality,"[13] is shared by armers and disarmers, chiefs of staff and chief negotiators. This rationality exhibits in near caricature the kinds of dichotomization and abstraction that, in other contexts, have been characterized as male. As Jean Bethke Elshtain points out, military theorists

portray themselves as clear-sighted, unsentimental analysts describing the world as it is . . . a world of self-confirming theorems invites fantasies of control over events that we do not have. . . . Through abstracted models and logic, hyper-rationalism reduces states and their relations to games which can be simulated. . . . One of the legacies of war is a "habit of simple distinction, simplification, and opposition." . . . One basic task of a state at war is to portray the enemy in terms as absolute and abstract as possible in order to distinguish as sharply as possible the act of killing from the act of murder. . . . It is always *"the enemy,"* a "pseudo-concrete universal."[14]

In her account of her sojourn among defense intellectuals, Carol Cohn tells of how she learned to speak, and then was trapped in, a military language marked by abstractions and euphemisms that protect the speaker and prohibit the listener from even imagining the physical suffering of nuclear holocaust.

"Clean bombs" [so-called because they release a higher proportion of energy through explosive blast than through radiation] may provide the perfect metaphor for the language of defense analysts and arms controllers. This language has enormous destructive power, but without . . . the emotional fallout that would result if it were clear one was talking about plans for mass murder, mangled bodies, and unspeakable human suffering.[15]

In this language, Cohn says, the reference points, the agents and the victims, are not people but weapons and weapons systems.

There is simply no way to talk about human death or human societies when you are using a language designed to talk about weapons. Human death just is "collateral damage" — collateral to the real subject which is the weapons themselves.[16]

Techno-strategic rationality is only an extension, albeit a stunning one, of the abstractness that characterizes military discourse as a whole. In militarist thinking, human bodies are subordinated to abstract causes, different bodies are organized around abstract labels of civilian or soldier, "the enemy" or ally, us or them. Weapons, positions, and targets have always been the primary referents of military strategy. When Olive Schreiner claimed that "no woman would say of a human body it is nothing," implying that militarists are committed to exactly this denial, she was contrasting women's speech with the strategic discourse of "conventional" militarists preparing for the first world war.[17]

If war is "masculine" and "abstract," peace seems "feminine" in exactly the way standpoint theorists predict. Women's peacefulness often begins in negation; alienated women insist that they stand outside men's wars and are repelled by otherwise respect-worthy men who have been transformed by war's rhetoric. Virginia Woolf's *Three Guineas,* a feminist antimilitarist tract from the fascist thirties, has assumed a central place in contemporary feminist peace politics:

Inevitably, we look upon societies as conspiracies that sink the private brother, whom many of us have reason to respect, and inflate in his stead a monstrous male, loud of voice, hard of fist, childishly intent upon scoring the floor of the earth with chalk marks, within whose mystic boundaries human beings are penned, rigidly, separately, artificially. . . .

Therefore if you insist upon fighting to protect me, or "our" country, let it be understood soberly and rationally between us that you are fighting to gratify a sex instinct which I cannot share; to procure benefits which I have not shared and probably will not share; but not to gratify my instincts, or to protect myself or my country. . . . As a woman I have no country, as a woman I want no country, my country is the whole world.[18]

For many women, a more or less conscious alienation from "men's wars" is positively grounded in a history of caring labor. Patriotic East German women declare their political identities maternally as they address their government:

We women do not regard military service for women as an expression of our equality, but as standing in contradiction to our existence as women. We regard our equality as consisting *not* in standing together with *those* men who take up arms, but in solidarity with *those* men who have like us recognized that the abstract term "enemy" in practice means destroying human beings. . . . We feel that as women we have a particular mission to preserve life and to give our support to the old, the infirm and the weak.[19]

A Soviet dissident writing from exile sounds a similar message:

It is natural for women, who give life, to be opposed to war and violence — war of any sort, be it in Vietnam or Afghanistan, and violence against any being. We do not distinguish between guns and nuclear bombs, because all are weapons used for the death and destruction of people.[20]

The Australian physician Helen Caldicott has made a similar maternalist position well known in the United States:

Women all over the world are mobilizing for disarmament. . . . As mothers we must make sure the world is safe for our babies. . . . Look at one child, one baby. . . . I have three children, and I'm a doctor who treats children. I live with grieving parents. I understand the value of every human life. . . . I appeal especially to the women to do this [peace] work because we understand the genesis of life. Our bodies are built to nurture life.[21]

The same point has been reiterated by so many women from so many nations over so many years that it is hard to hear it afresh. Nor is it only women who expect peacefulness from mothers. Some men attribute to mothers a romantic peacefulness that few who know them would dare to match. American physician and writer Lewis Thomas provides an exuberant example:

All the old stories, the myths, the poems comprehended most acutely by young children, the poking and nudging and pinching of very young minds, the waking up of very small children, the learning what smiles and laughter are all about, the vast pleasure of explanation, are by and large the gifts of women to civilization. . . . Put the women in charge I say. . . . Place the single greatest issue in the brief span of human existence, the question whether to use or get rid of thermonuclear weapons of war, squarely in the laps of the world's women. I haven't any doubt at all what they will do with this issue, possessing as they do some extra genes for understanding and appreciating children.[22]

There is a sober basis for this rhetoric. All of women's work — sheltering, nursing, feeding, kin work, teaching of the very young, tending the frail elderly — is threatened by violence. When maternal thinking takes upon itself the critical perspective of a feminist standpoint, it reveals a contradiction between mothering and war. Mothering begins in birth and promises life; military thinking justifies organized, deliberate deaths. A mother preserves the bodies, nurtures the psychic growth, and disciplines the conscience of children; although the military trains its soldiers to survive the situations it puts them in, it also deliberately endangers their bodies, minds, and consciences in the name of victory and abstract causes. Mothers protect children who are at risk; the military risks the children mothers protect. What Chinua Achebe sees in a Biafran mother's "ghost smile" and "singing eyes" is war's perversion of preservative love:

No Madonna and Child could touch
that picture of a mother's tenderness
for a son she soon would have to forget

The air was heavy with odors
of diarrhea of unwashed children
with washed out ribs and dried up
bottoms struggling in labored
steps behind blown bellies. Most
mothers there had long ceased
to care but not this one; she held
a ghost smile between her teeth
and in her eyes the ghost of a mother's
pride as she combed the rust-colored
hair left on his skull and then —
singing in her eyes — began carefully
to part it. . . . In another life this
would have been a little daily
act of no consequence before his
breakfast and school; now she
did it like putting flowers
on a tiny grave. [23]

Women's war narratives — fictional or remembered — draw
on the power of Kollwitz's *mater dolorosa*. Through her eyes war
is a catastrophic destruction that swamps whatever purposes lie
behind it. While the staunchest militarist knows that war brings
suffering, the *mater dolorosa* stands for the refusal to subordinate
pain to tales of victory and defeat. As in the best war stories, "The
cold *brutality* of the deeds of war is left undisguised; neither victors
nor vanquished are admired, scorned or hated."[24] The vision of
war as suffering amid the ruins takes on new poignancy as we
imagine wars worse than any we have known. Anne Marie Troger
is among those who have noted a surprising continuity between
stories German women now tell about their experiences in World
War II and the political rhetoric of the disarmament movement.
As she notes:

Women's memories of the inferno of burning cities under carpet bombing
allows one to imagine nuclear war: destructive forces operating beyond
interference, with no visible enemy of front.[25]

The tales of Hiroshima survivors speak in our century for war itself:

I heard her voice calling "Mother, Mother." I went towards the sound. She was completely burned. The skin had come off her head altogether, leaving a twisted knot at the top. My daughter said, "Mother, you're late, please take me back quickly." She said it was hurting a lot. But there were no doctors. There was nothing I could do. So I covered up her naked body and held her in my arms for nine hours. At about eleven o'clock that night she cried out again "Mother," and put her hand around my neck. It was already ice-cold. I said, "Please say Mother again." But that was the last time."[26]

Mothers need not wait for war to become antimilitarist. Although I only occasionally alluded to war in Parts 1 and 2, I believe that everyday maternal thinking contrasts as a whole with military thinking. Just-war theories control our perceptions of war, turning our attention from bodies and their fate to abstract causes and rules for achieving them. Nuclear thinking gives an illusion of control over events that are profoundly unpredictable. For mothers too the dream of perfect control is dangerously seductive, but in identifying humility as a virtue they relinquish the fantasy of dominating the world. The analytic fictions of just-war theory require a closure of moral issues final enough to justify killing and "enemies" abstract enough to be killable. In learning to welcome their own and their children's changes, mothers become accustomed to open-ended, concrete reflection on intricate and unpredictable spirits. Maternal attentive love, restrained and clear-sighted, is ill adapted to intrusive, let alone murderous, judgments of others' lives. If they have made training a work of conscience and proper trust a virtue, if they have resisted the temptation to dominate their children and abrogate their authority, then mothers have been preparing themselves for patient and conscientious nonviolence, not for the obedience and excessive trust in authority on which military adventures thrive.

Indeed, as I will argue in detail in the next chapter, if military endeavors seem a betrayal of maternal practice, nonviolent action can seem a natural extension. Maternal "peacefulness" is not a sweet, appeasing gentleness that gives peace a bad name and has little to do with living peacefully in the world. When mothers fight with their children or on their behalf, when they teach their children ways of fighting safely, without being trampled on or trampling others, they engage in nonviolent action. Since children are vulnerable and the vulnerable are subject to abuse and neglect, mothers may be more than usually tempted by sadism, self-indulgent aggression, and self-protective indifference to the real needs of others. If mothers refuse to abandon or assault their children but, whatever their disappointment and anger, learn ways to live without giving up on the connections they have fostered or the lives they have tended, they exemplify the commitments of nonviolence.

In the glare of war's destruction and the light of women's hope, what mother would hesitate to "cast her lot" with peacemakers? As suffragist Anna Shaw asked several wars ago:

Looking into the face of . . . one dead man we see two dead, the man and the life of the woman who gave him birth; the life she wrought into his life! And looking into his dead face someone asks a woman, what does a woman know about war? What, what friends, in the face of a crime like that does a man know about war?[27]

Complications

Men's wars, women's peace; a warrior's murder, a child's birth. "It's up to women to change the world." "Put women in charge, I say!" Both the rhetoric and the theory run up against two facts: men are not so warlike and women are certainly not peaceful.

Consider first the "masculinity" of war. There is, undeniably, a disproportionate male presence in defense councils and on battlefields as well as a masculinist military ideology to justify it. The manliness of war is an outcome of many factors. Considered as a biological class, men *may* have a greater propensity toward aggressiveness than women, and this aggressiveness, which is given license in wars, *may* also motivate some of the men who engage in them. On the other hand, warfare, especially in its contemporary forms, seems to require, as much as physical aggression, a tolerance of boredom or the ability to operate a computer under stress, characteristics that are neither distinctly "masculine" nor heroic. Freudian theorists explain why men tend to need and be comforted by the abstract thinking that creates enemies and the abstractions and fantasies of control expressed in rules of war. But these same Freudians point out that the tendencies toward abstraction and control vary in historical circumstances and that, in any case, men differ from each other as much as women do. A legend of heroically violent manliness is taught in patriotic homes, neighborhood movies, schools, and boot camps. There is, too, the sheer weight of history, of Fathers and Fathers before them who marched away, fought, and, if they returned, were set apart by their knowledge of the mysteries of danger and death. I would not deny that cumulatively, biological, psychological, and historical conditions provide partial and modest explanations of men's greater propensity for war. The problem is that men's compliance in war or active pleasure in battle has been confidently explained in so many ways that we are likely to forget that the masculinity of war is in large part a myth that sustains both women and men in their support for violence.

Very few of the men who take part in war can be said to "make war." Most are foot soldiers and workers in the service of grand campaigns they did not design, about which they were not consulted, and which they rarely comprehend. Even within the military, the proportion of suppliers and bureaucrats to active fighters is high. Those soldiers who do engage in combat are usually very young men. Many are conscripted for battle; others fight only to escape intolerable civilian life. Some boys fight eagerly; many of the eager boys are as deluded by patriotic fervor and duty to others as they are by masculinist myths. That they often fight for "national interests" and "causes" from which they derive no benefit and which they barely understand should not detract from the principles and loyalty that motivate them.

If men were so eager to be fighters, we would not need drafts, training in misogyny, and macho heroes, nor would we have to entice the morally sensitive with myths of patriotic duty and just cause. Indeed, history suggests that men have an even more ambivalent relation to the fighting expected of them than women do to the mothering work for which they are said to be "naturally suited." Some men thrill to battle and to the sexually predatory violence it allows. Others partake with mixed feelings but minimal questions simply because fighting is expected of them. Some of these men later report that they took pleasure not only in excitement and camaraderie but also in destruction, cruelty, and the bizarre deaths around them. But there are others, as well as these same men on other days, who are ashamed and disgusted by the killing. Then, in every war, are men who with clear-sighted courage refuse to fight, often at great cost to themselves.

It would be ironic if women were to accept a central, heroic image from military mythology: the male soldier on the battlefield of soldiers, a killer who can be killed. If the soldier is an executioner, he is also victim. As he makes war, war makes and often maddens him. Before she wrote *Three Guineas,* Virginia Woolf created Septimus Smith, a romantically patriotic, white working-class Englishman who "had gone through the whole show, friendship, European War, death, had won promotion" and thus had also "developed manliness."

For now that it was all over, truce signed, and the dead buried, he had, especially in the evening, these sudden thunder-claps of fear. He could not feel.[28]

Toni Morrison's Shadrack, a Black American soldier "blasted and permanently astonished by the events of 1917," is also haunted by memory. While Septimus kills himself, Shadrack establishes a national suicide day to control death. His near hallucinatory memory of "the soldier" is quite specific:

He ran, bayonet fixed, deep in the great sweep of men flying across the field. Wincing at the pain in his foot he turned his head a little to the right and saw the face of a soldier near him fly off. Before he could register shock, the rest of the soldier's head disappeared under the inverted soup bowl of his helmet. But stubbornly, taking no direction from the brain, the body of the headless soldier ran on, with energy and grace, ignoring altogether the drip and slide of brain tissue down its back.[29]

Shadrack's memory is worth clinging to: a headless soldier, running with energy and grace, as his brain drips and slides down his back. War's manliness.

Women's peacefulness is at least as mythical as men's violence. Women have never absented themselves from war. Wherever battles are fought and justified, whether in the vilest or noblest of causes, women on both sides of the battle lines support the military engagements of their sons, lovers, friends, and mates. Increasingly, women are proud to fight alongside their brothers and as fiercely, in whatever battles their state or cause enlists them. There is nothing in a woman's genetic makeup or history that prevents her from firing a missile or spraying nerve gas over a sleeping village if she desires this or believes it to be her duty.

War is exciting; women, like men, are prey to the excitements of violence and community sacrifice it promises. War offers personal adventure and economic advantage to men and women. It may be, however, that women are especially enlivened by war's opportunities just because they are traditionally confined by domestic expectations in peacetime. Nonetheless, women usually justify their militarism as men do, in terms of loyalty, patriotism, and right. Even peace-loving women, like most men, support organized violence, at least in "emergencies." Like some men, some women are fierce and enthusiastic militarists; others, also like some men, see war as a natural catastrophe but collude with it, delegating to leaders political and military judgments they do not intend to understand. Most women, like most men, believe that violence must be met by violence and that the virtue of a cause justifies the horrors done in its name.

Although women and men support war for reasons that transcend gender, war also excites women in gender-related ways. It is sometimes forgotten that to the extent that it is masculine, war is also distinctly feminine. As Virginia Woolf exclaimed in 1941, "No, I don't see what's to be done about war. It's manliness; and manliness breeds womanliness — both so hateful."[30] War offers its own redescription of the work that standpoint theorists celebrate. Doing the wash keeps the home fires burning, a kiss inspires a soldier, and daily child care is suffused with a patrio-erotic glow.

Even as it excites its distinctive brand of self-congratulatory heroism in feminine women, war also offers the adventurous — or the same woman in her adventurous moments — real and imagined freedoms from feminine duty. In wartime a woman may lead a charge up palace steps, carry secrets behind the lines, blow up the troop train, free prisoners, or torture them — and thereby enrich the romantic imagination of all women.

Perhaps many women do not succumb to the romance of war and are instead horrified by "giving over living sacrifices in the bodies of male children for the survival of the homeland."[31] Yet war affords even horrified women the opportunity "to engage in deeds that partake of received notions of glory, honor, nobility, civic virtue."[32] Not surprisingly, even regretful mothers often construe their military service in maternal terms. A German munitions maker in the second world war, like many of her counterparts elsewhere, pithily described her war acts as a plausible extension of peacetime love and duty: "Earlier I buttered bread for him, now I paint grenades for him, and think 'this is for him.' "[33] Similarly, an English woman working in an armaments factory during the Falklands war explained her military activities as a widening of peacetime maternal concern:

Our attitude was that although it was unfortunate we were involved [in the war], once it was upon us we had to get on and do everything to back our boys. People were very willing to work overtime and do whatever was necessary, whether you've got a son involved or not, when it's the English, it's your boys isn't it? I mean it could be your boy next time.[34]

When war ends, mothers nurse the survivors just as, at first, they painted grenades and then put gold stars in their windows. How could they do otherwise? In a time of crisis, would they foster dissension within a family or community whose connectedness it has been their responsibility to sustain? Having applauded their children's efforts from the first somersault to their latest high school test, would they undermine their resolve when legal force combines with community excitement to draft them for war? If her son is killed while killing, should his mother deny herself the consolation of giving his "sacrifice" a point? For her own sake, for her children and family's sake, isn't it a mother's duty to accept, hopefully, justifications for violence?

Listen again to Adrienne Rich:

> I have to cast my lot with those
> who age after age, perversely
>
> with no extraordinary power
> reconstitute the world.

These lines are preceded by lines that speak of "the fibers of actual life / as we live it now," symbolized by incomplete, interrupted, unfinished weaving:

> this fraying blanket with its ancient stains
> we pull across the sick child's shoulder
>
> Or wrap around the senseless legs
> of the hero trained to kill[35]

It is the same blanket that mothers wrap around a sick child and a wounded killer. A pure maternal peacefulness does not exist and cannot be invented.

The Hope

A pure maternal peacefulness does not exist; what does exist is far more complicated: a deep unease with military endeavors not easily disentangled from patriotic and maternal impulses to applaud, connect, and heal; a history of caring labor interwoven with the romance of violence and the parochial self-righteousness on which militarism depends. Nor for all her power to move us is the *mater dolorosa* a reliable instrument of peace. In many Western cultures women are portrayed as strong and brave victims of circumstances over which they have little control. Their sufferings and sacrifices are expected; they persevere in a violent world — but they bear no responsibility for it. Although she reminds us unrelentingly of war's suffering and the loving connections she persistently sustains, the *mater dolorosa* also equates war to natural catastrophes, like hurricanes, and peace to a normal quietness that catastrophe interrupts. It is the beginning of peace politics to realize that war is an activity for which human beings plan, in which they consciously engage, and in which, therefore, they can anticipate the suffering they later mourn. If it is essential for developing a peace politics to keep one's eye on suffering, it is equally important to identify the actions that knowledge of suffering requires.

The dilemma of women's peacefulness is the dilemma of peace politics itself. Peacemakers must make people look closely and persistently at the myriad horrors of war; peace requires standing in solidarity with war's victims. Yet the victims' part can too easily be the part of despair and apolitical perseverance. It is good to persevere and right to admire those who do. But the peacemaking woman has to become as active, inventive, and angry as an ordinary, harassed, coping mother. Yet unlike that mother she must find a way to see and to resist the organized violence that "befalls" her and her people. She must identify threats to the protectiveness that in an ordinary way she has valued and created, starting with threats to her own children and then including as many other children as her imaginative knowledge allows.

Although mothers are not intrinsically peaceful, maternal practice is a "natural resource" for peace politics. For reasons both deep and banal it matters what mothers say and do. Women, and perhaps especially mothers, have serviced and blessed the violent while denying the character of the violence they serve. A peacemaker's hope is a militarist's fear: that the rhetoric and passion of maternity can turn against the military cause that depends on it. Mothers have supported their boys and their leaders, but in the contradiction of maternal and military aims there is a dangerous source of resistance. Because mothers have played their military parts well, their indifference, their refusal to endorse, could matter now. The question peacemakers face is how the "peacefulness" latent in maternal practice can be realized and then expressed in public action so that a commitment to treasure bodies and minds at risk can be transformed into resistance to the violence that threatens them.

Käthe Kollwitz's lithographs and sculptures of loving, protective, and mourning mothers are hauntingly illuminating emblems of war's brutality and of the tenderness that might be peace. But in a poignant memoir,[36] Sara Friedrichsmeyer reveals that it was only after a painful struggle that Kollwitz realized that "the values she espoused as a woman and mother could in no way be interpreted to support war." Kollwitz had to *learn* to stand against the German state and to reject its abstract military ideals.

Kollwitz sent her younger son to the first world war with flowers and a copy of *Faust*. It was partly her son's death that made her increasingly skeptical of military honor and loyalty to *patria*. But it was also the memory of his "sacrifice" and her desire to honor it that made it nearly impossible for her to accept her own growing antimilitarism. According to Friedrichsmeyer, Kollwitz's diaries reveal "an almost paralyzing bewilderment as she tries to balance loyalty to her son's memory with the horrible reality of the fighting." She *sees,* Kollwitz writes in her diary, only the "criminal insanity" of war, but thoughts of her son lead her to *feel* loyal to the army and the state for which he fought.

Friedrichsmeyer traces Kollwitz's halting, vacillating progress to antimilitarism. At first she can copy into her diary only the antimilitarist remarks of others; slowly she dares to criticize in her own words the abstract ideals of sacrifice and patriotism that she once found so moving. By the end of the first world war, Kollwitz was joining public demonstrations and writing open letters, first attacking the government's last desperate efforts of recruitment, then protesting German militarism, and finally renouncing war itself. Shortly after the war, Kollwitz declared herself committed to nonviolence, which, as she wrote to her daughter-in-law, "was not passive waiting" but "work, hard work." This new commitment provoked new conflicts as Kollwitz tried to reconcile her long-standing fervent support of revolutionary movements with her distrust of the violence they endorsed. Because of her public antimilitarist, socialist, and anti-Nazi sentiments, Kollwitz lost her teaching position and atelier when Hitler came to power and was forbidden to exhibit her works. But she couldn't prevent her grandson's fighting and dying in Nazi Germany's army, nor do we know that she even tried to persuade him to refuse to serve or to attempt to escape.

In 1938, when she was seventy-one years old, Kollwitz created a small bronze sculpture called *Tower of Mothers* that depicts a circle of defiant mothers, arms outstretched, joined to protect the children massed behind them. This sculpture epitomizes the maternal antimilitarist works that have made Kollwitz a heroine of feminist peace politics. But none of the lithographs or sculptures adequately expresses their creator's internal conflicts and intellectual as well as emotional struggles to see and to act. It is Kollwitz's conflict, learning, and hard work, even more than her achievement, that I find inspiring.

CHAPTER SEVEN

Maternal Nonviolence: A Truth in the Making

ALTHOUGH MOTHERS MIGHT wish it otherwise, conflict is a part of maternal life. A mother finds herself embattled with her children, with an "outside" world at odds with her or their interests, with a man or other adults in her home, with her children's enemies. She is spectator and arbiter of her children's battles with each other and their companions. If there were a job description for mothers, written in the style of the government report I cited in Chapter 2, it might read in part:

Teaches her children — and herself — when to fight and when to make peace. When battles occur, she prevents her children — and herself — from deliberately or predictably perpetrating or submitting to techniques of struggle that are damaging. Learns to distinguish serious harm from permissible hurt and teaches her children this. Names violence when it occurs and teaches her children to take responsibility for their violent assaults. Maintains conditions of peacefulness so that her children may grow in safety. Is available, when called on, to help her communities develop policies for minimizing and strategies for resolving conflict.

This description of a "good enough" mother is also a description of a person whose work is governed by ideals of nonviolence.

The defining activity of nonviolent activism is peacemaking, that sustained effort to create conditions of "peace" in which people can self-respectfully pursue their individual and collective projects free of the structural violences of poverty, tyranny, and bigotry. Nonviolent peacemaking is governed by four ideals: renunciation, resistance, reconciliation, and peacekeeping. Nonviolent activists renounce violent strategies and weapons. They resist, nonviolently, the violence of others, including their policies of bigotry, greed, and exploitation. The aim of nonviolent battle is responsible reconciliation in which crimes are named and responsibility for them is assigned. Peacekeepers find ways to avoid battles whenever possible and to halt necessary nonviolent battles as soon as aggression is turned back and the aims of justice are secured.

In examining maternal practice through the lens of nonviolence, I look for evidence of an ongoing attempt to renounce and resist violence, to reconcile opponents, and to keep a peace that is as free as possible from assaultive injustice. That is, I ask if there are principles in the practices of mothering that coincide with the four ideals of nonviolence. In attributing ideals of nonviolence to peacemaking mothers, I speak about what they *aim* to teach children, but I say nothing about their pedagogical success. Mothers have little control over the decisions their draft-age children make about when or how to fight. Children are provoked to, encouraged in, and sometimes conscripted for violence by friends, public officials, and counselors, as well as by the frustrations and injustices of their lives. I do not intend to blame mothers once again for others' policies or their children's actions. In saying that mothers are governed by ideals of nonviolence, I am not talking primarily about mothers' effects on children but about the ideals that determine how mothers themselves think about anger, injury, conflict, and battle.

Those governed by an ideal can be identified by the efforts they make, by their shame, guilt, and determination to change when they fail to follow the ideal, and by their pleasure in their own and others' success. Mothers who beat and tyrannize their children or passively watch others do so and who show no signs of remorse or attempts to get help cannot be said to be governed by ideals of nonviolence. Nor is remorse sufficient to show such governance; indifferently abusive people can apologize many times over without seeking help or determining to change their violent ways. To say that an ideal governs is to say, at the least, that in an ordinary way, much of the time, the ideal is nearly fulfilled. Otherwise, ideals only mystify, as a sentimental mother-speech generally mystifies the realities of maternal life. In the peacemaking practices I describe, nonviolence is honored not in the exception but as the rule.

In speaking of those maternal practices that are governed by ideals of nonviolence, I am not attributing success to mothers. Almost all mothers remember actions of theirs that were violent, that is, actions which if repeated often would have damaged their children. As in maternal thinking as a whole, to say that an ideal governs is to identify a kind of struggle, not to record an achievement. The question is whether mothers count failure as a nonviolent activist would count it, not whether they fail. In speaking of mothers' failure to be nonviolent, I do not refer to pathological abuse or neglect but to the failures of "good enough" mothers who only imperfectly fulfill the ideals that govern them. When I speak of temptations to assault and abandon and of the passivity, timidity, vengeance, and battle lust that are liabilities of maternal work, I am talking about temptations and liabilities that are part of maternal nonviolence, not exceptions to it.

My description of maternal practices governed by ideals of nonviolence does not include all mothers everywhere. Considerable maternal violence, collective and individual, exists. In most cultures certain accepted maternal practices elicit from outsiders surprised disapproval if not outright horror — for example, tightly swaddling infants, circumcising female children, or denying teenagers the information about sexuality that is necessary to their safety. Many individual mothers are pathologically violent — they abuse their children deliberately and regularly, apparently indifferent to damage. It is difficult even for trained investigators to assess the extent of maternal nonviolence. If a mother is violent ten minutes out of ten waking hours or one day out of seven, it is the violent act rather than the nonviolent practice that is remembered. Given the vulnerability of children, this is as it should be. On the other hand, children accept abuses done to them if they become routine, especially if an abusive mother claims to be acting for the good of the child.

In my discussion, I put these socially critical questions to one side. I aim to identify principles of maternal nonviolence that I believe could contribute to collective, public understandings of peacemaking. For my purpose, it is sufficient that there are *some* maternal practices actually governed by the ideals I articulate. Because I am not measuring statistical extent but rather articulating governing ideals, I refer only to those peacemaking maternal practices — atypical as they may be — that I have seen. When for stylistic ease I revert to the idiom of achievement — "mothers do . . . mothers say . . . mothers believe . . ." — I always mean only that what *some* mothers do, say, and believe is evidence of a maternal effort and that this effort is characteristic of at least some maternal practices of nonviolence.

I am aware, however, that my epistemological restraint is often betrayed by my rhetoric. In the past years I have watched mothers intensively in a variety of circumstances and neighborhoods. I have seen slaps and pulling and heard shrieking abuse — especially when children endanger themselves or others by sticking their heads out a closing subway door, running into the street, or sending a skateboard skidding into a passer-by. I know that children suffer from their caretakers far worse violence than anything I have seen and that the epidemic of drug addiction makes abuse increasingly likely. Yet I have found myself repeatedly struck not by maternal violence but by resilient, nonviolent mothering under considerable provocation in difficult circumstances. While poverty and isolation make nonviolence a miracle, the miracle seems to occur. After several years of thinking about these issues, I believe that there are many voices of maternal nonviolence, with different mothers and cultures of mothers pursuing nonviolence in their own flawed and imperfect ways. Hence it is out of respect as much as stylistic laziness that I revert to the idiom of achievement: "Mothers do . . . mothers say . . . mothers try."[1]

Ideals of Nonviolence

The most controversial and distinguishing ideal of nonviolent action is the renunciation of "violent" strategies and weapons. Simone Weil defined "force" — roughly her term for "violence" — as whatever "turned a person into a thing," treating that person as if he counted for nothing.[2] Gandhi spoke of "ahimsa," noninjury, a refusal to harm.[3] More prosaically, I take a violent act or policy as one that is either intended to damage or can predictably be expected to damage a person against whom it is wielded and for which there is no compensatory benefit for the person damaged. By damage, I mean serious and apparently long-lasting harm or injury. By compensatory benefit, I mean some good that the damaged person may expect from her injuries, as, for example, a patient hopes to benefit from assaultive chemotherapy.

Although damage is painful and harmful, not all pain and harm are violent. If I fall and break my arm I have not suffered violence. Violence is almost always coercive, inflicted without a person's consent, but people also inflict violence on themselves. The drug addict and anorexic are not, typically, coerced into the behavior that damages them. Someone violent to herself or cooperating in her own violence treats herself as a "thing" of no value, says to herself "I do not count." Damage can be psychological as well as physical and can be indirectly as well as directly visited on the violated person. A person whose loved one is killed or tortured is an indirect victim of violence. However, the clearest case of damage is physical injury or harm to the violated person. Other kinds of damage are understood by analogy to this central case, in which the human body becomes the place of pain and domination.

Whether in the midst of action or in moments of calm reflection, it is often very difficult to identify violence. The most elaborate definitions cannot substitute for judgment and indeed must be altered in its light. Who is to say whether damage could have been predicted? How serious is "serious," how long "long-lasting"? Who is to determine compensatory benefit? Although I worry over these questions in other discussions of nonviolence, for my purposes here I have clear enough cases of violence to anchor a definition. Torturing a person, burning her with napalm, destroying her home and provisions, killing her loved ones — all these routine acts of tyranny and war are clearly violent. So are painful and extensive beatings, sexual assault on vulnerable young people, and humiliating practices of shaming — the routine acts of domestic tyranny and violence.

In the renunciation of violent weapons and strategies, it is customary to distinguish those who are relatively weaponless and powerless from those who believe they could, if they chose, use violence effectively. Mothers, as we have seen, often feel powerless in respect to their children and, typically, are actually powerless in respect to men in their home and social group. Minority or poor mothers are also powerless in respect to men and women of governing classes and races.

Like other powerless people, mothers resort to nonviolent strategies because they do not have weapons — guns, legal clout, money, or any other tools with which to work one's will on others. Like the powerless everywhere, mothers are often enraged. Officials callously neglect or deliberately injure their children. Mothers feel as if they relinquish pleasures and ambitions to do important human work only to find that their work is taken for granted and their word for naught. Fantasies of revenge must thrive among mothers. Yet they are rarely capable of violent revenge on their own or their children's behalf. Officials — teachers, welfare workers, landlords, doctors and the like — can retaliate against the children as well as the mothers themselves at the hint of maternal violence. Even maternal anger is apt to be punished or trivialized (the "hysteria" of an "overinvolved" or "embittered" woman). Nor, ideally, can mothers turn against their children whom they are pledged to protect. To get their way, mothers engage in nonviolent techniques that are familiar from more public struggles: prayer, persuasion, appeasement, self-suffering, negotiation, bribery, invocation of authority, ridicule, and many other sorts of psychological manipulation. These techniques may go to the edge of violence — of real damage — without endangering either a mother, her children, or the people they fight against.

From the perspective of nonviolent activism, what is striking about mothers is their commitment to nonviolent action in precisely those situations where they are undeniably powerful, however powerless they may feel — namely, in their battles with children. Children are vulnerable creatures and as such elicit either aggression or care. Recalcitrance and anger tend to provoke aggression, and children can be angrily recalcitrant. Typically, the mother who confronts her children is herself young, hassled if not harassed by officials in an outside world, usually by her own employers, and often by adults she lives with. She brings to confrontations with her children psychological and physical strengths which are potentially lethal. Her ability to damage her children increases the more alone she is with them, the less others are available to go to the children's aid. Yet it is these same circumstances of frustration and loneliness that will tempt her to violence when faced with her children's recalcitrance. I can think of no other situation in which someone subject to resentments at her social powerlessness, under enormous pressures of time and anger, faces a recalcitrant but helpless combatant with so much restraint. This is the nonviolence of the powerful.

It might be thought that, like other powerful people, mothers only appear to renounce violence while actually maintaining control by the fear they inspire. It does not follow, however, that because mothers are fearsome, their control is typically and primarily a function of fear. Control by fear and threat is always fragile. Threats must be sufficiently frightening to deter but not so frightening to have undesired effects. When adults are frightened, they may react by deceiving those who frighten them, resenting and abandoning them, resisting them courageously out of self-respect, or becoming so terrified that they no longer can play or work. Young children, only barely able to distinguish the illusory from the legitimate fear, are still more likely to respond unpredictably and destructively when frightened. Although many mothers threaten, often ritualistically, their threats are often limited not only in number but, more important, by the context of protectiveness in which they occur. Those mothers who are governed by ideals of nonviolence know this and ensure that their threats occur amid effective, trustworthy means of nonviolent control.

Because they are powerful, mothers can also discipline a child by deliberately inflicting pain through measures that do not risk damaging a child, such as controlled "spanking," a deliberate use of pain quite distinct from damaging beatings or angry blows. Frequently, mothers who threaten or resort to the infliction of pain draw their children into the discipline, requiring them to pick a switch from the yard or to agree on and then count the number of strokes. I have heard such mothers defend their discipline as a measured expression of justice that prevents less worthy, capricious expressions of anger. Mothers (like me) who criticize the infliction of pain point out the danger that controlled violence will escalate into uncontrolled abuse, especially if a child becomes actively resistant. Moreover, both mothers and children can become sexually excited by the conjunction of pain, domination, and submission. Most generally, the social construction of a child's body as a vulnerable locus of pain seems a preparation for later public domination and submission, even if it does not humiliate or sexually confuse the young child.

Although I believe that the deliberate infliction of pain is predictably, though not invariably, damaging to a child, my point here is that it is within practices governed by ideals of nonviolence that mothers argue about pain in the ways I report. In my experience of maternal arguments, mothers do not advocate bullying, capriciousness, or any sort of physically damaging violence. Despite deeply felt generational, cultural, or temperamental differences among mothers, they seem to agree that a practice, *if damaging*, should be renounced and then go on to argue about damage. If my experience is at all typical, these maternal debates about the benefits and dangers of inflicting pain do not contradict but rather actually reflect an ongoing maternal effort to be governed by the ideal of renunciation, however differently the ideal is interpreted.

As their discussions about pain make clear, mothers who renounce violence must find some acceptable ways to train and
control. This requires recognizing violence in its many forms.
Beyond certain clear and visible acts of physical damage, the distinction of what actions seriously harm and injure varies from
family to family and from culture to culture. There is a tendency
among pacifist theorists to escalate the requirements for "ahimsa,"
or noninjury, considering even thoughts and wishes as damaging
acts. Gandhi's description of ahimsa provides a striking example
of such an inclusive definition:

Not to hurt any living thing is no doubt a part of ahimsa. But it is its
least expression. The principle of ahimsa is hurt by every evil thought,
by undue haste, by lying, by hatred, by wishing ill to anybody.[4]

Ahimsa really means that you may not offend anybody, you may not
harbor an uncharitable thought even in connection with one who may
consider himself to be your enemy.[5]

Impatience is a phase of violence.[6]

Mothers who embrace the Gandhian ideal will be in for sleepless
nights. It would be nearly impossible for mothers to renounce
uncharitable thoughts and angers, let alone impatience. Rather,
their task is to determine which hurts, hates, impatience, and lying
are damaging and which strategies are effective and consonant with
safety, development, and conscientiousness. Maternal conversations, heard in a certain spirit, are as filled with controversy about
the morality and effectiveness of strategies as are the meetings of
war cabinets. By my definition, any strategy of fighting or resisting that does not actually damage an opponent is nonviolent.
The trick is to distinguish permissible hurt from damaging harm,
nonviolent coercion from damaging force. "Forcing" a child to
go to bed or grabbing a knife from his hand is, in almost all
contexts, nonviolent though coercive. An inoculation is a permissible hurt. But many bribes, threats, lures, reprimands, and
other manipulative nonviolent techniques become questionable
when development and conscientiousness are at stake.

Of the many controversial techniques of nonviolent manipulation, the uses of "self-suffering" are especially prominent because of the role they played in the public nonviolence associated with Gandhi and Martin Luther King, Jr. A self-sufferer takes upon herself the pain involved in fighting. Willingness to suffer is considered a condition of endurance and a testament to seriousness and courage. To assume rather than to inflict suffering is also, for both King and Gandhi, an expression of love. In the midst of the brutal violence of the civil rights movement, King promised:

Send your hooded perpetrators of violence into our community at the midnight hour and beat us and leave us half dead, and we shall still love you. [7]

This echoes his mentor Gandhi:

Love ever suffers, never resents, never revenges itself. . . . The test of love is *tapasya* and *tapasya* means self-suffering. [8]

Self-suffering is also a weapon that induces guilt and shame in the conscientious opponent and sympathy in the "whole world [that] watches." The famous nonviolent, unarmed assault on the salt mines in India, where Satyagrahi marched in unbroken ranks against soldiers who beat them, was an instance of self-suffering and, proleptically, a fulfillment of King's promise: "Be ye assured we will wear you down by our capacity to suffer." [9]

Whatever its public uses, in maternal nonviolence self-suffering is morally and practically limited. Self-suffering is sometimes a prominent maternal strategy. Mothers may manipulatively display the pain their children cause them, adeptly employing the tears and tones of suffering. Yet mothers often realize that children are not and cannot afford to be too long and deeply affected by maternal tears. The limits of self-suffering are part of a general limitation on provoking children's guilt and shame. A child's conscientiousness develops slowly and unpredictably. While the capacity for shame and guilt may be necessary for conscientiousness, excessive guilt leads to anger, indifference, or inhibition while humiliating shame damages a precariously developing self.

Like any other nonviolent strategy, techniques of self-suffering may be evaluated in terms of an insistence, central to pacifism, on the inseparability of means and end. Although Gandhi spoke of ahimsa as the means to truth, saying that "without Ahimsa it is not possible to seek and find Truth," he undermined this distinction conceptually and practically:

Ahimsa and Truth are so intertwined that it is practically impossible to disentangle and separate them. They are like two sides of a coin, or rather a smooth, unstamped metallic disc. Who can say which is the obverse and which is the reverse.[10]

To paraphrase Gandhi, if the preservation and growth of children is truth, then a criterion of its realization is that it be achieved nonviolently. However closely an outcome resembles an original goal — a child asleep or in school — a method that damages a child has failed. Drugging a child to sleep or dragging her into a school room is not a means to but a perversion of the end they allegedly achieve.

Although the ends of mothering cannot be achieved violently and still remain maternal ends, nonviolence is not a mother's only goal. Mothers aim to nurture and train an adult capable of work and love. They also typically have aims for their children that are related to their religious, political, or intellectual groups. These long-range goals inform some intermediate choices and help a mother to make sense of her work as a whole. Nonetheless, they must be pursued flexibly, with attention to particular challenges and circumstances. Gandhi held on to the distant aim of home rule through years of actions, compromises, and settlement. Yet in the course of struggle, the long-range goal was too general to dictate strategy. Rather it was the nonviolence of ongoing struggle that gradually, over time, gave meaning to the goal. Similarly, a mother cannot decide what to do with a bullying or frightened child by appealing to models of adulthood. It is the nonviolence of daily life that is itself a goal to which longer-range aims must be adapted. Gandhi never gave up the goal of home rule. Mothers, by contrast, may be called on to relinquish religious or political aims that are dear to them. All the more important for mothers to learn to interpret long-range goals flexibly as they attend to the specific tasks at hand. As Gandhi would say, "The way is the truth"; or as feminists put it, "The process is the project."

There is nothing simple about a commitment to nonviolence. A mother often finds herself confronted with seemingly untenable choices. Either she gives her child sleeping pills or he will go sleepless and become increasingly unable to sleep; either she locks a child in her room or she continues to beat on her brother, all other means of prevention having failed; either she drags him sobbing into the classroom or reinforces his fear that school is indeed a dangerous place. Mothers have to do *something* — nighttimes and school days arrive, siblings must live together. Relief comes when a difficult day or phase has passed. The issue again is what counts as success. To the extent that a child is damaged, i.e., controlled violently, the ends of preservation and growth are compromised.

Partly because nonviolent fighting is exhausting and peace and quiet are such a relief, most mothers avoid battles when they can and end unavoidable battles quickly. To be sure, some mothers seem to thrive on battle with or among their children. The perception of a child's separateness, central to fostering growth and conscientiousness, is needed to prevent mothers from taking their children's part in battles with an inappropriate enthusiasm. Although she may be tempted to fight more often and with more fervor than children require, it is in a mother's self-interest to limit battles. Most of her children's "enemies" are members of her neighborhood and school community, often indeed children of close friends. Typically a mother will be held and will hold herself responsible for any damage her children cause or suffer if nonviolence turns to violence. In children's battles, as in adults', escalation can be swift — a shouting child stomps on the baby's stomach, an insulting taunt is met with a brick to the head. Moreover, even nonviolent battle has its cost. Hurting and being hurt are part of fighting. Scraped knees and feelings usually mend with astonishing speed, but they can also be stubbornly immune to aid; even the most nonviolent strategy can go awry and leave its scars.

Peace is the more secure, the fewer weapons at hand. In domestic as in public life, there is no substitute for disarmament. Ideally, a mother keeps her house and yard as weapon-free as possible, despite the advertising of toys far more lethal than play pistols and the increasing popularity in the United States of keeping real, dangerous guns at home. She also tries to disarm her neighbors' children. It would be unrealistic to leave weapons about, let alone to pile them up deliberately, and then to expect children not to use them when provoked. But as in public life, disarmament can never be complete. Even if real guns are banned, there are always weapons available to the weak as well as the strong — blocks, rocks, play trucks, and sewing needles, for example. Moreover, bigger children are often as physically capable of seriously injuring a smaller child as is a mother herself. Although weapons should be eliminated wherever possible, there is no substitute for the renunciation of violence. By example and precept a mother has to train children not to stamp on the baby, throw a rock at the head, push a toddler in the river, or squirt insecticide in an enemy's face.

To keep the peace, a peacemaking mother, as best she can, creates ways for children and adults to live together that both appear to be and are fair. She distributes goods and privileges, listens carefully to complaints, and respectfully explains the unavoidable differences in powers and rewards that are inevitable among adults and children of different ages. Faced with rivalry, tyranny or greed, nonviolent mothers do not sit passively by, letting a stronger or older child annex the possessions or exploit the smaller or more vulnerable one. Arbitrating and restraining, mothers appeal to interests the children share — or invent them. In reinforcing the fragile affections that survive rivalry and inevitable inequality, mothers who are guided by ideals of nonviolence work for the day that their children will come to prefer justice to the temporary pleasures of tyranny and exploitation.

A mother who aspires to nonviolence makes a peace worth keeping. But the best peace should not entirely prevent battle. Premature appeasement or totalitarian techniques of controlling conflict, though comforting, prevent children from learning how to recognize what they want, articulate their desire, and set out to achieve it. Such evasive techniques leave them unpracticed in victory or defeat and therefore unmindful of the necessity for and ways to achieve reconciliation. They encourage those who are treated unjustly to despair of change and allow those who dominate, either through strength or oppression, to remain oblivious to the cost their dominance exacts on themselves and others. To put the matter starkly, children whose conflict is always managed for them are trained both to submit to power and to exercise abusive power over others.

Mothers are often accused of appeasement and totalitarian control. They walk away from the scene, lie to make a child feel better, insist on the appearance of affection where there is none, bribe or threaten children into denying their anger and hurt, or create small rituals of disorder — shouts, slaps, and tears — that appear to express conflict while burying it in noise. Most mothers have sometimes done these things. The belief dies hard that children will be so good, or an order so artful, that fighting will disappear. Yet for the most part, mothers appreciative of nonviolence know that "peace and quiet" can mask many kinds of violence; some battles with and between children should and must take place.

Even more important than her attitude toward children's battles is a nonviolent mother's commitment to resist authorities and policies that are unjust or harmful. Like anyone else, in the face of superior power, mothers often succumb to fearfulness and despair. But they also often name and encourage, in themselves and their children, the duty to resist, and they recognize their lack of resistance as failure. Most striking is the courageous resistance, in the face of danger, against enormous odds, by mothers who live in poverty, tyranny, and slavery. In quieter times, more fortunate mothers exhibit their own barely visible courage as they get for their children what they need and learn to say no to those who hurt them. When they identify resistance as a virtue, mothers try to teach children to stand up for themselves and others, knowing that mothers themselves may be the first authority a child resists and that those around them, including other mothers, may criticize the spiritedness they have fostered. An unusually spunky mother, Grace Paley's Faith, the same character who took it to be part of her work to raise children "righteously up," faces the consequences of another mother's disapproval:

How can you answer that boy?
   "You don't," says Mrs. Julius Finn. . . . "You answer too much, Faith Asbury, and it shows. Nobody fresher than Richard."
   "Mrs. Finn," I scream in order to be heard, for she's some distance away and doesn't pay attention the way I do. "What's so terrible about fresh. EVIL is bad, WICKED is bad. ROBBING, MURDER, and PUTTING HEROIN IN YOUR BLOOD is bad."
   "Blah, blah," she says, deaf to passion. "Blah to you."[11]

Peacekeeping is the art of avoiding battle; the challenge is to recognize when peacekeeping should end and battle begin. Resistance is the art of discerning, and then having the courage to fight, violences. The challenge is to recognize when fighting is no longer justified but is motivated by vengeance, battle pleasure, or inertia. In peace campaigns there is often a tension between those gifted in nonviolent fighting and those adept at peacekeeping. A peace politics must coordinate and reward the efforts of both kinds of work. Similarly, some mothers will be more adept at peacekeeping, others at resisting. In maternal conversations, mothers often help each other develop both gifts while using their special talents on behalf of each other's children.

Nonviolent battles are meant to end quickly, but not any end will do. People who have fought must be reconciled; harder, once nonviolent battle is won, people who have been abused must forgive. King's views are not atypical:

Forgiveness does not mean ignoring what has been done or putting a false label on an evil act. It means rather that the evil act is no longer a barrier to the relationship. . . . The evil deed of the enemy-neighbor, the thing that hurts, never quite expresses all that he is. . . . We must not seek to hate or humiliate the enemy but to seek his understanding. . . . Hate multiplies hate, violence multiplies violence. . . . Hate scars the soul. . . . Like an unchecked cancer, hate corrodes the personality and eats away its vital unity.[12]

In public battles, where peoples and nations are hatefully and violently abused, to forgive is as intellectually confusing and morally controversial as is renunciation of violence at the outset. For mothers, by contrast, the ideal of responsible reconciliation is a routine aspect of training and education. Mothers name the evils that are done to or by their children. It is wrong (usually) to lie, bully, or humiliate, although children -- and mothers — do these things. It is also wrong to suffer such insults in silence or to forgive perpetrators before the deed is named and the agent held responsible. Mothers, like children, are tempted to patch up prematurely, make do, and forget. After all, many "crimes" by and against children are trivial, and some cheerful forgetting is necessary to get through the day. But nonviolence is not simple. There is no rule for distinguishing the trivial "childish" escapade from more serious hurt. While moralism has its clear limits, cheery forgetfulness is no morality at all. Truthful, responsible reconciliation protects children from their own or others' hatred, which "scars the soul," and also from forgetful indifference to pain that they have inflicted or suffered and that, like hate, "corrodes the personality and eats away its vital unity."[13]

Assigning and taking responsibility comes fairly easily to mothers, even when they themselves have become violent. Maternal "forgiveness" is a more complicated phenomenon. Mothers often forgive their children even for serious crimes of violence and bigotry despite their clear harm. If a passionate loyalty overcomes her ability to name her child's crime and to urge upon him responsibility for it, then a mother has failed to live up to the ideal of responsible reconciliation. While mothers may forgive their children too easily, many find it difficult to forgive themselves. A responsible reconciliation would require of mothers a clearsighted, resiliently cheerful appreciation of their own imperfections as well as their children's. It is probably most difficult for mothers to forgive people they perceive as their childrens' enemies — hard enough when opponents are children, almost impossible if the enemies are adults. Often children's "enemies" are also a mother's — Father, mate, grandparent, or friend who have treated both mother and child badly. In their harshness, mothers are not wrong. If mothers can name and take responsibility, it is much more likely that the peace that follows battle will be sturdy. Yet hatred does "scar the soul," frequently also imposing on the injured children a vengeance they no longer need. Often mothers realize this. After the bitterest divorce or most divisive neighborhood or school battle, there are mothers who let combatants and even outright offenders make amends and resume relationships in the interest of the active connectedness that is "peace."

The four ideals of nonviolence — renunciation, resistance, reconciliation, and peacekeeping — govern only some maternal practices of some mothers. Yet it is also true that to elucidate these ideals is to describe, from a particular perspective, maternal practice itself. Peacemaking mothers create arrangements that enable their children to live safely, develop happily, and act conscientiously; that is, they preserve, nurture, and train, exemplifying the commitments of maternal work.

Public Peacemaking

Nonviolence arises out of maternal practice, even if only some mothers in some practices are effectively governed by its ideals. Looking through the lens of nonviolence, I see instances of practice governed by ideals of renunciation, resistance, reconciliation, and peacekeeping. If I am right about the existence of maternal nonviolence, it is possible to ask whether this domestic achievement has any import for political conflict.

There is no evidence that mothers more or less automatically express domestic ideals of nonviolence publicly. In their daily lives they may renounce damaging strategies, resist the violence of others, prevent battles where possible, end them quickly, and aim for responsible reconciliation. They may even consciously, through story and parable, articulate their principles so children can learn them. Yet however adept they may be in domestic nonviolence, these same mothers often do not endorse or contribute in any way to public nonviolence. Many mothers consciously teach their children to renounce violence unless and until it is enlisted in a collective enterprise, such as a war, and sanctioned by authorities.

Others reluctantly or inauthentically comply in the violence required of acceptable children in their social group.

Maternal nonviolence is more seriously limited by distinctive and virulent forms of self-righteous hatred and fear of the outsider, sometimes issuing in a racism that fuels and is fueled by violence. Mothers work with life-gripping passion on behalf of particular children and kin. Often they are fiercely committed to the values and survival of their people or their neighborhood. It is not surprising that mothers who practice nonviolence at home nonetheless sometimes teach their children to hate "all the people their relatives hate." Political or religious allegiance, fear of the different stranger, misguided desire for purity and order, the sheer lust to see one's own children privileged, all may fuel a violence toward outsiders that would not be tolerated at home. Unfortunately, the contorted faces of white mothers shouting at Black children seeking to enter previously white schools are faces of maternal practice. Many an embattled or frightened mother may be relieved when her state provides her with "enemies" she can blame, hate, and kill.

This is the underside of maternal nonviolence, but it is not the only side. Greeting card sentiments about women and children belie the tensions and fragility of the best efforts of mothers to identify with each other's work. It is an ongoing struggle for mothers to sustain the tension between passionate loyalties to their particular children and a less personal imaginative grasp of what other children mean to other mothers. Nonetheless, those mothers who make the work of training a work of conscience extend the range of their nonviolence when they identify proper trust and distrust of allegedly legitimate authority virtues and develop habits of resistance. Although susceptible to self-righteous protection of their own, mothers also develop distinctive ways of combating their fear and ignorance. Frequently, mothers widen their vision by finding in other particular mothers, children, and families passions and responsibilities akin to their own. They justify an injunction against killing and mutilating by pointing to the particularities of lives and life connections, to the many kinds of past work and present hope that violence destroys.

Whether or not mothers themselves explicitly extend principles of nonviolence, in their domestic practices they have developed a conception of conflict and its resolution that can serve as an alternative to a conception that dominates public negotiation and is now familiar through decades of treaty making and arms negotiation. The philosopher W. B. Gallie has given this dominant conception a name — "conflict resolution through mutual concessions," — and an ancronym CRTMC.[14] A comparison of CRTMC with its maternal analogue reveals that each has distinctive and contrasting assumptions about human "nature," community, and conflict. If, as Gallie suggests, CRTMC is a dangerous and exploitative form of peacemaking, then it is useful to articulate alternatives, whatever their origin.

In its ideal form, CRTMC consists of negotiation between equals, each of whom gives up as little as seems necessary to get what he wants. (Optimally, they give up nothing except the bargaining chips that were invented to be given up.) CRTMC is allegedly successful when each partner is free from fear of the other and can live alone, independently, in "peace."

Even when no visible agreement results, the mere practice of CRTMC serves to preserve the status quo, providing the occasion for public competitive bargaining that both expresses and contains the desire to dominate. This exercise may well prevent, or at least postpone, outright violence. It is, however, both exploitative and inherently unstable. It is exploitative because the "equal," strong partners bargain over the heads and with the lives of persons or nations they consider weak enough to be excluded. Although sometimes those who are excluded are promised safety or a particular form of government in return for submitting to protection, often they are not even consulted. CRTMC is unstable because economic, political, and technological conditions change and the excluded develop effective forms of resistance and reject the "peace" that turned on exploiting their labor, armies, crops, and land. Moreover, it is not only the excluded who change. Among the actively negotiating participants, equality is rightly perceived as fragile; anyone's power is dependent on physical, political, and economic conditions difficult to control. Consequently, each partner must increase her or his strength, in fear of the possibilities of increased strength of the other. "Equality" is in any case an abstraction blind to the context and history of power relations. The search for quantitative measures of strength ignores the meanings people attribute to their own and others' needs and strategies. Actual people and nations have histories; power — the ability to pursue individual and collective projects — is not a possession but a changing relation people have to and with others in particular social and political contexts.

The presuppositions of CRTMC are remarkably like those of "realist" justifications for defense and conquest. Realists claim that people and nations will, if they can, dominate and exploit those who are weaker. In Thucydides' words, "They that have odds of power exact as much as they can, and the weak yield to such conditions as they can get."[15] The weaker are not less domineering than the strong but only people who have not yet gathered the strength needed to retaliate and dominate in turn. Moreover, at least some realists claim that the strong should get what they can, so long as what they get is in the interest of state or cause. In this view, the relentless pursuit of greater strength and the domination of others which strength allows serve the good of the whole.

Although in the realist view, as in CRTMC, the other's strength is perceived as a threat, one's own greater strength is taken to be unthreatening. Either it is required for minimal safety or it is justified, as the other's is not, by the needs of cause or state or even by the well-being of those whom one dominates. It is only part of peacemaking to build up strength for defense or justified domination. Given that the partners share perceptions of the other's strength as dangerous and their own as harmless or justified, strategic stability is not a resting point but an invitation to preemptive increases of economic or military armament or even, if the other seems to be getting stronger, "preemptive deterrence."

When it works, CRTMC is essentially negative: partners, moved by fear and frustration, concede and compromise so as to be left alone in safety. At its best, CRTMC leads to a stasis of separate but equal partners each with cause to doubt whether the other will persist in renouncing violence if and when he becomes able to profit by it. Its best, then, is, in its own terms, only second best to outright domination and is inherently unstable.

Maternal thinking articulates an opposed and superior conception of conflict resolution rooted in a maternal view of relationships. This maternal perspective is expressed independently and is therefore confirmed in "different voice theory."[16] In this alternative conception, the ideal of equality is a mystifying phantom. Mothers are not equal to their children; siblings and childhood friends are not equal to each other. Differences in strength cannot be wished away — they are the stuff of childhood and of family life. Power relations are shifting and complex. Weakness in one context — say physical strength — may be irrelevant in another. In any case, the weak have powers to resist and seduce that belie any absolute division between strong and weak. Because they live through and witness shifting power relations, because they watch firsthand the anxieties of children driven to be "equal," mothers would be slow to wish on themselves or those they love the fearful pursuit of equality. In the maternal view of conflict it is not necessary to be equal to resist violence. Most mothers try to teach their children when self-respect demands a fight. Their own peacemaking — their attempt to create conditions of peace — includes training for active, engaged nonviolent fighting. Rather than depending on an illusory state of equality, they aim to fight as they live, within communities that attend to and survive shifting differences in power.

Maternal practice includes many moments of CRTMC, between parents and children, between parents, between parents and authorities, between siblings and friends. But these are only moments in an ongoing practice of peacemaking that is radically different. Peace is not a precarious equilibrium in which everyone is somewhat warily left alone — though this certainly describes many "peaceful" respites in maternal life. Battles provoke and are provoked by fear and rage, lust, greed, jealousy, shame and guilt, and certainly by loyalty and love. Peace, like the maternal life that it blesses, includes ambivalences and compromise. Many mothers go through long nights of disappointment, distrust, hurt, and rage. Though temporary distances between children and mothers are useful for both, mothers tend not to exit, but to speak, even where speech is a quarrel. They struggle to resist the temptation to abandon, struggle to stay in the fight and on the scene, a goal almost the opposite of the "safe" independence of CRTMC.

Peace is a way of living in which participants counting on connection demand a great deal of each other. The peacemaker asks of herself and those she cares for not what they can afford to give up, but what they can give, not how they can be left alone, but that they can do together. It is all too easy to sentimentalize maternal peacemaking. It is *not* easy to give what can be usefully received or to receive what can be willingly given. Mothers become addicted to giving, create addicted receivers, misperceive others' desires, refuse to say what they want and then attribute their wishes to others, demand from others what they cannot give while refusing to receive what can willingly be given. In short, mothers, like other humans, fail. But the task of making peace by giving and receiving while remaining in connection is radically different from and less dangerous than CRTMC.

From a maternal perspective, CRTMC seems partly a sweet dream of "objective," impersonal, rule-governed reason, partly a nightmare in which reason's failure betokens violence and death. Negotiators of dangerously armed, vast bureaucratic states trust each other to be restrained, if not by contracted agreements, at least by prudence. It would indeed be "mad" to detonate weapons that would result in a war that would be catastrophic for everyone — though it is not much crazier than to divert national and world resources to manufacturing such suicidally destructive weapons in the first place. Usually, however, where conflict exists, even if the participants are few and well known, it is not wise to count on rule-governed "sanity." Mothers, long used to the "mad" envies and passions of children, are also likely to recognize the "mad" child in the adult, not least herself. Even doting or fearful mothers will likely suspect the nuclear statesman's trust in a reason that obscures rather than clarifies the passion that fuels conflict. Taking an "objective" distance from the rage and fear of battle, CRTMC negotiators are left without resources to understand the failure that leads to war and preparations for war; nor can they manage the emotions of peace, that is, of life. Given their realist assumptions about strength, weakness, and unstable equality, for them to look at fear, anger, loyalty, and love, to look at history, is to see violence. And indeed, they are not deluded. Violence is everywhere to be seen, a public, documented, "realistic" nightmare.

Mothers know another history. Passion is often destructive, but it is the material for a discipline of love and for a maternal thinking that is love's reason. A mother learns firsthand, as agent and spectator, in the position of the stronger and of the weaker, that the cost of dominating is paid in the fear and hatred of the dominated and anyone who sympathizes with them. Mothers have many dominating moments and therefore experience in their own person what it means to lose the trust of the dominated and to watch those they dominate lose pleasure in themselves. Most mothers also know what it is to be dominated. They watch as their children stumble in their efforts to learn to love, suffering the pain and loss that comes from dominating or the humiliation that comes from being dominated. But pain is not the only history a mother tells. Even siblings and rivalrous children learn to take strength from each other's strength rather than primarily from their weakness. And the radical inequality of mother-child relations does not preclude a mutuality and respect for another's lively being. Without being atypically unselfish, a mother may measure her power in terms of her ability to nurture a child whom she *cannot* dominate, a child lively with her own desires and projects.

It would be sentimental foolishness to claim for all mother-child relations such mutuality. It would be equally sentimental cynicism to deny that many mothers and children create together an ongoing, changing approximation of mutuality. Out of their failures as well as successes, mothers develop a conception of relationships that undermines the dominant conception of individuality that fuels conquest as well as provocative "defense." They not only modify aggression in the interest of connection but develop connections that limit aggression before it arises.

Maternal peacemakers both depend on and foster conceptions of the self and "human nature" that Carol Gilligan and others have heard in the "different voices" associated with women. According to these conceptions, human nature is not an enemy, humans change and learn to welcome change, and responsible reconciliation is a permanent possibility, however improbable at the moment. Individuals are not primarily centers of dominating and defensive activity trying to achieve a stable autonomy in threatening hierarchies of strength, although this does describe some individuals and some moments in most lives. They are also and equally centers of care, actively desiring other selves to persist in their own lively being, judging their own well-being in terms of their capacity for a love that "struggles toward definition." This is the "mother knot" and its resolution:

Love? I had not [always] loved him [my son] any more than I had always loved myself. In both cases, love had struggled toward definition, grown out of confusion, knowledge, misery and necessity.[17]

At its best, maternal nonviolence is a reality in the making, or, to borrow a phrase attributed to the French philosopher Maurice Merleau-Ponty, a *vérité-à-faire,* a truth-to-be-made.[18] The reality is only in the making because failures are many and the ideal marks a struggle that is often lost. Nonetheless there is a reality: there are maternal practices in which ideals of nonviolence actually govern. Mothers can, and often do, renounce the violence to which they are tempted, fight back against the violence done to them and their children, name and insist on responsibility for damages done, yet forswear a scarring hatred in favor of a peace in which they can love and work.

Peacemakers can learn from maternal nonviolence even when mothers themselves do not extend or publicize the nonviolence they imperfectly practice. Conversely, whether or not they take on public militarism, mothers should find it illuminating to look at the ordinary tasks and temptations of their work through the lens of nonviolence. Maternal struggles to achieve nonviolence parallel and illuminate the struggle to achieve a sturdy peace. Whatever their public antimilitarist commitments, nonviolent mothers offer an invigorating image of peace as an active connectedness.

All participants resist others' violence and their own temptations to abandon or assault, persisting in relationships that include anger, disappointment, difference, conflict, and nonviolent battle.

CHAPTER EIGHT

Histories of Human Flesh

WOMEN AND MEN have made war together. Most women, like most men, thrill to or reluctantly support the organized violence in which their cause or state enlists them. Nonetheless, throughout history some women have insisted that, as women, they have distinct reasons for rejecting war. This does not mean that women are innately or inevitably peaceful. As the American social critic Jane Addams put it during the first world war:

The belief that a woman is against war simply and only because she is a woman and not a man, does not, of course, hold. In every country there are many, many women who believe that War is inevitable and righteous, and that the highest possible service is being performed by their sons who go into the Army.[1]

Nor are women afraid to fight, unable to fight, or morally superior to fighters. In the words of the white South African novelist, feminist, and critic Olive Schreiner, written a few years after Addams's comment:

It is not because of woman's cowardice, incapacity, nor, above all, because of her general superior virtue that she will end war when her voice is finally and fully heard.[2]

Rather, to quote Addams again,

The women do have a sort of pang about it. . . . That curious revolt comes out again and again, even in the women who are most patriotic. . . . Even those women, when they are taken off their guard, give a certain protest, a certain plaint against the whole situation which very few men I think are able to formulate.[3]

Both Addams and Schreiner traced women's "curious revolt" against war to their experience as mothers. Addams compared a mother to "an artist who is in the artillery corps, let us say, and is commanded to fire upon a wonderful thing, say St. Mark's at Venice, or the Duomo at Florence, or any other great architectural and beautiful thing. I am sure that he would have just a little more compunction than the man who had never given himself to creating beauty and did not know the cost of it."[4] Schreiner spoke of "so many months of weariness and pain while bones and muscles were shaped within; so many hours of anguish and struggle that breath might be; so many baby mouths drawing life at woman's breasts; all this that men might lie with glazed eyeballs, and swollen bodies, and fixed, blue unclosed mouths, and great limbs tossed."[5] Neither Addams nor Schreiner believed that women became generally wise from being mothers. Schreiner did however attribute to women a quite specific knowledge:

No woman who is a woman says of a human body, "it is nothing." . . . On this one point, and on this point almost alone, the knowledge of woman, simply as woman, is superior to that of man; she knows the history of human flesh; she knows its cost; he does not.[6]

In this chapter, I take Addams and Schreiner seriously: women tend to know, in a way and to a degree that many men do not, both the history and the cost of human flesh. Their knowledge derives from the work of mothering, which, though it can be shared equally with men, has been historically female. It also derives, at least in part, from an experience or appreciation of female birthing labor on which all subsequent mothering depends. Their maternal conception of the history of human flesh sets women at odds with militarist endeavors. This does not mean that an antimilitarist maternal "history of the human flesh" exists, waiting to be told. Maternal thinking includes conceptions of the body more militarist than antimilitarist. Moreover, women, whether or not they are mothers or identify with them, learn the language of their cultures. If they are educated or influenced by Western philosophy, they learn to minimize and fear birthing labor, which I believe should stand at the center of a maternal history of the flesh. Yet maternal thinking already includes a latent conception of bodiliness that is potentially a resource for those who reject militarism in the hope of inventing peace.

I begin by considering "the body" as it appears in Western popular and philosophical thinking, including some versions of Western feminism. Because it is a dominant conception, this view may seem simply true; it often represents my own "common sense." Yet this popular and philosophical understanding is also part of the militarist conception of the body, which I discuss next. Then I turn to a maternal history of the flesh, where I relinquish my own defensive efforts to separate a potentially genderless work of mothering from the female birth on which it depends. Recasting the "truths" of "common sense"* and philosophy that have shaped my thinking, I offer a conception of the bodily that is centered in birthing labor and the unique relation of birthgiver and infant. Throughout, in speaking of "the body" I focus on three of its attributes: natality, sexuality, and mortality. This abstract tripartite characterization of the body in terms of its most dramatic entrances, exits, and connections slights the variety of ordinary bodily activities — sleeping, listening, eating, running, and other transactions of daily life. One task of maternal thinking is to reclaim this ordinary bodily variety from the sort of dramatic abstractions I resort to here.

---

*I put "common sense" in quotation marks because the commonality of the views I report is in part illusory and in part imposed by philosophical and ideological considerations. The common sense views on which I report have been my own, but I have also been alienated from my experiences by them. I will now leave out the quotation marks for ease of reading.

Reason's Body

Surely the soul can best reflect when it is free of all distractions such as hearing or sight or pain or pleasure of any kind — that is, when it ignores the body and becomes as far as possible independent, avoiding all physical contacts and associations as much as it can in its search for reality. In despising the body and avoiding it, and endeavoring to become independent, the philosopher's soul is ahead of all the rest. . . . The body provides us with innumerable distractions in the pursuit of our necessary sustenance; and any diseases which attack us hinder our quest for reality. Besides the body fills us with loves and desires and fears and all sorts of fancies and a great deal of nonsense. . . . If we are ever to have pure knowledge of anything, we must get rid of the body and contemplate things by themselves with the soul by itself.
— *Plato*[7]

In some philosophical texts and in many popular representations, "the body" is like an erratic computer or a spirited horse. Like any machine, the body breaks down; like the best horse, it is subject to mishap and failures of control on the part of its rider. Although we can do nothing without our bodies, we can't count on them either. Despite our best efforts to feed, rest, and train our machines or mounts, we are afflicted by failures of sense, breakdowns of function, and compulsive physiological desires. If few people are as disenchanted with the body as the dying Socrates, in many versions of Western thinking, popular and philosophical, the body is considered a recalcitrant adversary, or at best a distraction from worthier "transcendental" pursuits. This adversarial body is marked by mortality and a troubling sexuality. Its natality — the fact and conditions of human birth — though ostensibly ignored or celebrated, is indirectly represented as a fearful counterpart of Reason.

To judge by philosophical and religious reflection, the human body is essentially characterized by its mortal end. Volumes have been written about fears of dying, struggles with death, and existential angst in the face of the nothingness that shapes the consciousness of a species that knows its own mortality. The moment of death is preceded by a lifetime's susceptibility to illness, accidental physical damage, decay, and, if we are lucky, "old age, the parody of life."[8] Sexual ecstasy has been thought of as a kind of "dying," sexual pleasure as a harbinger of mortal disease. Even birth is associated with death and, accordingly, death with the female who creates life: "Man that is born of woman has but a short time to live."

In the dominant view of common sense, sexual desire seems nearly as worrying as death. Except where women have access to artificial insemination, sex is necessary for any body to enter life. Sexual sensations are so ineluctably enjoyable that they compel repetition. Sexual activity is a primary source of recreation, and sexual relations can be a model for and serve as the occasion of deepest intimacy. Nonetheless, it is difficult in most cultures to take sexuality at its simple best. Like Plato, both contemplatives and activists fear that sexual desire will undermine their long-term projects, whether writing philosophy, conducting a military campaign, or running for president. Many people fear that their own or others' adulterous or uncontrolled sexual desire will interfere with more stable intimacy. In cultures where sexuality is believed to be entwined with the threat of (mostly male) violence, many people — especially women and Fathers of daughters — also fear that sexual desire makes the desiring or desired person vulnerable to abuse. Sexual activity is also alleged to be unhealthy, giving rise to general debilitation, diseases, or, at worst, mortal illness. Even when heterosexual desire serves what is meant to be its "function," it produces children who are often seen as a portent of pain, danger, and onerous economic and social obligations.

Unlike sexuality, or certainly illness and death, birth seems to common sense a welcome event. A successful birth is at the least a profound relief to a birthing woman, whether or not she desired the infant or will assume its care. At best birth is a cause for celebration: "Unto us a child is born." Oddly, there is barely an echo of this celebratory aspect in philosophical writing. Although we are a species that knows its own natality, in philosophical texts we are "thrown" into the universe somehow, appearing at the earliest when we can talk and read. Since birth is hardly uninteresting, this silence suggests that something troubling is being kept at bay. Indeed, I believe that in the dominant view of common sense and Western philosophy, birth is as troubling as sexuality and as psychologically provocative, if not as unhappy, as death.

Suppose we look at birth, as I believe the Man of Common Sense does, with a suspicious eye. It is not difficult to see how birth itself and the female bodies who engage in it might get a bad name. Giving birth is painful and, throughout most of history and for many women even today, dangerous. To be sure, the degree and details of pain are mediated by numerous factors such as technological and medical expertise and the financial or social ability to acquire it. Nonetheless, despite propaganda to the contrary, birth often remains a painful, frightening, and sometimes humiliating experience for women. This can make birthing labor a source of fear not only for birthing women but also for those who love them. The pain and danger of birth may also provoke in men and nonbirthing women a sense of guilt and of exclusion from a primary experience of human suffering.

The gaze of the suspicious eye of common sense can extend itself over the entire female body, ambivalently fascinated and repelled by its reproductive activities. In many cultures birthing labor, the menstruation associated with it, and at times even breast-feeding evoke disgust. Regarded ungenerously, a woman's birthing body — bloody, swollen out of shape, exposed in its pain, its otherwise concealed parts broken open — is repellent. It is disturbing in itself and because it forces on any onlooker the intimate knowledge of his or her own fleshly beginnings. The nursing couple is disturbingly sexual, while the milk of a nursing mother is usually out of even the mother's control, coming when it's not needed, staining, and dribbling, or "drying up" despite a baby's hunger. Like urine and feces, menstrual blood is bodily excretion that must be socially regulated. Unlike the other bodily excretions, however, menstrual "discharge" is not subject to voluntary regulation by the menstruating woman. In fact, except for women who want to conceive, each month's blood is a welcome sign: the body is healthy; unwelcome pregnancies have been avoided; the blood hints at a promise that *might* be acted on if one chose. Yet in the popular view menstruation also puts the menstruating woman in the company of the incontinent — the infant, seriously ill, or frail elderly — who must bind, hide, or have hidden for them the expressions of their bodies. Regarded suspiciously, menstrual "incontinence" is closely allied with irregularity, and therefore unreliability. Unlike other repetitive bodily activities such as breathing, the "regular" cycle, over a lifetime and for many women in a monthly way, is unpredictable. Even when the cycle is regular, menstruation makes the body "irregular," a fact that has excluded women from psychological experiments as well as employment or posts that require stability.

It is the experience of birthing *bodies* and birthing labor that apparently disconcerts the philosopher. Yet for all its brute and sometimes brutal physicality, birthing is indelibly a social relation, a fact that only a radical distinction between mind and body can disguise. I would guess that the social relations of birth are also troubling to the philosopher or Man of Common Sense. Birth, more than any other experience except perhaps sexuality, undermines the individuation of bodies. The growing fetus, increasingly visible in the woman's swelling body, an infant emerging from the vagina, a suckling infant feeding off a breast, the mother feeding with and of her body express in dramatic form a fusion of self and other. Any man or woman might fear the obliteration of self that such an experience suggests. More prosaically, the dramatic intimacy of birthing foreshadows a milder but nonetheless life-shaping tie to a particular, dependent person. Unlike a sexual act or death, birthing labor is not complete of itself. Its peak, climax, or discharge is another life that requires for its continuance somebody's mothering. The bodies of birthing laborers are resonant with this responsibility, which inspires resentment and fear in both birthing women and those allied with them.

Most troubling of all its social aspects, birthing labor is uniquely female; only women can suffer its burdens or share in its powers. No other division — of class, race, religion, or culture — has been as ineradicable as that between the sex that can bear children and the sex that cannot. To be sure, unless artificial insemination is effective and widely accessible, men's sexual activity is as necessary to conception as women's. Even where men are bypassed by artificial insemination, every birth is dependent on male sperm. Yet a man's participation in birthing, no matter how eagerly and responsibly he engages in the process, is in no way comparable to a woman's — physically, sexually, emotionally, socially, or politically. Birthing most likely provokes in nonbirthing women as well as men envy, awe, and fear of the unknown. But it is only men who learn that they were excluded at birth from birthing labor.

And indeed, philosophers and psychologists[9] have revealed time and again men's fear and envy of birthing labor and of the female bodies responsible for it. From at least as early as Aristotle, who attributed spirit, form, and activity to the sperm for which he said women provided mere matter, to the latest legal and medical experts, who equate the uterus with a "container" available for rent, some men have claimed equal, or perhaps even superior, participation in birthing labor. These men might be thought to honor a work by insisting (mistakenly) that it was theirs. In fact, the reverse is true. When the active "seed" is compared with the matter in which it rests, birthing labor is ignored. Similarly, a claim that a child is genetically as much a male as a female creation, though true, simply passes over the pregnancy and birthing labor on which that child's existence depends.

Feminists have also shown that as men minimize women's birthing labor they claim for themselves a higher creativity. "Thrown" into the world, they turn their back on the dependencies that formed them. Accepting no presuppositions but those they stipulate, they sail away, disown what went before, begin anew as Fathers of themselves. While women (and many men) are engaged in bodily creation of physical children, some men (and a few women) are able to create Truth and Beauty with their souls. Again it is Plato who most hauntingly urged this view:

Those whose creative instinct is physical have recourse to women, and show their love in this way, believing that by begetting children they can assure for themselves an immortal and blessed memory hereafter for ever; but there are some whose creative desire is of the soul, and who long to beget spiritually, not physically, the progeny which it is the nature of the soul to create and bring to birth. If you ask what that progeny is, it is wisdom and virtue in general. . . . Everyone would prefer children such as these to children after the flesh.[10]

The minimization of birth is not only a masculine or misogynist fantasy. Some feminists have promulgated their own version of the distinction between merely physical procreativity and the worthier creations of artists and intellectuals.[11] Where men may envy procreative powers, feminists fear that women will be defined by them, in the worst case forced into birthing labor they do not choose. It has been an effort to assert the obvious: women are as capable as men of "higher" endeavors that, unlike birthing labor, require active, independent, focused, ordered discipline. No person, just because she has a female body, is necessarily inclined to engage in birthing labor or obligated to do so.

Not surprisingly, feminists have found themselves minimizing the female exclusiveness of birthing labor to ward off envy and share responsibility. Some include men in every way physically possible in the birthing process — as coaches, witnesses, comforters — and then exaggerate the equality achieved. Others minimize the importance of birthing labor to women or men. I have distinguished birth from mothering and then have described maternal work as potentially genderless, active, and disciplined, requiring the ability to separate as well as connect and at its best exhibiting the independent judgment of conscientiousness. In other words, mothering is quite unlike female birthing labor, which looks, in contrast, to be an essentially passive waiting in which growth takes care of itself, requiring of the birthgiver at most the discipline of a good, and perhaps informed, patient. In this construction the distinctive act of giving birth is blandly assimilated to the gestation that preceded it. In short, my treatment of birthing labor has been entirely consistent with at least the more benign versions of philosophical suspicion and denial of female bodies.

Once I actually looked at birthing labor, it seemed to me that the compulsion to control and minimize birth was expressed in the ideals of reason that dominate Western philosophy. I have in mind here certain feminist readings of Western philosophy that reveal that the body and ideals of reason are reciprocally and oppositionally defined. This relation can be represented in a series of "Big Dichotomies."[12] Reason is associated with mind, objectivity, detachment, culture, impersonal concern, public order, and agreement. The body in turn is associated with subjectivity, passion, nature, particular affections, domestic confinement, parochial prejudice, and irresolvable difference. A rational person is one for whom the capacities and values associated with reason control and order the properly subordinated capacities represented by the body. So, for example, a reasonable person's controlled body is subordinated to his or her controlled mind, his or her passions are controlled by impersonal, detached, objective judgment, and his or her particular, private affections are subordinated to public concern.

There is nothing intrinsically masculine about mind and objectivity or anything feminine about passion and physicality. Nonetheless, philosophers have tended to associate, explicitly or metaphorically, passion, affection, and the body with femininity and the mind with masculinity. That is, the body is associated with a female biological condition, the mind with an achieved masculinity that males are more likely than females to attain. We are so accustomed to this association that we may be insufficiently puzzled by it. In those cultures in which women are excluded from schools and the institutions where intellectual achievement is rewarded, it is not surprising if rationality has, historically, been associated with men. Nor is it surprising, given the work women have done, that they should be associated with affectionate ties to individuals and domestic practices — though it is not at all clear why these should be opposed to, rather than, say, made a requirement for, public responsibility and transcendental reflection. On the other hand, no possible biological difference between males and females could make one sex more "bodily" than the other.

How did it happen that Western philosophers came to think that some bodies were more "bodily" than others? The answer is obvious but it may be useful to make it explicit. Bodily mortality is not specifically female except by its association with birthing labor: "Man *that is born of woman* has but a short time to live."

Both male and female bodies are sexual. Women are sometimes thought to be aflame with ensnaring and incontinent desire; yet it is male desire that they ensnare. In any case, it is equally likely that a culture will represent active sexual desire as specifically male rather than female. Clearly, it is birthing labor and its attendant menstruation and nursing that distinguish female bodies. Thus in opposing reason and masculinity against the body and femininity, it is birthing labor and what it represents against which reason sets itself.

This can be shown by reversing the Big Dichotomies, attributing to reason those characteristics that are opposed not merely to physical bodies but specifically to birthing labor as it is conceptualized by the suspicious philosopher. Since the relationship of birth is taken to exemplify merging or the failure of individuation, reason would require and promise autonomy, which in turn would be defined in terms of separation and detachment. Since giving birth is a female activity, and therefore exclusionary and mysterious, reason must be simultaneously masculine and open to any person who could take a distance from the affective ties and particular passions that birth portends. Deliberately distant from the unsettling irregularities and stark physicality epitomized in birthing, reasonable people would be expected to provide and count on stability and regularity. Where birth implies life-shaping responsibilities to particular vulnerable others, reason enables people to act together with strangers in public or, if they choose, to contemplate without responsibility in rooms of their own. Whether active managers and rulers or reclusive contemplatives, reasoners are excused from serious domestic responsibility *for* others and, ideally, *count on* others for the material services on which any mind depends.

What I am suggesting is that the idealization of reason in Western philosophy may be in part a defensive reaction to the troubling complexities of birthing labor, that Western conceptions of what it is to be reasonable are intertwined with a fear and resentment of birthing female bodies. This is a matter of reciprocal definition. Just as the Man of Reason is nearly the opposite of a birthing woman–infant couple, so too her birthing labor has been conceptualized in opposition to him. My characterization of birthing labor as incontinent, repetitiously irregular, insufficiently individuated, and vulnerable to pain, confinement, and onerous responsibility reflects the dominance of reason, which is idealized as active, autonomous, controlling, progressive, and socially powerful yet exempt from unwanted social responsibilities.[13]

To be sure, it is not only the birthing labor that is taken to be inimical to active human projects. As I have suggested, mortality and sexuality are nearly as troubling, though not as conceptually determinative, as natality. Fear and resentment of birthing bodies shape and shade into a general distrust of bodily life. What reason needs is to be free of bodies. Second best, it needs a body suitable to its purposes. Concretely, reason's body is a controlled instrument of reason's purposes, such as Plato envisioned. Plato's Socrates drinks more than most but never lets intoxication divert his mind from its lively purposes. He is subject to passionate sexual desire and is glad of it, but he controls, and eventually frustrates, desire in the service of reason's passion for an abstract Good. In Plato's *Republic,* women and men who are destined to become rulers are schooled in gymnastics and music; their bodies are trained to become harmonious instruments of a will that is itself an instrument of reason. In the post-Cartesian world, Plato's controlled body becomes fundamentally abstract, a characterless, colorless, sexless extension of matter in space. But when it comes to earth again in affluent sections of the United States, this body continues to manage itself in Platonic fashion though with less than Socratic confidence. Working out, shaping up, controlling what it ingests, it makes physical life bend to reason's chosen projects.

When reason sets itself against a body that is epitomized by birthing labor, the relationship of birth stands outside speech. Bodily beginnings, and some women's participation in them, stand for all that reason is not. When birth figures in reason's story only as an absence, the birthing woman is silent.

There is no ready feminist and woman-respecting response to this condition of silence. There is, for example, no "woman's reason" to reflect rather than oppose birthing labor. Although distinctive rationalities may arise out of women's lives and work, the idea of an exclusive or singular *woman*'s reason repeats in reverse a mythical dichotomy between men's and women's minds. A reason that thrives on dichotomy is one that looks for a female to oppose to the male, a "natural" woman to oppose to man's "culture," a subjective mind to oppose to his objectivity. It certainly is not antimilitarist to reject men's "reason" in the name of femininity. It is militarists who benefit from the equation of women with the emotional, physical, and subjective, who then call Cassandra mad and defense intellectuals people of reason. The struggle to be "rational" — to see what is real in all its complexity and ambiguity — is a peacemaker's struggle.

Nor is it possible for feminists to see the errors of their abstraction and reaffirm "natural" connections of mothering to birthing labor. Women's powerlessness both when they are pregnant and later in custody cases lends emotional credence to the angry claim of a birthing woman's rights to care for her children. But mothering really isn't much like birthing labor. I now recognize that my characterization of mothering as an active, disciplined, human work resonates with Western ideals of reason. But having noticed the minimization of birthing labor that my concepts reveal, I nonetheless continue to believe that mothering is a focused work that can be undertaken by men as well as women. Nor is it only a philosophical fantasy that the experience of giving birth has been ineluctably female, even though scientific fantasies of test tube babies promise to put an end to the fears such exclusivity provokes. Whether giving birth is the activity of a woman or a laboratory scientist, it is not necessary or sufficient for mothering happily and well.

The reconceptualization of birthing labor and therefore of reason, the reconceptualization of reason and therefore of birthing labor are ongoing collective feminist tasks. It is necessary for feminist philosophers to tell the story of birth again, reconnecting the work of mothering to the female labor in which it begins. Human birth, when it is seen with a realistically celebratory rather than a suspicious eye, lies at the beginning and the center of antimilitarist maternal stories of human flesh. Before I suggest this maternal, revisionist history I turn directly to the militarist elaboration of Reason's body that it is intended to combat.

War's Body

If in some smothering dreams you too could pace
Behind the wagon that we flung him in,
And watch the white eyes writhing in his face,
His hanging face, like a devil's sick of sin:
If you could hear, at every jolt, the blood
Come gargling from the froth corrupted lungs,
Obscene as cancer, bitter as the cud
of vile, incurable sores on innocent tongues —
My friend, you would not tell with such high zest
To children ardent for some desperate glory,
The old lie: Dulce et decorum est
Pro patria mori.
— *Wilfred Owen*[14]

Reason's body, created where the birthing woman is not, is ready to become an instrument of military will. Socrates was a soldier who stood his ground, aided his wounded friend and lover, then retreated in orderly, confident fashion. Although the Cartesian abstract body lends no racist or other support to social division, it too serves military purposes. It is particularly appropriate for the "techno-strategic rationality" that characterizes the nuclear mentality. In the "rational world of defense intellectuals"[15] abstractions multiply as speakers obscure for themselves and their listeners the intense and extensive sufferings wrought by monstrously destructive and self-destructive strategies. Techno-strategic rationality is only an extreme version of any militarist theories that divert attention from what actually happens to real bodies and toward the causes and strategies that justify their abuse.

It is not abstractions but actual bodies that show up for basic training, drive tanks, and staff missile silos. These actual bodies are also creatures of Reason, controlled, hardened instruments of "higher purpose."[16] Numerous civilian exercises from weightlifting to self-starvation are designed to produce a hard, compliant body. The basic training of a soldier, with its potent mix of macho pride, punishing physical ordeals, and humiliating rituals, is the epitome of this effort to mold flesh in authority's image. The military body must be obedient to the soldier's will, even as that will is obedient to the rules and rulers of war. This military body is the perfect instantiation of philosophical fantasy. Abstract, ready to be counted, yet not counting; when under control, a reliable mount or machine.

From these "philosophical" beginnings, militarists construct and depend on a rich ideology of the body — of its sexuality, mortality, and even of its birthing. The business of war is a trafficking in bodies. Soldiers achieve their aims by threatening to damage bodies or actually doing so — burning, cutting, blasting, pounding, breaking flesh and bones. As Elaine Scarry puts it:

Injury is the thing every exhausting piece of strategy and every single weapon is designed to bring into being: it is not something inadvertently produced on the way to producing something else but is the relentless object of all military activity.[17]

In strategic terms a body is the place where pain and damage are inflicted.

It has been shown by Carol Cohn[18] that in the language of high-tech war, it is weapons that are targeted, put at risk, and survive or are wasted. Damage to human bodies not only is described as "collateral" but is genuinely taken to be a lamented secondary effect of the contest between weapons. Yet we outsiders recognize these machines as weapons because with them it is possible to sicken, mutilate, and burn human bodies. Soldiers are killed and kill with weapons that are meant to be cruel. Radiation sickness and chemical poisons are not merely the fallout of "clean" explosions but are predictable effects. Napalm purposely includes an ingredient, white phosphorus, that increases the adhesion of burning petrol to human skin. Explosive (dumdum) bullets, the metal cubes of claymore mines, the fiberglass fragments (fleshettes) of cluster bombs are deliberately designed to tear bodies apart not only with pain but precisely in ways that defeat medical skill.

Militarists are not alone in exploiting the body's capacity for pain. Torturers and enslavers dominate others through the imposition of suffering, inflicting pain in excess of what is needed to impose their will. In contrast to the torturer or violent bully, individual soldiers and in some cases whole armies are restrained, reluctant killers. Many would rather hide than injure others or risk injury to themselves. Some recognize in their "enemy" a "brother," a fellow victim rather than an executioner of plans neither understands. But however restrained its executors, war's business is hurting or threatening to hurt. The salient feature of war's body is its susceptibility to pain and damage that lead to surrender.

Whether inflicting or suffering damage, war's body is almost always sharply marked as either male or female. In most armies, in most of history, a soldier is male. Women may take up the sword or gun when men have fallen, but they do not set out to "carry the battle" to the enemy. Men and women may fight to- gether outside of state power, but once violence is "legitimately" organized, it is usually only male bodies that are deemed suitable for combat. Even in the United States, where the armed forces are atypically integrated and where some women are qualified to turn the keys that launch the missiles, combat is officially, and command is actually, a male privilege and responsibility. Military requirements cannot account for such a stringent association of war with masculinity. Many weapons and battle plans do not require the upper body strength that recruiters celebrate and that men, on the average, display. "The male's greater vital capacity, speed, muscle mass, aiming and throwing skills, his greater pro- pensity for aggression and his more rapid rises in adrenaline" may indeed make him on the average "more fitted for physically intense combat."[19] Such specifically masculine strength has little to do with the computer centers, missile silos, bomber cockpits, and armored tanks at the center of modern battle plans.

Although there is wide agreement that soldiers must be men, there are at least two competing views of manliness — the beastly male and the just warrior. Both serve to legitimate war's mur- derous mutilation and death. The beastly male is a man who is "naturally" suited by his "beastliness" to become a soldier. In civilian life he is under only the shaky, fragile control of his own reason and others' force. Basically he is all body and his body is all aggression and sex. A beastly man accepts the discipline of battle because it also includes or promises predatory and sadistic sexuality. He roars, rapes, castrates, and murders, and when he's killed he shrieks and dies. Since rape, assault, and murder are in his nature, civilized men and women needn't bewail his death. They need only ensure that his killing is controlled by obedience to reasonable officers and governments.

Reports from the battlefield sometimes sustain the myth of the beastly male soldier. There seems little doubt that, for many soldiers and strategists, injuring is sexualized and sexually exciting; soldiers themselves often describe their sexuality as compulsive and predatory. Military speech is imbued with masculinist heterosexual metaphor: war is a "pissing contest"; to disarm is "to get rid of all your stuff"; "spasm attacks" release "70 to 80 percent of our megatonnage in one orgasmic whump"; military lectures are filled with references to "vertical erectory launchers, thrust-to-weight ratios, soft lay downs, deep penetration"; an invasion of a small island becomes a "pre-dawn vertical insertion"; a new missile replaces a recent rather than an outmoded one because the former missile is "in the nicest hole."[20] Suspected or captured soldiers, male and female, are tortured in specifically sexual ways. Penises and testicles are objects of abuse; anal and genital rape and humiliations are standard instruments of pleasure and revenge; breasts and vaginas are mutilated; "conquered" women are predictably raped, and women from all quarters are hired, seduced, or forced into subservient sex. Even children and the elderly are not immune to sexual abuse. These well-known facts about war and sexuality can be cited to explain both the cruelty of soldiers and the popularity of warmaking, with its direct and, for civilians who are far from battle, vicarious sexual-aggressive gratification.

No doubt there are predatory, rapist men who welcome the opportunity to become soldiers. It is also likely that most men trained and licensed to kill may be at least temporarily sexually intoxicated by injuring others. But the evidence is also strong that the rapist-predator is a minority among soldiers, that the excitement of sexualized injuring is a momentary episode in many soldiers' lives. Judging from their published memoirs and their actual or later fictional letters home, soldiers experience an unpredictable mix of courage, fear, rage, lust, cruelty, loyalty, love, tenderness, and exhaustion and are often shocked by the vengeful fantasies of civilians. The "beastly male" seems the projective creation of women's and men's fantasies. War, like racism, both excites and focuses on the "other" fears and desires that would be disruptive if read into the bodies of men of one's own social group.[21] Although much has been written about the projection of desires and fears on to women's bodies, too little note is taken of women's and men's fearful, racist construction of men's bodies.

Whatever is true of most soldiers, there are clearly many fighters and reluctant loyal militarists who lament the cruel injuries of war. Rather than being sexually excited by the violence around them, they struggle to keep their eyes averted from suffering and fixed on the cause. There is a gap — moral and conceptual — between the aims of war and its outcome—the "glazed eyeballs, and swollen bodies, and fixed blue unclosed mouths, and great limbs tossed" that Olive Schreiner saw. The righteousness of a cause is disconnected from the capacity to outinjure. As Elaine Scarry has shown in some detail, military thinking provides identifiable techniques of description and evasion that focus the mind on strategy rather than suffering, sacrifice rather than killing, and the cause rather than the bodies torn apart in its name.[22] Primary among these conceptual strategies is the creation of the manly just warrior, which interlocks myths of masculinity, sacrifice, and heroic death.

The just warrior is the romantic double of the beastly male. He embodies the abstract restraints articulated in rules of war, fulfilling the fantasy of an armed and masterful yet quintessentially vulnerable sexuality. The just warrior is at once homo- and heteroerotic and sexual. In their planes and ships, as on their battlefields, just soldiers participate in a homoerotic romance ("bonding") with other soldiers whose sensual intensity suffuses war memoirs and poetry. The just comrade turned heterosexual is no rapist. Required by war to be celibate, he is by "nature" the masterly sexual lover of the woman and women he excites and defends. As women's literature and memoirs make clear, the potentially violent yet vulnerable, dangerous yet restrained protector and warrior is luringly erotic. Such a warrior may have to dwell among cruelties and mutilations, but he is essentially their victim or avenger, not their perpetrator. When he kills, he is swift and discriminate, harming only the dangerous combatant, the "enemy" whom he would rather embrace as brother.

The just soldier's sexual allure is partly a function of the danger he faces and his controlled courage in facing it. Facing death, the warrior transcends bodily passion and particular affection to identify with cause or state; while relinquishing particular sexual union for the "universal," he is also poignantly exciting for particular men and women.[23] When the just warrior dies, he "falls," his life a sacrifice to the cause he represents and also to the women and men whose desire he excites. Such a soldier's body is never ugly in its mutilation; even if the casket must be closed, the sacrificial body is welcomed home.

The just soldier is meant to die heroically, instantiating an ideology of death and sacrifice that masks crude injury. This ideology sits uneasily with the bodily realities it is intended to conceal. Ideologically, military dead are courageous under extraordinary fire, yet soldiers are at least as able to flee death as the citizens of the villages and cities they bomb and burn. Military deaths are meaningful; the best battlefield death is a chosen testament to individual valor and a just cause. In fact, numerous military deaths are accidental or fratricidal, and an individual's death is rarely of military consequence. A soldier's death is meant to be swift and clean, a sharp sacrifice. In fact, even as death by hemlock is messy and painful in ways philosophical fantasy must obscure, so too dying soldiers, like their victims who outnumber them, vomit, sob, shit, and scream their life away.

Real battlefield deaths are acceptable only for beastly males and enemies. It is an ongoing task of militarists to create a fiction of death to satisfy the emotional demands of ordinary soldiers and anyone who identifies with or mourns their "sacrifice." In the fragility of military ideologies of death lies a peacemaker's hope. It is thus a peacemaker's task not only to deconstruct that fiction but to provide an alternative, nonmystifying account of bodily death. Because military abstractions divert attention from bodies, it is a time-honored antimilitarist strategy merely to speak the details of war's suffering and to force listeners to hear them. "If you too could pace behind the wagon," "if you could hear," "if you could see."

A distinctive and joint creation of philosophical abstraction and sexual fantasy, war's body kills and suffers; it does not give birth. Warriors are male; victims are mutilated or dying; there is no space for birthing labor. Yet, although war is more antagonistic to the children of flesh than even philosophy, birthing imagery and fantasies recur in accounts of military experience. Soldiers and their interpreters speak romantically of a "second birth" for men whose normal sociality is radically ruptured by danger and killing and who live "homeless," entirely among men, in deprived yet ecstatic camaraderie.[24] We know from soldiers' memoirs that what the philosopher J. Glenn Gray called "preservative love" flourishes on battlefields and in barracks.[25] This love is at least associated with birthing labor and the mothering it gives rise to. Like its domestic counterpart, military preservative love is expressed in tender concern for whatever "home" survives homelessness — a foxhole, trench, or missile silo — as well as for stray animals, fragile natural life, vulnerable civilians, and frightened or ill soldiers. This love, according to Gray, is poignantly bittersweet because it is surrounded by death and destruction. Gray even suggests, perversely, that preservative love flourishes only in starkly contrasting surroundings of danger and destruction. If so, this military version of preservative love is a sick reflection of the ordinary protective work that is marked by unexciting dailiness and a matter-of-fact acceptance of vulnerability and the threat of loss.

As the French feminist Nancy Huston points out, since Heraclitus war has sometimes been thought of "as the mother of all things," "a virile form of regeneration," the "matrix of society."[26] Birth appears prominently and perversely in the service of death in the language of defense intellectuals who, like philosophers far from battle, simultaneously minimize and appropriate birthing labor. According to Carol Cohn, "the denial of women's role in the process of creation and the reduction of 'motherhood' to the provision of nurturance . . . seems thoroughly incorporated into the nuclear mentality."[27] Nonetheless, the language Cohn heard from defense intellectuals is rife with images of birth. The atom bomb was known as "Oppenheimer's baby," the hydrogen bomb as "Teller's baby." "In early tests, before they were certain the bombs would work, the scientists expressed their concern by saying they hoped the baby was a boy, not a girl — i.e., not a dud." Winston Churchill was informed of the scientists' success: "Babies satisfactorily born." In what may be the ultimate perversion, the bomb dropped on Hiroshima was known as Little Boy, celebrating at once a new age of destruction and an ancient and lethal link between the boy child and murder.[28] In this language of war, birthing laborers are male, the "child" a damaging, injuring weapon, the birth a grand destruction rather than individual creation. Even in birth, war's body is in the service of death.

War contains still another image of birth. A birthing woman with her crying infant, bereft amid the ruins and mangled bodies of war, a recurrent image in antimilitarist art, stands in for the promises of life and birth that have been shattered by war. Throughout history, this birthing woman has been mute, prone, passive, and suffering — a victim on the other side of action and speech. It is a primary task of a distinctly antimilitarist maternal thinking to hear in her labor a voice of reason loving and fierce enough to speak for peace.

A History of Human Flesh Under the Aspect of Natality

Darkness replaced the white light then, a darkness so narrow she had to keep her body utterly stiff in order not to be bruised by the black walls. She slipped downward, eyes closed, mouth opened, feeling the silky slipping as the dearest comfort she had ever known. . . . Low in the black hole a steel shelf inside her began to push itself down, out of her, the bottom half of her body tearing away from the top like the discarded part of a spacecraft that has served its purpose and blown away. . . .

They placed him on her chest and she raised her hand slow as a low-

tide wave rolling onto his tiny head. She tried to breathe evenly to comfort him. She felt the wet satin of his body against hers and at the same time felt as if she were he, finding firm ground after what must have been his trial as much as her own.
— *Jane Lazarre*[29]

In maternal practice there is a real, unromantic, material basis for a revisionist history of the body, both realistic and celebratory. To tell a maternal history, it is necessary to look again, with trusting eyes, at sexuality and birth. The history begins at the beginning, with a birthing woman and infant, whose relationship, however disturbing, is also emblematic of promise. In this history, a body is a testament to hope. Every body, and therefore every death, counts; the promise of birth includes a dying well tended and a death well mourned.

Like militarists, mothers work through and with bodies. Mothering begins in some woman's intense physical experience. Early mothering is done amid feces, urine, vomit, and milk. Children are complex and physically at risk; their bodies must be tended as they are, not as they might become. Instead of "the body," there are bodies that come in various shapes and colors with distinctive chemistries and styles of being. In myriad ways, the youngest infants assert themselves: this physical being is here; whoever cares for me cares for this.

Soon children's bodily lives reveal elaborate, imaginative play. Genitals, limbs, toes, and fingers may acquire distinctive personalities and names. Torsos and faces painted; secret scars and individual oddities as well as "private parts" exposed to gaze and touch; elaborate games of dressing, undressing, making up, masking, and revealing; eating and refusing to eat according to ritual and individual taste; courting and inflicting minor pains; building up and slimming down; jumping, shouting, singing, cycling — these and many other activities make up children's daily fare. Mothers, in turn, respond to these bodies, cleaning, feeding, soothing, exciting, doting. Neither children nor their mothers could distinguish in their bodily lives between rich elaborate mental play and the "merely physical."

The omnipresence of bodies and the richly elaborated bodily experience of childhood and maternal life do not guarantee for mothers, any more than for militarists, respect for the bodily. Many mothers have too little time, insufficient space, too many children, too many worries, and too much work for any but the minimal protective tasks. They are unlikely to acquire a welcoming conception of bodies to match the richness around them. Even with time and space, the capacity to enjoy bodily pleasures does not come easily in cultures that are either repressive or sexually exploitative.

Some mothers, preoccupied by suffering, actively resist bodily pleasures. For them, pain, danger, and illness — certainly real enough — morbidly overshadow the exhilaration of painful childbirth, the erotic experiences of nursing and holding, the wonder of children's healthy bodies, and the poignant beauty of even frail or dying bodies. When suffering and danger infuse maternal fantasy, birth itself becomes a soldier's sacrifice. "*All* women who bear children are committing, literally and symbolically, a blood sacrifice for the perpetuation of the species."[30] Other mothers see only a dangerous vulnerability — imperfections, assault, disease, unwanted pregnancy, social ostracism — in their own and their children's, especially their daughters', sexuality. Since they are blamed for their own or their children's "unruly" sexual lives, they long for bodies whose gender is sharply defined, that are well behaved but not erotic. More aggressively, if a training mother comes to consider "nature" as an enemy, she will, like a general or philosopher, deny or twist a body to suit her purposes. In the worst case, children are victims of maternal sadism and domination through pain; then their physical life is at its core terrifying.

The primary obstacles to a maternal respect for bodily life are the insult and abuse that the female body suffers. A dismal tale of the mistreatment of female bodies, from the murder of infant girls to the trimming and contorting of adult women's bodies, has been told many times over throughout the world. Blamed for lasciviousness, yet not expected to act on autonomous sexual desires, women in the United States, especially lesbian women, often struggle to name and act safely on their desires. Mothers, especially lesbian mothers, must often brook internal conflict and external convention to be considered or even to feel both sexual and good.

In recent decades feminists have developed subtle and resilient understandings of female bodily life, teaching women new ways to take care of themselves and to resist violence, whether from strangers, friends, lovers, Fathers, or mothers, and to claim for themselves the pleasures to which all humans are heir. These efforts to respect a female sexual body are closely allied with campaigns to create for female bodies the ecological, economic, medical, and social conditions in which birthing women can thrive. The "abstract idea of paternity," as Mary O'Brien dubs it, has been used by men to control women's birthing and the children they bear.[31] Feminists are determined to wrest that control from a politico-medical system that interprets and intrudes on the female body in all of its birthing aspects. Envisioning birthing as a voluntary labor that no one should be denied or forced to undertake, feminists have spoken eloquently of the right to a fertile body[32] and the corresponding duties of employers and pharmacists, environmental agencies, and legislators to devise regulations of work and commerce that protect that right without sacrificing other rights to job security and fair wages. At the same time, they have looked with an increasingly critical eye at the technological and commercial manipulations of women who are unable to conceive. Aware of the radically disparate conditions in which women of different cultures, classes, and races give birth, they have set themselves to protect all birthing bodies from medical or social abuse and neglect. Only when female birthing bodies are nourished and protected can birthing women themselves afford to celebrate birth.

Only in the context of respect for female sexuality and female bodies can women and men tell a maternal history of human flesh. Such a history should begin by looking at the "facts" of birth with a welcoming, hopeful eye. Philosophers are of little help in this revisionist enterprise since they have written so little on birth directly and have indirectly taken the female birthing body as a source of irrationality and disorder. An exception among philosophers, Hannah Arendt developed a concept of birth as natality that Jean Bethke Elshtain later put to antimilitarist use. Elshtain cites this passage from Arendt's *The Human Condition:*

The miracle that saves the world . . . is, in other words, the birth of new human beings and the new beginning, the action they are capable of by being born. Only the full experience of this capacity can bestow upon human affairs faith and hope, those two essential characteristics of human existence . . . that found perhaps their most glorious and most succinct expression in the new words with which the Gospels accounted their "glad tiding": "A Child has been born unto us."[33]

Elshtain then comments:

Placed alongside the reality of human beginnings, many accounts of political beginnings construed as actions of male hordes or contractualists seem parodic in part because of the massive denial (of the "female") on which they depend. A "full experience" of the "capacity" rooted in birth helps us to keep before our mind's eye the living reality of singularities, differences, and individualities rather than a human mass as objects of possible control or manipulation.[34]

In their celebratory conception of natality, Arendt and Elshtain focus on the child who has been born more than on the woman who has given birth. Natality, like mortality, is a condition of all human life. Unlike mortality, natality is expressed in a distinctive relation to a particular woman. For every human, to experience fully the "capacity rooted in birth" requires imaginatively comprehending that particular relationship. Central to natality as Arendt and Elshtain conceive it are interwoven notions of beginning, action, difference, singularity, and promise. To these we can add maternal concepts of humility, trust, vulnerability, and protection, which characterize the birthing act. Birth is a beginning whose end and shape can be neither predicted nor controlled. Since the safety of human bodies, mortal and susceptible to damage, can never be secured and since humans grow variously, but always in need of help, to give birth is to commit oneself to protecting the unprotectable and nurturing the unpredictable. A woman giving her child to another to raise acts out that commitment when she carefully transfers the task of protection to others who assume the responsibilities to which birth gives rise. To engage actively in giving birth is an expression of trust in others and a determination to become trustworthy. It is an expression of hopefulness in oneself and in "nature," one's own and that of the child to whom one has given birth.

In the language of natality, "birth" signifies a reciprocal relationship of woman and infant. This relationship is indeed marked, as the philosophers suspect, by the dissolution of boundaries — a living being inside another, emerging from another, a body feeding off another body. The experience of self-loss through merging with others is sometimes ecstatic. Male bonding in battle, sexual union, communal religious fervor, and shared celebration of athletic victories are among the better known instances when, in excitement and danger, individuated, separate, bounded selves feel and act as one. Birth is not like these. Although it has its ecstatic — and certainly erotic — moments, birthing labor does not dissolve a woman's self-consciousness in fusion with others. A birthing woman is bound within herself through unsharable pain and overwhelming sensation, alone in a solitude perhaps best appreciated by a lover who would, if she or he could, fully share her experience. Birth is singular, in outcome as well as in process. In being birthed an infant is becoming one and singular. To breathe, an infant must breathe alone; with an infant's first breath, a child is beginning to walk away. The differences and singularities that threaten merging not only survive birth but are its point.

Regarded in the light of hope rather than suspicion, the entangling of self and other in birth — physical union in metaphysical separateness — is a crystallizing symbol not of self-loss but of a kind of self-structuring. The birthing woman is actively herself and her activity is a giving to, a creating of another who could not live without her. Her creation fails unless the infant takes up the singular life, breathing, crying, kicking, sucking her or his own way into the world. Giver and recipient are engaged in mutual, active, interdependent creation. The particular connectedness of the birthing couple is momentary. A pregnant woman's body begins to hint at a separateness to come; a nursing infant and mother hint at a union past. Only birth itself, singular and unrepeatable, expresses the metaphysical paradox of singularity and bodily conjunction. In this birth moment of mutual and utter dependency conjoined with incipient singularity are crystallized both the possibility and the necessity of "development" and the "nurturance" that developing, vulnerable separateness requires.

Although a birthgiving woman and an infant are intensely coupled, they cannot survive alone. While confrontations with death and philosophy might promise to raise a person above mere affections, birthgiving presupposes an expanding network of affectionate, sturdy dependencies. Every infant requires at least one mother. A birthgiving woman's labor comes to nothing without someone to adopt, protect, and nourish her infant. Even when birthgiver and adoptive mother are the same, mothering represents a new commitment quite different from that of the birthgiver, who cares for a gradually emerging infant primarily by caring for herself.

Any man or woman's mothering depends upon partners, friends, and helpers. These mothering associates, like the mothers they work with, depend on courts, economic policies, work schedules, medical practices, schools, and other institutions. Although cultures differ enormously in the social arrangements for supporting mothers, they fail to the degree that they leave mothers who must protect their children without protection. "A 'full experience' of 'the capacity rooted in birth' " includes an understanding of these dependencies and a commitment to sustain them.

Even as birthgiving depends on mothering, all mothering depends on some woman's birthing labor. Mothering women and men cannot repeat birth; they can only deliver on its promise. As I said in Chapter 2, I do not believe that any one relationship between birthgiving and mothering is mandated by morality or nature. What I do believe is that to divide new life from the life on which it depends — the hopes and aims of a particular woman — is to violate the connectedness symbolized by birth and aimed for in maternal nurturance and nonviolence. Without predicting in advance a particular birthgiver's actual hopes and ambitions for herself or her infant, mothers can listen to and respect the passion in which bodily promise begins. By contrast, to wrest from the birthgiver, by law or by force, the child she intends to mother or to require her to care for a child she wants to entrust to other adoptive mothers punishes rather than rewards her gift-giving labor and denies the lived conditions of the gift.

Birthgiving is fraught with complex social and moral relationships. Birth clearly is not merely a physical event. Yet whatever else it is, birth is physical, a transaction of bodies. In the Christian language to which Arendt alludes — "glad tidings," "a child is born" — the physical realities of birth are at best passed over. The infant, quickly "wrapped in swaddling clothes," is quite unlike the crying, shitting, burping, sometimes colicky babies that I have known. His mother is even less bodily. Sexually innocent, clothed in spotless robes, she sits serenely with her child after a birth apparently attended only by her husband, a birth whose dangers and pains require no mention. Such a conception of birth denies the bodily realities on which the birth relationship depends, and this renders natality sentimental.[35]

Remembering the body depends on a welcoming conception of the sexuality in which birth almost always begins. Bodies are sexual; sexual pleasure in its many varieties is, in human lives, a primary source of relief, ecstasy, play, recreation, imaginative invention, and intimacy. For some women, giving birth and nursing are intensely erotic experiences. In Margaret Walker's words, birthing experiences involve "the willing or grateful surrender of 'I' to flesh." Nursing and even erotic holding are also occasions for "direct sensuous congress" with another in which boundaries of self are temporarily suspended.[36] A child's erotic responses are at most inchoate and primitive, yet they portend the rich and confusing pleasures that shape human development. To reject sexuality is tantamount to rejecting the eroticism of birth and the bodily promise, necessarily sexual, of the infant.

No one can count on a welcoming maternal conception of eros in cultures in which mothers are expected to regiment their own and their children's sexuality to suit social requirements. Yet within maternal practice as I have known it, possibilities of welcoming sexuality exist. Mothers witness and are frequently the object of infants' and children's erotic desires. They themselves experience and control their own erotic responses to children.

Whatever their actual inhibitions and rigidities, as participants in and witnesses to infant-child erotic life, mothers have the opportunity to welcome eros where it begins. This means acknowledging rather than denying the existence of surprising desires in themselves and their children. It also means welcoming rather than repressing playful, expansive ways of being masculine and feminine. Maternal narratives are filled with the lore of children's efforts to experiment with prevailing mores of masculinity and femininity. Such playfulness, often a source of maternal delight, is also often greeted with fearful conventionality or even outright homophobia or sexist misogyny. As they watch their children's playful experimentation, mothers could resist their own and their culture's rigid insistence that boys be boys, girls subservient to them, and both entwined in exclusively heterosexual romance.

If a fair proportion of maternal thinkers developed a welcoming conception of sexuality, its public expression might have an antimilitarist effect. For example, if mothers deliberately and publicly opposed a sharp division of masculine and feminine by insisting that such a dichotomy was at odds with the vicissitudes of children's sexual identities, they would be challenging the rigid division of male and female bodies characteristic of military ideology. A welcoming maternal eros could also oppose the predatory license of the "naturally" aggressive male soldier. No matter how open they were to varieties of sexual identity and pleasures, conscientious mothers would control in themselves and discourage in children the sexualization of injury and destruction. The alluring helplessness of a child who is also stubborn and disobedient can be a powerful stimulus to sadistic excitement for a mother or a larger child. But sadism, however understandable, should not be visited on vulnerable children. More generally, the most welcoming maternal eroticism cannot justify abusive sexual behavior in the name of beastly male or "natural" impulse. Small children, like anxiously sexual adolescents, demand restraint. Despite the temptation to abuse or seduce, mothers can, and often do, discipline their own desires and resist the predatory sexuality of others who threaten their children. If mothers' predictable advocacy of sexual restraint were newly combined with a welcoming eros, it might become more difficult to attribute a maternal rejection of the militarization of eros to a frustrating and prudish mom.

A welcoming maternal eros, publicly expressed, might even undermine the romantically mystified allure of the just warrior. While the marauding male soldier is a fearful apparition, the just defender is a quintessential nursery hero. Mothers do not stop desiring an armed yet vulnerable warrior simply by learning to acknowledge the complexities of their own and their infants' erotic lives. The lifting of repressive denial offers more modest hopes. In recognizing the complexity of any desire, mothers could subject military romance to critical reflection. Moreover, if they were allowed and accorded themselves desires of their own, women who are mothers might be less in need of the heightened and distant eroticism the warrior figure provides. Taking pleasure in bodily pleasures, one's own and others', makes sacrifice and transcendence less attractive.

Although a realistic celebration of birth requires taking pleasure in bodily pleasures, welcoming pleasure is not sufficient for welcoming birth. As the philosophers warned, to welcome female or male bodies requires welcoming incontinence, irregularity, discharge, pain, decay, and, finally, death. But these are part of bodily life and cannot be relegated to the female. Aches, flushes, and multiple failures of function and sense afflict both male and female human bodies. The conception of the normal body as a controlled and steady (and therefore male) instrument of human will is a fantasy not even realized among healthy men.

The pain of birthing labor likewise represents the manifold pains to which human flesh is heir. However exhilarating "natural" childbirth may be and however solacing the drugs medicine offers, birth cannot be rescued from philosophical suspicion by denying its pain. Rather, birth's distinctive conjunction of erotic excitement, physical pain, and social promise can provoke reflection on the place of pain in life. Emily Martin has reported on birthing women's efforts to invent, in the midst of alienating medical language, images appropriate to painful birth.[37] These images attempt to "assert wholeness in the face of being broken apart"; they do not purchase wholeness by denying the physically real and dramatic experience of breaking in pain. Wholeness means accepting the interlacing of promise and suffering, suffering and comfort, breaking apart and creation — and of each new life with some particular woman's painful labor.

Human beginnings include their end. To tell the history of human flesh under the aspect of natality, to weight birth over death, is not to deny death's realities. A full appreciation of the capacity rooted in birth includes an understanding that death must be tended and cared for. A death that is cared for is actively non-violent. Those who mitigate pain and assuage fear are engaged in a discipline of intellect and action contradictory to the planned cruelty of a claymore mine or napalm bomb. Tended deaths, like war deaths, are neither romantic nor heroic. Dying bodies stumble, smell, forget, leak, fester, shake, and gasp. But whereas military ideology masks these realities, those who protect and sustain dying bodies depend on grasping them accurately. And whereas military strategies note the body's vulnerabilities merely to exploit them and philosophers acknowledge bodily realities to transcend them, caretakers perceive pain and decay accurately to comfort an embodied being.

Like giving birth — or, for that matter, being born — dying is an experience quintessentially one's own and unshared. Yet dying, like birthing labor, is also a social experience, engaging the intense feelings and often the demanding care of the living. It is the living — those who have cared and those who have killed — who are bequeathed the task of remembering the history of human flesh. Soldiers, especially victorious ones, may be consoled for the injuries they have suffered and inflicted by reflecting on the necessity and virtue of the cause. Or they may forget, since the "ache of guilt" is frequently the price of memory.[38] Caretakers likewise have witnessed, though usually they do not contribute to, the pain of the dying. Even the most "natural" death is, for its subject and for those who love her, a culturally mediated, social end to a human story. Those who minister in kindness must learn to remember in sorrow, to tell, and thereby continue, the story of the dead.

The critic Celeste Schenck has identified an elegaic tradition among women poets which differs from that of men poets and which seems appropriate to care.[39] She writes of women poets who reject ceremonies and myths of consolation — even "the dead are bored with the whole thing" — in favor of "more crazy mourning, more howl, more keening," "mourning without end." In the midst of sorrow, they also celebrate continuity rather than separation. Refusing "to render up their dead," they imagine forms of mourning "that arise from a distinctly feminine experience of attachment and loss." Drawing on Gilligan's work, Schenck ascribes to women a desire for "separation based on attachment and recovery, rather than a severing of ties."[40] Such a resurrection of the dead as a real and benign presence among the living depends on unsentimental remembering adequate to the ambivalence and complexity of love.

Conceptions of natality and a well-tended death determine the organizing themes of the history of human flesh that I imagine mothers telling. This history, as Olive Schreiner, Jane Addams, and so many other women have foretold, stands against the militarist conceptions of a body whose fate is excused by heroic death, a body that is counted but doesn't count, a body whose vulnerability is not an occasion of protection and welcome but of conquest. To be sure, mothers who fear an uncontrolled "nature" and simplify sexuality play into military hands. When wills, bodies, and desires appear uncontrollable, then military discipline can bring them to heel. When sexuality is denied or simplified, the predatory assaultive sexuality of soldiers can be concealed while the allure of the warrior (like the desire of the women who serve him), goes unexamined.

Nonetheless there is in maternal thinking a sturdy antimilitarist conception of the body. In this conception the body is not fearful, either in its pleasures or its suffering. Birth is privileged over death and with that privilege comes a commitment to protect and a prizing of physical being in its resilience and variety. Bodies are at least as important as the causes that use them. When they are damaged — exploded, burned, poisoned, irradiated, or cut up — no heroic phrases come to the rescue. Dying bodies are tended and comforted. Those who survive them create ways of mourning that allow the dead to be included among the living as the real, complicated people they were. Real, complicated people, caring and cared for, do not make good heroes or good enemies.

The Promise

Then the baby whimpered and Sethe looked. Twenty inches of cord hung from its belly and it trembled in the cool evening air. Amy wrapped her skirt around it and the wet sticky women clambered ashore to see what, indeed, God had in mind.

Spores of bluefern growing in the hollows along the riverbank float toward the water in silver-blue lines hard to see unless you are in or near them, lying right at the river's edge when the sunshots are low and drained. Often they are mistook for insects — but they are seeds in which the whole generation sleeps confident of a future. And for a moment it is easy to believe each has one — will become all of what is contained in the spore: will live out its days as planned. This moment of certainty lasts no longer than that; longer, perhaps, than the spore itself.

On a riverbank in the cool of a summer evening two women struggled under a shower of silvery blue. They never expected to see each other again in this world and at that moment couldn't care less. But there on a summer night surrounded by bluefern they did something together appropriately and well. A patroller passing would have sniggered to see two throw-away people, two lawless outlaws — a slave and a barefoot whitewoman with unpinned hair — wrapping a ten minute old baby in the rags they wore. But no patroller came and no preacher. The water sucked and swallowed itself beneath them. There was nothing to disturb them in their work. So they did it appropriately and well.
— *Toni Morrison* [41]

Maternal peacefulness is a myth. At its center is the promise of birth. To threaten bodies — to starve, terrorize, mutilate, or deliberately injure them — is to violate that promise. Every body counts, every body is a testament to hope. The hope of the world — of birthing woman, mothers, friends, and kin — rests in the newborn infant. The infant's hope resides in the world's welcome. As they take up the life that birthing labor has given, infants express what Simone Weil described as "this profound and childlike and unchanging expectation of good in the heart" — an expectation that she called sacred:

At the bottom of the heart of every human being, from earliest infancy until the tomb, there is something that goes on indomitably expecting, in the teeth of all experience of crimes committed, suffered, and witnessed, that good and not evil will be done to him. It is this above all that is sacred in every human being.[42]

To respond to the promise of birth is to respect a birthing woman's hope in her infant and her infant's hope in the world. I concluded the last chapter with an image of "peace" as an active connectedness in which all participants resist others' violence and their own temptation to abandon or assault. This connectedness, in its mutual dependencies and singularities, can now be symbolized by the relationship of a birthing woman and her infant and the relation of both to the mothers on whom they depend. Birth is both in the world and a world's beginning. A mother completes a birthing woman's labor by adopting her infant and thus protecting in the world the physical promise and vulnerability she has created. To "adopt" is to respond to an infant's trust that "good and not evil will be done to him." To adopt in and for the world means resisting "in the teeth of all experience of crimes committed, suffered, and witnessed" anyone or any policy that cruelly or carelessly violates that trust. To adopt is to make a space, a "peace" where the promise of birth can survive. In this myth of peacemaking, birth is the beginning of a world; all mothers-in-the-world are adoptive; all adoptive persons are peacemakers.

CHAPTER NINE

Notes Toward a Feminist Maternal Peace Politics

Whenever a poet employs a figure or story previously accepted and defined by a culture, the poet is using a myth, and the potential is always there that the myth will be revisionist: that is, the figure or tale will be altered for appropriate ends, the old vessel filled with new wine, initially satisfying the thirst of the individual poet but ultimately making cultural change possible.
— *Alicia Ostriker* [1]

MATERNAL PEACE POLITICS begins in a myth: mothers are peacemakers without power. War is men's business; mothers are outsiders or victims; their business is life. The myth is shattered by history. Everywhere that men fight, mothers support them. When powerful men have not discouraged them, women, and sometimes mothers, have fought as fiercely as their brothers. As feminists insist that women and men share fairly the burdens and pleasures of battle, many young women expect their lives to include, without contradiction, both fighting and mothering.

Yet the myth remains intoxicating. The contradiction between violence and maternal work is evident. Wherever there are wars, children are hurt, hungry, and frightened; homes are burned, crops destroyed, families scattered. The daily practice and long-term aims of women's caring labor are all threatened. Though mothers may be warlike, war is their enemy. Where there is peace, mothers engage in work that requires nonviolent battle, fighting while resisting the temptation to assault or abandon opponents. The connectedness of maternal nonviolence is symbolized in the relationship of a birthing woman to her infant and of the infant to her adoptive mother. Although mothers may not be peaceful, "peace" is their business. Despite clear historical evidence, the myth of maternal peacefulness survives.

Like revisionary poets, peacemakers set themselves to alter the myth so that it can survive contemporary realism about women and still serve the ends of peace. The contemporary mythmaker can point to the usefulness of mothers and maternal thinking to peace politics. Although a group of mothers, like any other group, includes ordinary militarists and peacemakers as well as fierce fighters and saintly pacifists, the practice of mothering taken as a whole gives rise to ways of thinking and acting that are useful to peace politics. Mothers might bring to *any* politics capacities honed in their work — for example, attentiveness, realism, and a welcoming attitude toward change. Some maternal characteristics, thought useful to any organized endeavor, seem specifically appropriate to nonviolent action. Nonviolent action, like maternal practice at its best, requires resilient cheerfulness, a grasping of truth that is caring, and a tolerance of ambiguity and ambivalence. For mothers, issues of proper trust, permissible force, and the possibility and value of control are alive and complex in daily work as they are in any nonviolent action. Peace itself can be conceived for both activists and mothers as depending on a connective "love" that still struggles "toward definition, grow[s] out of confusion, knowledge, misery and necessity."[2] None of this makes most mothers peaceful. Rather, those mothers who are already committed to public peacefulness — to fomenting suspicion of violence and inventing nonviolent action — can contribute distinctively to a collective peacemaking effort.

It is all to the good, from a peacemaker's perspective, that individual mothering women and men bring distinctly maternal abilities to peace work. But this is less than the revisionist myth needs. The promise of maternal peacefulness lies in the work and love to which mothers are committed. The mythical peacemaking mother does more than bring distinctive gifts to peace projects. By virtue of her mothering she is meant to be an initiator of peace and a witness against war. She represents a practice whose aims and strategies contradict those of war, which, like mothering, is also an organized human activity with moral pretensions. It is this potentially painful and lively contradiction between war and mothering as human activities that might motivate individual mothers to resist. Similarly, the principles of nonviolence by which ordinary mothers judge themselves govern a practice; it is the nonviolent aspirations of the practice, persisting through continuous and sometimes catastrophic individual failure, that suggest a wider, more public peace. Women and men whose maternal identity is central to their self-respect should, as mothers, be uneasy militarists and self-possessed peacemakers, whatever their individual proclivities.

It is here, at its deepest promise, that the myth of maternal peacefulness is most seriously challenged. It is no great surprise that many mothers love war and many more play their parts in military scripts. But it is troubling that the very demands of maternal practice often inspire a militarist politics. Maternal nonviolence is rooted in particular tribal, often racial, loyalties; the defensive and defended state celebrated by just-war theory is often the most likely object of an extended maternal love; maternal inclinations to dominate whatever is unruly threaten a vision of the body as a testament of hope. The many kinds of parochialism, denial, and inauthenticity to which maternal thinkers are prey often prevent them from seeing, let alone resisting, militarist violence.

How then can the myth of maternal peacefulness be revised? What actions or understanding can transform mothering itself? If there is no way to make the leap from mothers to peace, is it possible to build a conceptual-political bridge between them? Individual women such as Käthe Kollwitz are exemplary in their courage to change. Are there also ways to transform the *practices* of mothering, and hence the public conception of mothers? Is it possible to create a new, real and symbolic, publicly acknowledged maternal identity? Are there collective enterprises or political movements that transform the practice of those mothers who engage in them? How does participation in these movements undercut specifically militarist elements typical of maternal practices?

Among the many political movements that might serve as agents of political change, I have been struck by two that strengthen the peacefulness of mothers who participate in them and crystallize for witnesses and sympathizers new possibilities of maternal power and peacefulness. The first I call a women's politics of resistance, the second feminist politics. Although neither a women's politics of resistance nor a feminist politics is inherently a peace politics, each instructs and strengthens peacemaking. Both politics are intricately connected to mothering, yet each also challenges just those aspects of maternal practice that limit its public, effective peacefulness. Hence separately and, even more, in combination, they transform maternal practice into a work of peace.

A Women's Politics of Resistance

A women's politics of resistance is identified by three characteristics: its participants are women, they explicitly invoke their culture's symbols of femininity, and their purpose is to resist certain practices or policies of their governors.

Women, like men, typically act out of social locations and political allegiances unconnected to their sex; women are socialists or capitalists, patriots or dissidents, colonialists or nationalists. Unlike other politics, a women's politics is organized and acted out by women. Women "riot" for bread, picket against alcohol, form peace camps outside missile bases, protect their schools from government interference, or sit in against nuclear testing. A women's politics often includes men: women call on men's physical strength or welcome the protection that powerful male allies offer. Nonetheless it is women who organize themselves self-consciously as women. The reasons women give for organizing range from an appreciation of the protection afforded by "womanliness" to men's unwillingness to participate in "sentimental" politics to the difficulty in speaking, much less being taken seriously, with men around. Typically, the point of women's politics is not to claim independence from men but, positively, to organize as women. Whatever the reasons for their separatism, the fact that women organize, direct, and enact a politics enables them to exploit their culture's symbols of femininity.

Women can also organize together without evoking common understandings of femininity. Feminist actions, for example, are often organized by women who explicitly repudiate the roles, behavior, and attitudes expected of "women." What I am calling a women's politics of resistance affirms obligations traditionally assigned to women and calls on the community to respect them. Women are responsible for their children's health; in the name of their maternal duty they call on the government to halt nuclear testing, which, epitomizing a general unhealthiness, leaves strontium-90 in nursing mothers' milk. If women are to be able to feed their families, then the community must produce sufficient food and sell it at prices homemakers can afford. If women are responsible for educating young children, then they resist government efforts to interfere with local schools.

Not all women's politics are politics of resistance. There are politics organized by women that celebrate women's roles and attitudes but that serve rather than resist the state. In almost every war, mothers of heroes and martyrs join together in support of military sons, knitting, writing, and then mourning, in the service of the military state. The best-known instance of women's politics is the organization of Nazi women in praise of *Kinder, Küche, Kirche*.[3] Today in Chile, a women's organization under the direction of the dictator Pinochet's wife celebrates "feminine power" (*el poder femenino*), which expresses itself through loyalty to family and fatherland.

A women's politics of *resistance* is composed of women who take responsibility for the tasks of caring labor and then find themselves confronted with policies or actions that interfere with their right or capacity to do their work. In the name of womanly duties that they have assumed and that their communities expect of them, they resist. This feminine resistance has made some philosophers and feminists uneasy. Much like organized violence, women's resistance is difficult to predict or control. Women in South Boston resist racial integration; mothers resist the conscription of their children in just wars.

Even where women aim to resist tyranny, their "feminine" protest seems too acceptable to be effective. As Dorothy Dinnerstein eloquently laments, women are *meant* to weep while men rule and fight:

Women's resigned, implicitly collusive, ventilation of everybody's intuition that the world men rule is murderously crazy is a central theme in folklore, literature, drama [and women's politics of resistance].

Think, for instance, of the proverb that groups woman with wine and song as a necessary counterpoint to battle, a counterpoint that makes it possible for men to draw back from their will to kill just long and far enough so that they can then take it up again with new vigor. Or think of the saying "Men must work and women must weep." Woman's tears over what is lethal in man's work, this saying implies, are part of the world's eternal, unalterable way. . . . [Her] tears serve not to deter man but to help him go on, for she is doing his weeping for him and he is doing what she weeps about for her.[4]

Christa Wolf expresses a related fear that women's resistance is as fragile as their dependence on individual men, loyalty to kin, and privileges of class:

I was slow on the uptake. My privileges intruded between me and the most necessary insights; so did my attachment to my own family, which did not depend upon the privileges I enjoyed.[5]

For whatever reasons, feminists are apt to be disappointed in the sturdiness and extent of women's resistance. Dorothy Dinnerstein expresses this feminist disappointment:

The absurd self-importance of his striving has been matched by the abject servility of her derision, which has on the whole been expressed only with his consent and within boundaries set by him, and which has on the whole worked to support the stability of the realm he rules.[6]

While some people fear that "feminine" resistance is inevitably limited — and their fears seem to me not groundless — I place my hope in its unique potential effectiveness, namely, women's social position makes them inherently "disloyal to the civilization"[7] that depends on them. Thus Hegel worries, and I hope, that ostensibly compliant women are on the edge of dissidence. The state, whose most powerful governors depend on women's work and whose stability rests on the authority of the Fathers, "creates for itself in what it suppresses and what it depends upon an internal enemy — womankind in general."[8] Underlining as Hegel does women's exclusion from power, Julia Kristeva celebrates a woman who is "an eternal dissident in relation to social and political consensus, in exile from power, and therefore always singular, fragmentary, demonic, a witch."[9] Yet like Kristeva, I find that the dissident mother, perhaps unlike other witches, is not only a potential critic of the order that excludes her but also and equally a conserver and legitimator of the order it is her duty to instill in her children. Kristeva expects from this dissident mother an "attentiveness to ethics" rooted in a collective experience and tradition of mothering. And I would expect from her the ambivalence that Jane Lazarre believes keeps the heart alive, even as it slows the trigger finger. This attentiveness to ethics can become effectively militant in a women's politics of resistance. Its ambivalence, while a spur to compassion, does not slow action if women are governed by principles of nonviolence that allow them to hate and frustrate oppressors they neither mutilate nor murder.

Women's politics of resistance are as various as the cultures from which they arise. Of the many examples I could choose, I select one, the resistance of Argentinian and Chilean women to military dictatorship, specifically to the policy of kidnapping, imprisonment, torture, and murder of the "disappeared." The resistance of the Madres (mothers) of Argentina to its military regime and the similar, ongoing resistance of Chilean women to the Pinochet dictatorship politically exemplify central maternal concepts such as the primacy of bodily life and the connectedness of self and other. At the same time, these movements politically transform certain tendencies of maternal militarism such as cheery denial and parochialism.

Although women's work is always threatened by violence and although women in war always suffer the hunger, illness, mutilation, and loss of their loved ones, the crime of "disappearance" is especially haunting. Kidnapping and rumors of torture and murder destroy lives and families. Yet because the fate of the disappeared person is unclear, because no one in power acknowledges her or his existence, let alone disappearance, even mourning is impossible:

To disappear means to be snatched off a street corner, or dragged from one's bed, or taken from a movie theater or cafe, either by police, or soldiers, or men in civilian clothes, and from that moment on to disappear from the face of the earth leaving not a single trace. It means that all knowledge of the disappeared is totally lost. Absolutely nothing is known about them. What was their fate? If they are alive, where are they? What are they enduring? If they are dead, where are their bones?[10]

Nathan Laks describes the Argentinian protest that began in Buenos Aires in 1976:

Once in power [in Argentina in 1976], the military systematized and accelerated the campaign of terror, quickly annihilating the armed organizations of the Left and the unarmed ones, as well as many individuals with little or no connection to either. The indiscriminate nature of the kidnapping campaign and the impunity with which it was carried out spread terror — as intended. Relationships among friends and relatives were shattered by unprecedented fear. Perfectly decent individuals suddenly became afraid even to visit the parents of a kidnap victim, for any such gesture of compassion might condemn the visitor to a terrible fate. In this terrorized society, a small organization of women, mothers and other relatives of kidnapped Argentines staged a stunning act of defiance. One Thursday afternoon they gathered in the Plaza de Mayo, the main square in Buenos Aires and the site of countless historic incidents beginning in 1810 with the events that led to Argentina's separation from the Spanish Empire. In the center of the Plaza de Mayo, within clear sight of the presidential palace, the national cathedral, and several headquarters of ministries and corporations, the Mothers paraded in a closed circle.[11]

The Madres met each other outside hospitals or prisons, where they took food and other provisions and looked for traces of the disappeared, or outside government offices, where they tried, almost invariably without success, to get some accounting of their loved ones' whereabouts. When they marched, the Madres wore white kerchiefs with the names of the disappeared embroidered on them. Often they carried lighted candles and almost always they wore or carried photographs of the disappeared. In Chile, women chained themselves to the steps of the capitol, formed a human chain to a mine, Lonquen, where a mass grave was discovered, and took over a stadium where disappeared people had been rounded up, later to be tortured and killed.

The Latin American women's movements are clearly politics of resistance. The women who engage in them court imprisonment and torture and in some cases have become "disappeared" themselves. Knowing what fearful things could happen to them, women in Chile trained themselves to name and deal with what they feared:

If they were afraid of facing police, they were told simply to find a policeman and stare at him until they could see him as a man and not as a representative of the state. [They] circled police vans on foot, until these symbols of the regime appeared as just another kind of motor vehicle. . . . The women also instructed one another how to deal with the tear gas . . . to stop eating two hours before demonstrations, to dress in casual clothing, to take off makeup but to put salt on their cheekbones to keep teargas powder from entering their eyes, . . . to carry lemon to avoid teargas sting and to get a jar with homemade smelling salts made up of salt and ammonia.[12]

The women talked among themselves about their terrors, found others who shared their fears, and marched with them in affinity groups. And thus they brought their bodies to bear against the state.

As in many women's politics of resistance, the Argentinian and Chilean women emphasize mothering among women's many relations. They are Madres, whether or not they are biological or adoptive mothers of individual disappeared; a later group is made up of Abuelas (grandmothers). Their presence and the character of their action, as well as the interviews they have given, invariably evoke an experience of mothering that is central to their lives, whatever other home work or wage labor they engage in. Repeatedly they remember and allude to ordinary tasks — clothing, feeding, sheltering, and most of all tending to extensive kin work. All these works, ordinarily taken for granted, are dramatically present just because they are interrupted; they are made starkly visible through the eerie "disappearance," the shattering mockery of a maternal and childlike "unchanging expectation of good in the heart."[13]

As these women honor mothering, they honor themselves. The destruction of the lives of their children, often just on the verge of adulthood, destroys years of their work; their loss and the impossibility of mourning it constitute a violent outrage against them. Yet there is something misleading about this way of talking. The women do not speak of their work but of their children; they carry children's photographs, not their own. The distinctive structuring of the relation between self and other, symbolized in birth and enacted in mothering, is now politicized. The children, the absent ones, are *not* their mothers, who have decidedly *not* disappeared but are bodily present. The singular, irreplaceable children are lost. Yet as the pictures the Madres carry suggest, the children are not, even in disappearance, apart from their mothers but, in their absence, are still inseparable from them.

For these Argentinian and Chilean women, as for women in most cultures, mothering is intuitively or "naturally" connected to giving birth. The Abuelas, especially, have made a political point of the emotional significance of genetic continuity. Since the fall of the military regime, one of their projects has been to form a genetic bank to trace the biological parentage of children adopted by people close to the ruling class at the time the military was in power. The insistence on genetic connection is one aspect of a general affirmation of the body. Indeed, the vulnerability, promise, and power of human bodies is central to this women's politics of resistance, as it is to maternal practice:

Together with the affirmation of life, the human body is a very important reference for these women. They often speak of physical pain, the wounds caused by the disappearances. It seems that wearing a photograph of the missing one attached to the clothing or in a locket around the neck is a way of feeling closer to them.[14]

Because they have suffered military violence — have been stripped naked, sexually humiliated, and tortured — children's bodies have become a locus of pain. Because the violation of bodies is meant to terrify the body itself becomes a place where terror is wrought. In resistance to this violation mothers' bodies become instruments of nonviolent power. Adorned with representations of bodies loved and violated, they express the necessity of love even amid terror, "in the teeth of all experience of crimes committed, suffered and witnessed."[15]

In their protests, these women fulfill traditional expectations of femininity and at the same time violate them. These are women who may well have expected to live out an ideology of "separate spheres" in which men and women had distinct but complementary tasks. Whatever ideology of the sexual division of labor they may have espoused, their political circumstances, as well as the apparently greater vulnerability and the apparently greater timidity and conventionality of the men they lived among, required that they act publicly as women. Women who bring to the public plazas of a police state pictures of their loved ones, like women who put pillowcases, toys, and other artifacts of attachment against the barbed wire fences of missile bases, translate the symbols of mothering into political speech. Preservative love, singularity in connection, the promise of birth and the resilience of hope, the irreplaceable treasure of vulnerable bodily being — these clichés of maternal work are enacted in public, by women insisting that their governors name and take responsibility for their crimes. They speak a "women's language" of loyalty, love, and outrage; but they speak with a public anger in a public place in ways they were never meant to do.

Although not a "peace politics" in a conventional sense, the Latin American protest undermines tendencies of maternal practice and thinking that are identifiably militarist. To some extent, this is a matter of shifting a balance between tendencies in mothering that support militarism toward tendencies that subvert it. In this

case, the balance shifts from denial to truthfulness, from parochialism to solidarity, and from inauthenticity to active responsibility. Writing about André Trocme and his parishioners in the
French village of Le Chambon during World War II, Phillip Hallie
identified three characteristics that enabled them to penetrate the
confusion and misinformation with which Nazis covered their
policy and then to act on their knowledge. *"Lucid knowledge, awareness of the pain of others,* and *stubborn decision* dissipated for the
Chambonnais the Night and Fog that inhabited the minds of so
many people in Europe, and the world at large, in 1942."[16] In the
transformed maternal practice of the Argentinian and Chilean
women, these same virtues of nonviolent resistance are at work.

Cheery denial is an endemic maternal temptation. A similar
"willingness to be self-deceived," as the resistance leader André
Trocme called it, also sustains many decent citizens' support of
war policy. It is notorious that few people can bear, except very
briefly, to acknowledge the dangers of nuclear weapons and the
damage they have done and could still do. Similarly, few citizens
really look at the political aims and material-emotional lives of
people affected by their own country's interventionist war policies.
By contrast, the Argentinian and Chilean women insist on, and
then disseminate, "lucid knowledge" of military crimes. "What
is so profoundly moving about them is their determination to find
out the truth."[17] They insist that others, too, hear the truth. They
are "ready to talk immediately; they need to talk, to make sure
their story, so tragic and so common, . . . be told, be known."[18]
In addition to talking, they make tapestries, "arpilleras," that tell
stories of daily life including workers' organizing, police brutality,
kidnapping, and resistance. The protests, tales, and arpilleras extend the maternal task of storytelling, maintaining ordinary maternal values of realism in the face of temptation to deny or distort.
In this context, their ordinary extraordinary work becomes a politics of remembering.

After fighting in World War II the philosopher J. Glenn Gray
wrote:

The great god Mars tries to blind us when we enter his realm, and when
we leave he gives us a generous cup of the waters of Lethe to drink. . . .

When I consider how easily we forget the millions who suffered un-
bearably, either permanently maimed in body or mind, or who gave up
their lives before they realized their purpose, I rebel at the whole insane
spectacle of human existence.[19]

After the junta fell, Argentinian women insisted that violated bodies be *remembered,* which required that crimes be named, the men
who committed them be brought to trial, and the bodies themselves, alive or dead, be accounted for and, where possible,
returned.

"Awareness of the pain of others." The Argentinian and Chilean
Madres spoke first of their own pain and the pain of relatives and
friends of other disappeared. Similarly, maternal nonviolence is
rooted, and typically limited by, a commitment to one's "own"
children and the people they live among. In Chapter 7 I spoke of
this limitation as a principal source of maternal militarism; the
parochialism of maternal practice can become the racialism that
fuels organized violence. This tribal parochialism was also broken
down in the Argentinian and Chilean protests.

As in mothering generally, women found it easiest to extend
their concern for their own children to other mothers "like them";
only in this political context likeness had to do not with race or
ethnicity but with common suffering. In Argentina, where protests are marked by the "singularity" of photographs, the women
came to wear identical masks to mark their commonality. In Chile
one woman said:

Because of all this suffering we are united. I do not ask for justice for
my child alone, or the other women just for their children. We are asking
for justice for all. All of us are equal. If we find one disappeared one I
will rejoice as much as if they had found mine.[20]

Concern for all victims then sometimes extended to collective
concern for all the people of the nation:

We are the women and mothers of this land, of the workers, of the
professionals, of the students, and of future generations.[21]

This is still "nationalism," though of a noble sort. Many of the
women went further as they explicitly identified with all victims
of military or economic violence:

In the beginning we only wanted to rescue our children. But as time passed we acquired a different comprehension. We understood better what is going on in the world. We know that when babies do not have enough to eat that, too, is a violation of human rights.[22]

We should commit ourselves to make Lonquen [the mine where a mass grave was discovered] a blessed spot. May it be a revered spot, so that never again will a hostile hand be raised against any other person that lives on the earth.[23]

It would be foolish to believe that every woman in the Argentinian and Chilean protest movements extended concern from her own children to all the disappeared then to all of the nation, and finally to all victims everywhere. Why should women whose children and loved ones have been singularly persecuted extend sympathetic protection to all victims, an extension that is extraordinary even among women and men who do not suffer singular assault? Yet many of these women did so extend themselves — intellectually, politically, emotionally. They did not "transcend" their particular loss and love; particularity was the emotional root and source of their protest. It is through acting on that particularity that they extended mothering to include sustaining and protecting any people whose lives are blighted by violence.

"Stubborn decision." As children remind us, stubborn decision is a hallmark of maternity. And mothers reply: what looks like stubborn decision may well be a compound of timidity, vacillation, and desperation. Women in resistance are (almost certainly) not free from ordinary mothers' temptations to inauthenticity, to letting others — teachers, employers, generals, Fathers, grandparents — establish standards of acceptability and delegating to them responsibility for children's lives. And like ordinary mothers, women in resistance probably include in their ranks *individuals* who in ordinary times could speak back to the teacher or organize opposition to the local corporate polluter. But "stubborn decision" takes on a new and collective political meaning when women acting together walk out of their homes to appropriate spaces they never were meant to occupy.

Like their counterparts in resistance elsewhere, these stubbornly decisive Argentinian and Chilean women, whatever their personal timidities, publicly announce that they take responsibility for protecting the world in which they and their children must live. These women are the daughters, the heirs, of Kollwitz's *mater dolorosa*. As in Kollwitz's representations, a mother is victimized through the victimization of her children. These women are themselves victims; moreover, they bear witness to victimization first of loved ones, then of strangers; they stand against those in power, in solidarity with those who are hurt. Yet there is also a sense in which, by their active courage, they refuse victimization. More accurately, they mock dichotomies that still riddle political thought. There is no contradiction between "playing the role of victim" and taking responsibility for public policies. It is possible to act powerfully while standing with those who are hurt. It is neither weak nor passive to reveal one's own suffering while refusing to damage or mutilate in return. The Latin American *mater dolorosa* has learned how to fight as a victim for victims, not by joining the strong, but by resisting them.

A women's politics of resistance is not inherently a peace politics. Women can organize to sabotage peace treaties or to celebrate the heroes and martyrs of organized violence. During the Malvinas-Falklands war, Argentinian and English women sought each other out at a women's meeting in New York to denounce together their countries' militarism and imperialism. Yet during that same war, the Argentinian Madres were reported to use patriotic rhetoric to reinforce their own aims: "The Malvinas belong to us and so do our sons."

Nonetheless, in their own contexts, the Argentinian protest had and the Chilean protest still has antimilitarist implications. The regimes against which the women protest were and are militarist; the omnipresence of the soldier as oppressor and the general as the torturers' commander was — and in Chile still is — sufficient to symbolize a contrast between women and war. Moreover, the generals' actions have not been accidentally related to militarism. As Plato saw, when he rejected militarist rule in his totalitarian state, torture, kidnapping and other physical terrorism infect the rule of fearful tyrants, just as atrocities infect the best organized war. In their deliberately and increasingly brutal strategies to ensure absolute control, the generals exemplify the excesses inherent in militarized tyranny. Hence in the women's protests, not only a particular government but military rule is brought to trial.

Whatever their militarist sentiments or rhetoric, the Argentinian and Chilean protests express to the world the ideals of nonviolence. Although effective protest inevitably hurts its opponents and those associated with them, the protesters did not set out to injure but to end injuring. None of their actions even risked serious, lasting physical damage. Their aim was steadfastly one of reconnection and restoration of a just community, even though and because those responsible for violence were held accountable and were punished. By providing an example of persistent, stubborn action, the Argentinian and Chilean women have offered a model of nonviolent resistance to other Latin American countries and to the world. They have therefore contributed to collective efforts to invent peace, whatever their degree of effectiveness within their own countries. Like the maternal practice from which it grows, a women's politics of resistance may remain racial, tribal, or chauvinist; we cannot expect of women in resistance the rare human ability to stand in solidarity with all victims of violence. Yet if these Latin American protests are at all emblematic, they suggest that the peacefulness latent in maternal practice tends to be realized as participants act against, and therefore reflect on, violence itself.

Feminist Politics

There is no litmus test for identifying a "feminist." Internationally and in the United States, feminism is a multifaceted social movement in the process of change and self-creation. When I speak of feminism I refer, minimally, to a politics that is dedicated to transforming those social and domestic arrangements that deliberately or unwittingly penalize women because of their sex. Second, whatever their other politics and interests, feminists focus seriously on the ways that gender — the social construction of masculinity and femininity — organizes political, personal, and intellectual life. The feminist assumption is that gender divisions of work, pleasure, power, and sensibility are socially created, detrimental to women and, to a lesser degree, to men, and therefore can and should be changed. Most important, though perhaps controversially, feminists are partisans of women,[24] fighting on their side, sometimes against, often with, men. As women, or in solidarity with them, feminists struggle against any social, racial, economic, or physical abuse that threatens women's capacity to work and to love.

This is a general and elastic definition that leaves open virtually every specific disagreement among feminists about policy or theory. It is a definition that in no way commits feminists to antimilitarism. In many parts of the world, feminist women organize to procure arms in defense of themselves and their people and in despair of getting powerful, violent men to disarm. Some feminists support military recruitment in less desperate circumstances, arguing that women benefit from the wages, work, travel, and education military life offers; moreover, they insist, if allowed to prepare for and participate in combat, women could acquire the courage and skills fostered by battle.

More politically, many feminists believe that it is a part of citizenship in a democratic society to assume the privileges and burdens a military state imposes on its citizens. In the United States, individual men have bought and begged their way out of combat; Black Americans and other men of "minority" races have had to fight to be included in combat and command; "minority" and poor men are selectively conscripted for unpopular wars. Nonetheless, despite these violations, many North American feminists endorse an ideal of civic virtue according to which no class of people, whether marked by race, sex, or ethnicity, should be excluded or exempted from military combat and command.

Whether they are sober liberals or struggling liberationists, feminists can take heart from a developing feminist *women's* militarist politics. The feminist soldier heroine may be most perfectly represented by a young woman with a baby in her arms and a gun over her shoulder, although an armed girl dressed as and sometimes passing for a comely man is a close second. The many distinctly feminine, and often distinctly sexy, soldier heroines of exemplary spirit simultaneously domesticate violence, expand women's imaginative aggressiveness, and rewrite, in a manner titillating and scary, the sexual scripts of battle.

Whether or not feminists are militarist, feminist politics transforms maternal militarism. Like a women's politics of resistance, feminism shifts the balance within maternal practice from denial to lucid knowledge, from parochialism to awareness of others' suffering, and from compliance to stubborn, decisive capacities to act. This transformation begins, paradoxically, in a tense relationship between feminists and women who are mothers. Mothers and feminists cannot leave each other alone. Almost every feminist had a mother; many are mothers; few think coolly about the institutions and passions of mothering that shaped their mothers' and often their own lives. For their part, many mothers, even those who are feminists, fear that feminism offers heartless or oversimple solutions to the social and personal dilemmas of mothering.

Nonetheless, the actual confrontation of mothers and feminists — whether practical or psychological — is deeply beneficial to mothering. Although some feminists have indeed been guilty of contempt for mothers, no other movement has taken so seriously or worked so effectively to ensure women's economic and psychological ability to engage in mothering without undue sacrifice of physical health and nonmaternal projects. Organizing women workers, fighting for day-care centers, adequate health care, and maternal and parental leave, demanding birthgivers' right to participate in mothering as and when they choose — in these and many other struggles feminists have proved many times over that, as partisans of women, they are sturdy allies of mothers. In this practical support of mothers in their daily work the feminist transformation of maternal militarism is rooted.

Either because of their own experience of sexual prejudice and abuse or because they are heartened by particular feminist policies and fights on their behalf, many previously skeptical mothers become feminists. That is, with varying degrees of conviction, they tend to become partisans of women, able to focus on the impact of gender on their lives and to set themselves to change the sexual and domestic arrangements that oppress them. In becoming feminists, mothers acquire a "feminist consciousness," a confusing, often painful, but irresistible recognition that the stories they have told themselves about "being a woman" are self-deceptive and do not serve their interests. With this new knowledge comes an unsettling conviction that certain realities of their lives are intolerable and must be changed.

Sandra Bartky's early account of feminist consciousness — suggestive of the later standpoint theory — is especially useful:

Coming to have a feminist consciousness is the experience of coming to know the truth about oneself and one's society. . . . The very *meaning* of what the feminist apprehends is illuminated by the light of what ought to be. . . . The feminist apprehends certain features of reality *as* intolerable, as to be rejected in behalf of a transforming project for the future. . . . Social reality is revealed as deceptive. . . . What is really happening is quite different from what appears to be happening.[25]

For a mother, "coming to know the truth" includes looking at the real feelings and conflicts of mothering. It is a feminist project to describe realistically the angers and ambivalences of maternal love. A feminist consciousness also requires mothers to look undefensively at women's social status and the political relations between men and women, which exact from mothers — even those who are men — unnecessary and unacceptable sacrifices of power and pleasures.

A feminist mother's growing ability to name and resist the forces ranged within and against her undermines many varieties of self-denial to which maternal thinking is susceptible. This does not mean that cheery denial, inauthenticity, or self-loss in attentive love — to take only three examples — can be "cured" by feminism. These are temptations endemic to maternal work. But a clear-sighted rather than mystifying apprehension of "oneself and one's society," combined with real increases in women's opportunities and self-respect, shifts the balance away from illusion and passivity toward active responsibility and engagement. A mother acquiring feminist consciousness ferrets out the meaning of dominant values, asking whose interests they serve and how they affect her children. To be a feminist mother is to recognize that many dominant values — including, but not limited to, the subordination of women — are unacceptable and need not be accepted.

These feminist habits of lucidity strengthen maternal nonviolence in distinctive ways. Although mothers are committed to resisting violence directed against their children, children themselves often remember being betrayed by mothers who blamed them for "provoking" the violence they suffered or who asked them to "understand" the violator. Nearly as frightening are memories of protective mothers unable to protect themselves from physical abuse or from silencing and contempt that borders on violence. Feminists name the many kinds of violence women suffer — from lovers, employers, husbands, and strangers — and recognize women's tendencies to "submit" or take the blame for men's violence, or, worse, get their children to do so.

Although feminists may be appalled when mothers abuse or neglect their children, and although feminist voices are prominent in protesting the poverty and desperation that often lie behind abuse and neglect, it is sometimes harder for feminists to see violence clearly and condemn it unequivocally when it is committed by women. Nonetheless, in scholarly works, fiction, and letters to the editors, feminists have insisted on looking at maternal violence in order to understand and take action against it. It is a feminist task to identify the violence involved when mothers take nature as an enemy, breaking the wills and sometimes the bodies of children. More generally, when feminists analyze the effects of repressive sexuality or a maternal rage for order born of fear and deprivation, they also write about and against maternal violence. Feminists do all this as partisans of women, not only analyzing but also creating policies and spaces that give women the economic possibility and physical safety to take care of themselves and those they care for — to start again.

In sum, a feminist mother becomes increasingly clear-sighted about the violences she has suffered or inflicted and increasingly able to resist them. As she develops a critical stance toward violences that she previously accepted, she is also likely to become suspicious of the fantasies and theories that dominate organized, public violence. Myths of beastly males, alluring warriors, omniscient defense intellectuals, conspiracies, emergencies, and nuclear protection are all vulnerable to the lucid, knowing gaze. When conjoined with the commitment to protect, lucid, suspicious knowledge may in itself be sufficient to inspire a mother's resistance to militarist plans and "strategic defense initiatives" that threaten her children.

But lucid knowledge cannot in itself inspire a mother's resistance to violence that threatens "other" children, not even when it is violence funded and perpetrated by her own government. For extended maternal antimilitarism, the best knowledge must be motivated and tested by a sympathetic apprehension of *others'* suffering as "intolerable, to be rejected in behalf of a transforming project for the future." I suggested in Chapter 7 that there is a basis in maternal practice for extending the range of domestic nonviolence through maternal identification with other mothers' particular commitments to protect and cherish lives. I have just celebrated the extension of sympathy in Argentinian and Chilean women's politics of resistance. Feminist politics too makes a distinctive contribution to transnational and transcultural solidarity among mothers.

Unlike maternal thinking, which is rooted in particular passions and loyalties, feminism explicitly proclaims an ideal of solidarity and loudly rues its failures to implement the ideal. The ideal of solidarity is a successor to an earlier ideal of "sisterhood," which some feminists espoused as recently as a decade ago.[26] The sisterhood of women was based on allegedly shared oppression and shared responsibility for caring labor. The romantic hope of sisterhood did not survive class and racial division, the marked disparity between the kind and degree of women's oppression, and the myriad cultural and individual varieties of women's participation in caring labor. Along with the ideal of sisterhood the idea that men were other and enemy briefly held sway. This militarist construction belied the alliances of women with men of their race and class and the affectionate camaraderie that often flourishes among women and men who are colleagues and friends. Nor could a feminism that identified men as enemies enlist the allegiance of

countless women who, whatever their sexuality, loved men —
brothers, fathers, sons, other kin, friends, and sometimes
lovers.

The feminist ideal of identifying with women's struggles quite
different from one's own survived romantic and militarized sisterhood. While feminists no longer claimed that all women shared
a common oppression or common experiences of mothering and
tending, they did develop an alternative ideal based on solidarity
with women who suffered from and resisted sexual, racial, intellectual, economic, or other abuse. The ideal of solidarity does not
reflect an attitude feminists have to any or all women. Most obviously, the subjects of feminist solidarity are women who suffer
abuse from individual men or from sexist and heterosexist institutions. Second, whatever their individual experiences, feminists
tend to ally themselves politically with women who are abused —
out of whatever combination of class, race, and sexual oppression — as birthgivers, mothers, or female kin. Solidarity extends
indefinitely with different emphases depending on the feminist.
But it does not extend to "women" in general, but rather to
women in particular situations of struggle.

A mother who is a woman acquiring feminist consciousness
will likely encounter the ideal of solidarity among women, especially if she finds herself in the company of other feminists.
Whether they meet in a shelter, reading group, health center,
union, or peace action, feminists proclaim ideals of solidarity in
explicit ideological statements, often through bitter recriminations
and acknowledgments of failure that attest to the force of the ideal.
To the extent that a mother herself acquires the ideal of solidarity,
the purview of her lucid knowledge will extend to "other"
women, including often mothers who are targets of her own government's violence. Solidarity with women in struggle tends to
undercut military loyalty to states. It eschews abstract labels of
cause or party — "communist," "fascist," "democrat" — in favor of a closer look at what women actually suffer and how they
act. Military loyalties require women and men to kill — or at least
to pay for and train killers — in the name of abstract enmity.
Feminist solidarity searches among these abstract enemies and al-

lies to identify with women's culturally specific struggles to work, care, and enjoy, to think and speak freely, and to resist abuse.

As feminism transforms the denial and parochialism that encourage maternal militarism, mothers are likely to act first against particular policies and forces of violence that threaten them and their children, then against those that are deployed by their own government against others, and finally on behalf of children anywhere who suffer violence. Mothers are not especially altruistic; nonetheless they are capable of responsibility and solidarity. Mothers engage in various kinds of action, from writing letters to blockading a military base, usually in concert with women and men who are not mothers, sometimes in groups that are specifically maternal or feminist. Insofar as they become publicly visible *as mothers* who are resisting violence and inventing peace, they transform the meaning of "motherhood."

It is also true that when mothers become publicly visible as peace activists, feminists may prove reluctant to support them. As many feminists have pointed out, women can act individually or collectively as women without making for themselves or for women generally typical feminist claims such as for the right to equal pay, promotion, and management, self-respecting sexual pleasure, control of the conditions of giving birth, or autonomy within marriage and the option of fair divorce. Any politics that does not make explicit claims about injustice to women will be seen by many feminists as diverting women's energies from feminist demands. Many feminists will be especially skeptical of a maternal antimilitarist politics that turns on women's identities as mothers, caretakers, kin workers, and shelterers. In drawing strength from women's work, this politics seems to ignore the exploitation of the workers and to reinforce a conception of women's responsibility that has boded ill for women themselves. Unlike a women's politics of resistance that proudly draws on traditional identities even as it transforms them, a feminist politics subjects all traditional womanly roles to critical reflection.

Nonetheless, despite these inevitable tensions I believe that feminists strengthen mothers' power to act whether as individuals, in mixed groups, or in a women's politics of resistance. Feminists themselves point out that whenever women act publicly or in conjunction with other women they tend to acquire the self-respect and skills that feminists wish for all women. Feminist literature and art celebrate these strengths and consequently legitimate them for the women themselves and often in the eyes of their culture, whatever the cause in which they are developed. Less happily, it is also true that women acting militantly, once they are at all effective, are invariably subject to misogynist insult from strangers and political opponents and often from the men they live among. Despite local variations in vocabulary and emphasis, there is a depressing redundancy in the vocabulary of abuse: women's judgment is impugned as "crazy," "hysterical," naive, and sentimental; their "castrating" anger arises from sexual envy or deprivation; they are witches, whores, and lesbians. It is feminists who have deconstructed these terms of abuse, revealing the ways in which psychiatric insult, sexual superstition, and homophobia have been tools of intimidation that separate women from each other and deny them confidence in their minds, angers, and desires. In a feminist culture, even without explicit feminist support, contempt that would otherwise be dispiriting can issue in appropriate anger and pride.

In sum, mothers who acquire a feminist consciousness and engage in feminist politics are likely to become more effectively nonviolent and antimilitarist. By increasing mothers' powers to know, care, and act, feminism actualizes the peacefulness latent in maternal practice. Feminism has these transformative powers whether or not feminists are antimilitarist. As I have insisted, in any generous understanding of feminism, it is possible to applaud organized violence without violating feminist commitments.

It does not, however, follow that feminism and peace politics are opposed. Indeed, it is my belief that feminism is already conjoined with a peace politics that is marked by its double origins in women's traditional work and feminist resistance to abuse against women. It should be obvious that insofar as feminist mothers are antimilitarist, so too is that part of the feminist movement made up of mothers and mother-identified men and women. Quite aside from its maternal membership, there are inherently antimilitarist features of feminism. In revealing connections between making "masculine" men and making war, feminists cut beneath the abstractions of just-war theory to the sexual fantasies and fears that sustain the allure of violence. Often feminists take violence against women both as emblematic of military and ecological violence and as causally responsible for them; to resist the one is to resist the other. Feminism is a global movement committed to a solidarity that respects differences despite anger and bitterness. Even in their efforts to support one another effectively, feminists have to invent the techniques of "peace."

It is not surprising that a distinctly *feminist* peace politics is one of the most vital parts of the international peace movement. If feminism at its most militarist challenges maternal militarism, is it unreasonable to hope that an antimilitarist feminism can effectively transform a latent maternal peacefulness into an instrument of peace? Feminist peace activists offer peacemaking mothers resources, theoretical insights, psychological support, and solidarity in action. The direction is not only one way. Mothers strengthen even as they are strengthened by feminism, bringing to a collective peace politics distinctive habits of mind and principles of nonviolence honed by daily use.

I do not want to suggest that feminism assimilates either to mothering or to peace politics. Many feminists are appalled by the conditions of mothering and by the women who submit to them; many feminist women are engaged in organized violence as part of their resistance to the unrelenting economic and racial violence they suffer. Nonetheless, there is truth — and hope — in the poster slogan "A feminist world is a peaceful world." A feminist consciousness can be both antimilitarist and maternal; the standpoint achieved in the feminist transformation of mothering is also a distinct and powerful antimilitarist vision. To paraphrase Sandra Bartky's account of coming to feminist consciousness that I cited earlier:

Coming to have an antimilitarist and feminist maternal consciousness is the experience of coming to know the truth about the social uses of organized violence and one's own excited or timid response to them. Social reality, the reality of organized violence is deceptive. . . . What is really happening is quite different from what appears to be happening. . . . Coming to have a maternal feminist and antimilitarist consciousness is the experience of coming to know what violence does to one's children and to oneself, as victim or perpetrator, and then casting one's lot in solidarity with women who resist violence. . . . The very *meaning* of what the maternal feminist antimilitarist apprehends, the brutality and costliness of violence, is illuminated by the light of the peace that ought to be, by the promise of birth that violence destroys. The maternal antimilitarist apprehends certain features of reality as intolerable, as to be rejected in behalf of a transforming project for the future.

Epilogue

A feminist maternal politics of peace: peacemakers create a communal suspicion of violence, a climate in which peace is desired, a way of living in which it is possible to learn and to practice nonviolent resistance and strategies of reconciliation. This description of peacemaking is a description of mothering. Mothers take their work seriously and create a women's politics of resistance. Feminists sustain that politics, devising strategies, celebrating strength, resisting violence and contempt. Together mothers, feminists, and women in resistance are members of an "imaginative collective."[27] As a collective, the group draws strength from the act and symbol of birth and from the passionate labor of women who, throughout most of history, have assumed the responsibilities of protection and care. Yet because it is feminist, this imaginative collective subverts the mythical division between men and women, private care and public defense, that hobbles both maternal and peacemaking endeavors. As men become mothers and mothers invent public resistances to violence, mothering and peacemaking become a single, womanly-manly work — a feminist, maternal politics of peace.

The "imaginative collective" of mothers, feminists, and women in resistance is an odd political entity. It is made up of a practice and two political movements, each element often at odds with the other two. Either political movement would, on its own, transform maternal practice; together they work on the imagination of mothers and anyone who identifies with preservative love. Actual coalitions of mothers, feminists, and women in resistance is rare. Yet the imaginative conjunction inspires a new political identity: the feminist, maternal peacemaker who draws upon the history and traditions of women to create a human-respecting politics of peace. The forms and ideologies of a feminist maternal peace politics are various and still being invented out of different combinations of maternal, feminist, and resistant women's commitments. Individuals participate in ways that their economic situation, political loyalty, temperament, and skill suggest. Yet even in its inchoate forms, this politics already contributes distinctively to the many-faceted, polymorphous inventions of "peace."

I have made the arguments; I believe them. Yet the idea of a feminist maternal peace politics inspires disbelief. War surrounds us. Everywhere, it seems, men and sometimes women are fighting. Everywhere, men and women support these fighters in causes that they believe justify violence. Everywhere, despite the best intentions of just warriors and those who love them, "atrocities follow war as the jackal follows a wounded beast."[28] Those who live in the absence of declared war — in what passes for peace — witness the tribal nationalism, racialism, domination, and imperialism that remind us why peace so often seems only a temporary cessation of hostilities.

The work of peace is always specific, a particular resistance to particular violences. In Argentina, the Madres, as a group, have not survived the victory that they achieved. Once the kidnappings stopped and military tyranny was replaced by a more democratic government, the women were not sure what to demand, how to resist. Women were divided by class and political differences; only some were interested in participatory democracy within their group. They could not collectively decide how long to hope for the return of their children or how to remember them and hold their murderers accountable. Yet the demands required of them even after the fall of the military junta seem clearer than those confronting peacemakers in the United States.

In the United States government officials meet with leaders of empires they used to call evil and, in optimistic moments, declare the "cold war" over. Yet these same officials continue to invoke a holy war against communism and in its name prepare "low-intensity conflicts" that rip the fabric of far-away societies, countenance murderous violations of human rights in "friendly" countries, and plan in detail nuclear destruction so vast and final that it eludes the imagination. Citizens of the United States live in a state of nuclear siege,[29] hostage to the weapons their government deploys, complicit in munitions manufacture that is widely recognized as "armed aggression against the poor,"[30] unable to think their way out of the theology of "peace through strength" — in other words, through violence. Nuclear weapons do not stand inert but function in a system of risk and of economic and military domination almost too complex to fathom. When torture and tyranny are tolerated in one country, while farms are overrun, cities bombed, or health clinics burned in another, it is possible to glimpse the effects of the wars we prepare for and fund. But it is easy to look away from the violences a nuclear state permits and risks, turning instead to past wars in order to revel in, or at least justify, the patriotic violence of earlier, more innocent times.

Yet despite the ubiquity of war, the central sustaining ideals of military honor and justice are now endangered by their own weapons. To be sure, the military romance was probably always an illusion (even The Iliad does not give a consoling picture of violence). Although there may have been battlefields where soldiers fought soldiers and hardly anyone else was hurt, as long as there have been wars there have also been "civilians" who have been injured, starved, raped, and enslaved as the soldiers passed by. Now, however, even the remnants of romance are fading. The strictest division between combatant and civilian cannot survive modern weapons. There is no "firebreak" between "conventional" and nuclear weapons;[31] they are economically, physically, and strategically inseparable. Together they epitomize the contradiction between ideals of chivalric, morally restrained military patriotism and the machines on which patriots are dependent. Now, in the nuclear light, all wars look sickly. Were there ever weapons good enough for the armed yet vulnerable, brave but restrained just warrior? Was the bayonet better than napalm, the rotting animals thrown over the walls of besieged towns to sicken inhabitants better than the chemicals sprayed over conscripted troops? Where did the unraveling of war begin? An American philosopher, ironically and perhaps parochially, places the turn at Gettysburg, where "the triumph of slaughter over chivalry gave rise to Sherman's horrifying march through Georgia and South Carolina, to total war, to the fire-bombing of Dresden, to Hiroshima and Nagasaki, to the rolled grenade in the full jetliner."[32]

Although countless women have been caught up in the romance of war, many others have refused the sexual-conceptual allure of military thinking. Like any just-war theorists, these women are able to tell the moral difference between the My Lai massacre and the Battle of Britain, Pickett's charge at Gettysburg and the grenade in the jet. What they refuse is a kind of thinking that outlaws some kinds of violence only to legitimate others: "We do not distinguish between guns and nuclear bombs." "We are against war of any sort and violence against any being." "The abstract term 'enemy' means in practice destroying human beings."[33] Whatever women do, the curtain is falling on the drama of victor and vanquished, soldier and civilian, hero and villain. Saturation bombing, nuclear missiles, and profiteering in small deadly arms were enough to stop that play. Women didn't put an end to war; many of them loved it. But as the Big Drama plays itself out, women are creating an alternative. In their vision, war is not a play of its own but a creation of the "civilization" which it only appears to interrupt. Virginia Woolf writes from the fascist thirties:

The public and the private worlds are inseparably connected; the tyrannies and servilities of the one are the tyrannies and servilities of the other.[34]

Her words are echoed today by Christa Wolf:

You can tell when a war starts, but when does the prewar start? If there are rules about that we should hand them on. Hand them down inscribed in clay, in stone. What would they say? Do not let your own people deceive you.[35]

In this alternative vision, the "beautiful brother," chivalric hero of every militarist sister and just-war theorist, is gone and all his rules are gone with him. As Christa Wolf's Cassandra, whom no one could hear, watches her brother Troilus murdered, ancient battle is linked to current danger, "naked hideous male gratification" to the abstract euphemisms of defense intellectuals:

Troilus stood his ground, faced his opponent, fought. He fought by the rules, as he had been taught was the way to fight between high-born men. . . . Achilles raised his sword high above his head, gripping it with both hands, and let it whistle down on my brother. All rules fell into the dust forever. So that's how it's done.[36]

Cassandra takes her wounded brother into the temple, removes his armor, and tends his wounds. Achilles follows her, leaving the designated "battlefield" for the sanctuary.

In what role was his enemy approaching my brother? As a murderer? as a seducer? Could such a thing be — the vuluptuousness of the murderer and the lover in one? Was that allowed to exist among human beings? The fixed gaze of the victim. The capering approach of the pursuer, whom I now saw from behind, a lewd beast. Who took Troilus by the shoulders, stroked him, handled him — the defenseless boy from whom I, wretched woman, had removed the armor! Laughing, laughing all over. Gripped his neck. Moved to the throat. His plump, stubby fingered hairy hand on my brother's throat. . . . My brother's eyes were starting out of their sockets. And the gratification in Achilles' face. The naked hideous male gratification. If that exists, everything is possible.[37]

So Christa Wolf, citizen of nuclear East Germany, writes of Troy. From the United States she is echoed by another woman, Leslie Marmon Silko, who created another just-war hero. Her hero, the Native American Tayo, was a soldier in the 1941–1946 Japanese war and has now returned to live in the United States. "Maddened" like Virginia Woolf's Septimus Smith and Toni Morrison's Shadrack, Tayo cannot forget:

He saw the skin of the corpses again and again, in ditches on either side of the long muddy road — skin that was stretched slimy and dark over bloated hands; even white men were darker after death. There was no difference when they were covered and swollen with flies. They had become the worst thing for Tayo; they looked too familiar even when they were alive. When the sergeant told them to kill all the Japanese soldiers lined up in front of the cave with their hands on their heads, Tayo could not pull the trigger. . . . In that instant he saw Josiah [his uncle] standing there. . . . So Tayo stood there, stiff with nausea, while they fired at the soldiers and he watched his uncle fall, and he *knew* it was Josiah . . . [even after] Rocky made him look at the corpse and said "Tayo, this is a *jap!* This is a *jap* uniform."[38]

The war Tayo fights "goes nuclear"; Tayo himself comes home to the Laguna Pueblo reservation, to the land where bombs are made and where crops and cattle were seized and destroyed long before the land was needed for bombs. In an abandoned uranium mine Tayo envisions the mad and global pattern of destruction, a vision that is almost the beginning of a vision of peace:

Trinity Site, where they exploded the first atomic bomb, was only three hundred miles to the southeast at White Sands. And the top-secret laboratories where the bomb had been created were deep in the Jemez mountains, on land the Government took from Cochiti Pueblo: Los Alamos, only a hundred miles northeast of him now, still surrounded by high electric fences and the ponderous pine and tawny sandrock of the Jemez mountain canyon where the shrine of the twin mountain lions had always been. There was no end to it; it knew no boundaries; and he had arrived at the point of convergence where the fate of all living things, and even the earth, had been laid. From the jungles of his dreaming he recognized why Japanese voices had merged with Laguna voices. . . . The lines of cultures and worlds were drawn in flat dark lines on fine light sand. . . . Human beings were one clan again, united by the fate the destroyers planned for all of them, for all living things; united by a circle of death that devoured people in cities twelve thousand miles away, victims who had never known these mesas, who had never seen the delicate colors of the rocks which boiled up their slaughter.
. . . He cried the relief he felt at finally seeing the pattern, the way all the stories fit together — the old stories, the war stories, their stories — to become the story he was being told. He was not crazy; he had never been crazy. He had only seen the world as it always was: no boundaries, only transitions through all distances and time.[39]

Anyone might despair of "peacefulness" amid a violence so pervasive yet often so invisible. Women, expected to be "peaceful" and powerless, are especially aware of the forces ranged against them. Among women it sometimes seems that mothers have the best chance of influence. Militarists still count on mothers to bless the plans of the violent, including the violence for which their children are recruited. It should matter if mothers, in the name of protection and acceptability, say no. Yet if among women, mothers are the most able to speak, they may also be the least liable to be heard.

In many ways, mothers are like soldiers. Like Wilfred Owen and other soldier-poets, they have created a literature against war, drawing on the authority of *their* experience to exhort us to see what they have seen: If you could hear the hopes and fears that I have heard, if you knew what I know about living and caring, "My friend, you would not tell with such high zest / To children ardent for some desperate glory, / The old lie." That soldiers continue to celebrate war despite what they have seen and mothers turn militaristic despite the conditions of their work and love does not discount the authority of their experience, though it does suggest that their continued support of war needs explaining. Interestingly, it is often the woman/mother whom the soldier accuses of ignorant patriotism, while she in turn accuses him of heedless destruction.

Yet finally mothers and soldiers are quite unalike. Soldiers know war, they have been there. They return from the land of dying, speak from privileged knowledge of war's horror and mysterious appeal, bearing witness to what most of us have not seen. Mothers, especially if they are from countries that fight their wars far away, have been nowhere special. What they know is something that any man or woman can know and from which no one should be excluded. Some people find soldiers' tales hard to hear, others take a perverse or sadistic pleasure in the confirmation of horrors they have long suspected. Almost no one is bored. Maternal tales are neither mysterious nor attractively horrible. When they speak against war, mothers say just what anyone expects to hear.

It may be, however, that in the political-acoustic conditions of techno-strategic reasoning, mothers are especially able to speak and make visible both the senselessness and the patterns of destruction. If wars really were fought between combatants, by rule, on battlefields from which ordinary folk were excluded, then only the soldier could understand, only he (or she) would have earned through suffering the right to bear witness. But in war, "homes" have always been battlefields; now "battlefields" can be brought home by soldiers high in the sky or behind computers miles away. It may be the soldier who is somewhere else, on the other side of the missile or bomb, when the cities burn, the food rots, and the children sicken and die. Or perhaps the glare of our latest rockets only reveals what we've long suspected. It is mothers and those who live with them on their side of the gun — the "population" that is raped, enslaved, starved and burned — who can tell us what really happened.

Mothers have always been the custodians of the promise of birth; it is they who have been meant to "make us feel with sharp regret what it is that violence kills and will kill again."[40] But their witness has been enfeebled by their own exploitation, unnecessary sacrifice, and political isolation. Birth is nothing without mothering, yet mothering as we have known it is not immune from, but rather is entwined with, the racialism in which war flourishes and the abstract hatreds and loyalties on which militarism depends. Now, so my story goes, a feminist maternal peace politics can transform maternal practice and the natality in which it begins. Of course, there is no simple way to unravel the destructiveness we have created, to dismantle its weapons, tease apart the allure of its concepts, and cure ourselves of its fearful romance. The story I have told is not the only one about mothers or about peace. Many politics are needed, many wills, many moral and intellectual inventions. A feminist maternal peace politics is one story. It makes a beginning that, like birth itself, revives human hopes as old and at least as indestructible as war.

Notes

Love's Reason

1. Plato, *Symposium,* 208e. I discuss Plato's views at greater length in Chapter 8.
2. Throughout these introductory remarks, as well as in Chapter 2 and especially in the discussions of Plato and Aristotle, I am greatly indebted to the readings of Elizabeth Spelman, *Inessential Woman: Problems of Exclusion in Feminist Thought* (Boston: Beacon Press, 1988). The quotations here are from Plato's *Republic,* cited by Spelman.
3. Plato, *Phaedo,* 60a.
4. I am attributing to Aristotle a view that Spelman finds implicit in his work, although part of her point is that Aristotle did not have the consciousness of class differences among women that would allow him to recognize or articulate the position he actually holds. For detailed citations to Aristotle, see Spelman.
5. Aquinas, *Summa Theologica,* I, Q.92 art. 1, vol. IV, p. 276. Cited by Genevieve Lloyd, *Man of Reason* (Minneapolis: University of Minnesota

Press, 1984), p. 36. I am greatly indebted to Lloyd's reading of Western philosophers.

6. Susan Bordo, "The Cartesian Masculination of Thought," *Signs,* vol. 11, no. 3, 1986, p. 451. Bordo is actually talking here of the masculine character of Cartesian thinking. In my introductory remarks to Part III, I consider the claim that the ideals of reason express an "abstract masculinity." I am indirectly suggesting here that the ideals can be found wanting, that one can look to women's experience for alternative ideals without making any claims about connection of the dominant ideals with a distinctly masculine subjectivity.

7. The phrase is from Spinoza, *Ethics,* part V, passim.

8. Evelyn Fox Keller, *Reflections on Gender and Science* (New Haven: Yale University Press, 1985), p. 174. Once I began reading philosophical texts with gender in mind, their contempt for women was clear. Philosophical attitudes toward women range from the explicit misogyny of Nietzsche and Schopenhauer to the assertion of masculine superiority by Aristotle and Spinoza to the complex assumptions of a misogynist feminist like Plato. Contemporary feminist intellectuals have suffered from the heirs of these men. For a particularly poignant account of the difficulty an intellectual woman has sorting her way through abuse, see Evelyn Fox Keller, "The Anomaly of a Woman in Physics," in *Working It Out,* ed. Sara Ruddick and Pamela Daniels (New York: Pantheon, 1977). There are egalitarian philosophers — Descartes and John Stuart Mill are examples. And Plato believed, notoriously, that women could be philosophers and as philosophers were as suitable to rule as male philosophers.

9. Virginia Woolf, *Three Guineas* (New York: Harvest/HBJ, 1966), p. 18. Some feminist philosophers influential in developing feminist critique do not endorse the attempt to derive alternative ideals of reason from women's experience. Genevieve Lloyd, for example, argues that it is dangerous to look for distinctive women's voices when the very content of "femininity" has been determined by the exclusion of women from reasoning. In *Reflections on Gender and Science,* Evelyn Fox Keller argues that there is insufficient basis for identifying a distinctive women's scientific perspective. Her point is that the dominance of a masculinist ideal of objectivity distorts scientific practice and disguises the actual thematic diversity of men's scientific practices.

10. Margaret Anderson, "Changing the Curriculum in Higher Education," *Signs,* vol. 12, no. 2, (Winter 1987), p. 223.

11. Adrienne Rich, *Of Woman Born,* (New York: Harper & Row, 1976), p. 283.

12. From J. Echergray, "Severed Heart," quoted in Jessie Bernard, *The Future of Motherhood* (New York: Dial, 1974), p. 4.

CHAPTER ONE
Maternal Thinking

1. The philosophers on whom I draw most closely are Ludwig Wittgenstein, especially *Philosophical Investigations* (New York: Macmillan, 1953) and *On Certainty,* ed. G. E. M. Anscombe and G. H. von Wright (Oxford: Basil Blackwell, 1969), and Peter Winch, especially "Understanding a Primitive Society," in *Ethics and Action* (London: Routledge and Kegan Paul, 1972). In my earliest work on maternal thinking I was directly indebted to Jurgen Habermas, *Knowledge and Human Interests* (Boston: Beacon Press, 1971), and influenced by Jean-Paul Sartre, *Being and Nothingness* (New York: Philosophical Library, 1956). In the last several years, there has been considerable philosophical discussion of the social construction of knowledge and its relation to relativism. An excellent account of some of this discussion is Richard Bernstein, *Beyond Objectivism and Relativism* (Philadelphia: University of Pennsylvania Press, 1983). I have found the following works and discussions of them useful: Richard Rorty, *Philosophy and the Mirror of Nature* (Princeton: Princeton University Press, 1979) and *Consequences of Pragmatism* (Minneapolis: University of Minnesota Press, 1982); Jean-François Lyotard, *The Post-Modern Condition: A Report on Knowledge* (Minneapolis: University of Minnesota Press, 1984). I do not, however, enter into the subtleties of philosophic argument here.

2. Winch, "Understanding a Primitive Society," p. 12.

3. The example is from Elisabeth Badinter, *Mother Love: Myth and Reality* (New York: Macmillan, 1980).

4. There is considerable controversy about parental attitudes toward children in different historical periods or in different subcultures of North America, particularly over the extent and degree to which children have been exploited and abused. What no one seems to dispute is that there is wide social as well as individual variation in the basic understanding of the needs and rights of children. Elisabeth Badinter, *Mother Love* is a good place to start reading about this issue. Lloyd De Mause has written extensively about the "nightmare" of childhood. See "The Evolution of Childhood," *The History of Childhood Quarterly,* Spring 1974, pp. 503–575. For a different perspective see John Demos, *Past, Present, and Personal* (New York: Oxford University Press, 1986).

CHAPTER TWO
Talking About "Mothers"

1. Philip Wylie, *Generation of Vipers* (New York: Rinehart, 1955); Edward A. Strecker, *Their Mothers' Sons* (Philadelphia: Lippincott, 1946).

2. Strecker, *Their Mothers' Sons,* p. 73.

3. Louise Kapp Howe, *Pink Collar Workers* (New York: Avon Books, 1977), pp. 233–42.

4. Howe, *Pink Collar Workers,* p. 237.

5. Monique Plaza, "The Mother/The Same: Hatred of the Mother in Psychoanalysis," *Feminist Issues,* vol. 2, no. 1 (Spring 1982), pp. 75–100. Feminists and psychoanalysts have offered several explanations for the "hatred of the mother." Dorothy Dinnerstein's *The Mermaid and the Minotaur* (New York: Harper & Row, 1976), has become a classic. I have found Eva Kittay's work on womb envy especially useful — and also delightful to read. See Kittay, "Womb Envy: An Explanatory Concept," in *Mothering: Essays in Feminist Theory,* ed. Joyce Trebilcot (Totowa, NJ: Roman and Allenheld, 1984). Julia Kristeva, critically adapting Lacanian language, explains why "the mother" must be abominated and her authority repressed. See especially *Powers of the Horror,* trans. L. Roudiez (New York: Columbia University Press, 1985). As Howe suggests, contempt for mothers cannot be separated from, but is an especially virulent form of, contempt for women.

6. For an eloquent, comprehensive discussion of children's fantasies of maternal power and their consequences, see Dinnerstein, *The Mermaid and the Minotaur.*

7. The phrase is Adrienne Rich's from *Of Woman Born* (New York: Norton, 1976).

8. Parental attempts to choose ambitions that suit both parent and child are discussed by William Ruddick, "Parents and Life Prospects," in *Having Children,* ed. Onora O'Neill and William Ruddick (New York: Oxford University Press, 1979), pp. 123–37.

9. Two moving essays that discuss this nostalgia fantasy for a mother-paradise lost are Elizabeth Abel, "Narrative Structure(s) and Female Development: The Case of Mrs. Dalloway," in *The Voyage In,* ed. Elizabeth Abel, Marianne Hirsch, and Elizabeth Langland (Hanover, NH: University Press of New England, 1983), pp. 161–85, and Madelon Sprengnether, "(M)other Eve: Some Revisions of the Fall in Fiction by Women Writers," paper delivered at the Modern Language Association, 1986. Manuscript courtesy of the author.

10. Monique Plaza's self-critical remarks (see note 5) are unwittingly reflected, I believe, in much feminist psychoanalytic theory. Perhaps it is impossible within the theory to hear mothers' voices, but if so, the usefulness of psychoanalysis to maternal self-understanding is limited. For references to feminist psychoanalytic theory, see notes to "Maternal Thinking as a Feminist Standpoint."

11. These beliefs are associated with certain French feminists, especially Helene Cixous and Chantal Chawaf, but they also surface in the work

of North American "cultural feminists" (including perhaps my own work). For an excellent discussion of the idea of a "woman's language" see Andrea Nye, *Feminist Theory and the Philosophies of Man* (London: Croom Helm, 1988).

12. Ynestra King, talk at Columbia Seminar on Women and Society, Spring 1983. King herself is a sympathetic and subtle critic of maternal thinking.

13. Mary Helen Washington, *Invented Lives* (Garden City, NY: Doubleday, 1987), p. 352. Washington adapts the language of Alice Walker, "In Search of Our Mother's Gardens: The Creativity of the Black Woman in the South," first published in *Ms.*, May 1974. Washington also cites Marianne Hirsch, "Feminist Discourse/Maternal Discourse: 'Cruel Enough to Stop the Blood,' " a talk given at the Bunting Institute, Cambridge, MA, Spring 1985. Among the several writers now attempting to articulate a maternal voice, the work of Marianne Hirsch is especially notable and will appear soon from Indiana University Press in a book entitled *Unspeakable Plots: Mothers, Daughters and Narratives*. There is also, in many of the writers I cite here, a respect for the mother's voice, such as in Jane Lazarre, Audre Lorde, Tillie Olsen, and Grace Paley.

14. Toni Morrison, *Tar Baby* (New York: Knopf, 1981), p. 281. I am indebted for this quotation and for many ideas about mothers to Maureen T. Reddy, " 'Maternal Thinking': Gaskell, Chopin, Lazarre and Walker," paper delivered at the Modern Language Association, Winter 1987. Manuscript courtesy of the author. The painter May Stevens has beautifully explored the mother/daughter relationship in a series of paintings entitled *Ordinary/Extraordinary*. These are reproduced in *Between Women*, ed. Carol Ascher, Louise de Salvo, and Sara Ruddick (Boston: Beacon Press, 1984), pp. 275–310. This book, a collection of self-reflective essays by women about women on whom they work, represents a sustained attempt to reconceive the daughter/mother relationship.

15. Mary Belenky, Blythe Clichy, Nancy Goldberger, and Jill Tarule, *Women's Ways of Knowing* (New York: Basic Books, 1987), p. 18.

16. Audre Lorde, "The Transformation of Silence into Language and Action," "Poetry Is Not a Luxury," in *Sister Outsider* (Trumansburg, NY: Crossing Press, 1984), pp. 36–45. Alicia Ostriker, *Stealing the Language: The Emergence of Women's Poetry in America* (Boston: Beacon Press, 1986), p. 211.

17. There is a superb discussion of the power/powerlessness of Fathers (and for that matter of mothers) in Carolyn Kay Steedman, *Landscape for a Good Woman* (New Brunswick, NJ: Rutgers University Press, 1987). A poignant description of a daughter's love for a powerless father and of her ambivalent relation to a psychologically stronger mother occurs

in Paule Marshall, *Brown Girl, Brownstones* (Chatham, NJ: Chatham Bookseller, 1972).

18. Bell Hooks, *Feminist Theory: From the Margin to the Center* (Boston: South End Press, 1984), pp. 138–39. In "Shaping an Acceptable Child," in *Learning for a Lifetime: Moral Education in Perspective and Practice,* ed. Andrew Garrod (Hanover, NH: University Press of New England, 1989), Nel Noddings offers the most thoughtful discussion I have seen on the issue of fathers' (or as I would say, male mothers') relation to maternal thinking. Noddings is particularly concerned with the possibility that men will offer distinct versions of parental thinking that are not maternal. I agree that maternal thinking will change when men are involved and also that feminists should maintain an agnostic attitude about the possible effects of physiological differences in a thoroughly egalitarian world.

19. Among the many essays dealing with the issues of shared parenting, three are particularly useful: Virginia Held, "The Obligations of Mothers and Fathers," Diane Ehrensaft, "When Women and Men Mother," and Susan Rae Peterson: "Against Parenting." All appear in *Mothering: Essays in Feminist Theory,* ed. Joyce Trebilcot (Totowa, NJ: Roman and Allenheld, 1984). I have also learned a good deal about how to think about family contexts of mothering from conversations with the philosopher Elizabeth Minnich and from her essay on stepparenting "Choosing Consciousness," to appear in a forthcoming anthology on stepparenting edited by Nan Bauer Maglin and Nancy Schneiderwind.

20. I take this phrase from Hilary Rose's remarks at the Feminist Theory Conference, Oslo, Norway, June 1986. Rose's theoretical understanding of women's work has been important in shaping my understanding of a "feminist standpoint," which I discuss in the introduction to Part III. See, for example, Hilary Rose, "Hand, Brain and Heart: A Feminist Epistemology for the Natural Sciences," *Signs,* vol. 9, no. 1 (1983), pp. 73–90. Carolyn Whitbeck provides a succinct statement of care as a collection of activities defined by "the (mutual) realization of people," in "A Different Reality: Feminist Ontology," in *Beyond Domination,* ed. Carol Gould (Totowa, NJ: Roman and Allenheld, 1983). In their critically important works on women's ways of knowing, both Carol Gilligan and Nel Noddings speak of care. Noddings, *Caring* (Berkeley: University of California Press, 1984), and Gilligan, *In a Different Voice* (Cambridge: Harvard University Press, 1982). I myself have often found it useful to speak of caring labor and the rationality of care.

21. I take the phrase "kin work" from a very useful article by Micaela de Leonardo, "The Female World of Cards and Holidays: Women, Families, and the Work of Kinship," *Signs,* vol. 12, no. 3 (1987), pp. 440–53.

22. I have discussed this point in "The Rationality of Care," forthcoming in *Women, War, and Militarism,* ed. Jean Bethke Elshtain and Sheila Tobias (Totowa, NJ: Roman and Littlefield).

23. I am indebted here to the classification of possible attitudes toward the fetus — gynecological, projective, or maternal — developed by William Ruddick, "Are Fetuses Becoming Children?" in *Biomedical Ethics and Fetal Therapy,* ed. Carl Nimrod and Glen Griener (Calgary: Calgary Institute for the Humanities, Wilfred Laurier University Press, 1988). I am also indebted to William Werpehowski, "The Pathos and Promise of Christian Ethics: A Study of the Abortion Debate," *Horizons,* vol. 12, no. 2 (Fall 1987), pp. 284–302. Though I disagree with Werpehowski's assumption that fetal life must be maternally interpreted and although I distinguish birthing labor from mothering, I found this article very useful in formulating my own questions and views.

I am skipping lightly over one of the central issues in feminist theory and politics today: How should women act in respect to the new reproductive technologies? I did not set out to write about birthgiving but to minimize its importance in relation to mothering. I am only now beginning to think again about the implications for women generally of female birthgiving. Joan Rothschild has generously shared with me her work, bibliographies, and insights. I have found her article "Engineering Birth: Toward the Perfectibility of *Man?*" in *Science, Technology and Social Progress,* ed. Stephen L. Goldman (Bethlehem, PA: Lehigh University Press, 1988) most helpful. Robyn Rowland, "Technology and Motherhood: Reproductive Choice Reconsidered," *Signs* (Spring 1987), pp. 512–28, is an excellent review essay. A classic collection is Rita Arditti, Renate Duelli Klein, and Shelley Minden, eds., *Test-Tube Women: What Future for Motherhood* (London: Pandora Press, 1984). Two recent collections are *Made to Order: The Myth of Reproductive and Genetic Progress,* ed. Patricia Spallone and Deborah Lynn Steinberg (New York: Pergamon Press, 1987), and *Reproductive Technologies: Gender, Motherhood and Medicine,* ed. Michelle Stanworth (Minneapolis: University of Minnesota Press, 1987). The literature on the politics of birth is vast. Readers will find further bibliographical references in the works I have cited. As even the titles of these works make clear, the literature as a whole assimilates mothering to birthgiving and accepts the language of *r*eproduction that I am contesting.

24. Simone de Beauvoir, *The Second Sex* (New York: Vintage, 1974), p. 301. Elizabeth Spelman has elaborately and persuasively made the point that "women" are never socially constructed only "as women" but always as particular women with particular social-historical locations. See Spelman, *Inessential Woman* (Boston: Beacon Press, 1988). In the last several years there has been an outpouring by feminists on the ways, if

any, in which it is philosophically possible, morally permissible, or politically useful to speak of or invoke the political category of "women." Bell Hooks's discussion of solidarity in *Feminist Theory: From the Margin to the Center* is directly relevant. I have also found Maria Lugones, "Playfulness, 'World-Travelling' and Loving Perception," *Hypatia,* vol. 2, no. 2 (1987), pp. 3–20, useful. Lugones is indebted, as I and my students have been, to Marilyn Frye's *The Politics of Reality: Essays in Feminist Theory* (Trumansburg, NY: Crossing Press, 1983). In "Shaping an Acceptable Child," forthcoming, Nel Noddings speaks in a useful, direct, and low-key way about taking up the "standpoint of women," seeing the world from a "woman's" perspective. Nodding worries that, given the differences among women, "the world of epistemological subjects will be broken down into many radical subjectivities." She looks for "bulwarks against fragmentation" but at the same time wants to respect the particularity of any woman's individual and social experience. Nodding offers the following description of her own practice of taking up the standpoint of women:

Writing as a woman, one can be careful to choose experiences that cut broadly across the lives of most women; note situations, opinions, or problems that are affected by membership in other groups; couch one's conclusions in language that is moderate and makes claims only to a contribution toward a cumulative universality — not for universality itself.

Most of this literature about "women" is directly relevant to the philosophical and moral issues involved in speaking about mothers. Nonetheless, the two literatures should not be confused. Since mothers can be men but have historically been disproportionately women, the relation of "mothers" to "women" or to the subject of gender difference is complex.

25. Sue Miller, *The Good Mother* (New York: Harper & Row, 1986). Phyllis Chesler's passionate *Mothers on Trial* (New York: McGraw-Hill, 1986) also suggests, indirectly, that women threatened with the loss of their children because of their sexuality would write with different emphases. The literature on lesbian mothers is rapidly developing. See especially *A Lesbian Parenting Anthology,* ed. Sandra Pollack and Jeanne Vaughn (Ithaca, NY: Firebrand Books, 1987). See also Sally Crawford, "Lesbian Families: Psycho-social Stress and the Family-Building Process," and Marjorie Hill, "Child-Rearing Attitudes of Black Lesbian Mothers," both in *Lesbian Psychologies: Explorations and Challenges,* ed. Boston Lesbian Psychologies Collective (Urbana: University of Illinois Press, 1987). I am grateful to Laura Benkov for discussing with me the

distinctive issues of lesbian mothering and for guidance to the relevant literature.

26. Rayna Green made these remarks in a public address at the National Women's Studies Association Conference, Minneapolis, June 1988. For a discussion of Argentinian resistance, see Chapter 9.

27. Several years ago I happened to read Buchi Emecheta's *The Joys of Motherhood* (New York: Braziller, 1979) at the same time that a colleague was teaching it. My colleague's pedagogical point was that the work and relationships of mothering varied not just between Nigerians and the various cultures of the students but also within Nigeria in particular decades of change. I, on the other hand, much to my colleague's consternation, saw in the experience of Emecheta's heroine elements of mothering work and maternal relationships which, though not universal, were both familiar and common. Emecheta surely meant to underline difference and change and to alert universalists like me to the specificity of my experience. Nonetheless, she dedicated the book to all mothers; I chose to count myself in.

28. Gloria Naylor, *Women of Brewster Place* (New York: Viking Penguin, 1983), p. 86. There are many mothers in this novel. It is not clear how sympathetic Naylor herself is with this remark of an affluent mother who lives in "Linden Hills."

29. Bernice Johnson Reagon, "African Diaspora Women: The Making of Cultural Workers," *Feminist Studies,* vol. 12, no. 1 (Spring 1986), p. 88. In "Mothering and Healing in Recent Black Women's Fiction," *Sage,* vol. 2, Spring 1985, pp. 41–43, Carol Boyce Davies confirms and explores Reagon's claim that in the African family tradition, mothering includes community responsibility. Rayna Green makes the same point about Native American tradition; see note 25. Numerous middle-class white women have made similar points about mothering and responsibility, such as Jane Addams and Olive Schreiner, whom I quote in Chapter 8.

Making It Up

1. The psychologists who have most directly influenced my articulation of maternal voices are Carol Gilligan, the *Women's Ways of Knowing* collective, and Jean Baker Miller, all of whom are cited in the next chapters. These women contribute to a vast feminist literature in psychology from which I benefit.

2. It was Nancy Goldberger of the *Women's Ways of Knowing* collective who coined the phrase "different-voice" theory, using Carol Gilligan's expression to designate those feminists who look to women's work and experiences to articulate alternative ideals of epistemology and moral

reasoning. I have cited different-voice theorists throughout the first two parts of this book. In addition, I am indebted to Jane Roland Martin for an illuminating discussion of the place of different-voice theory within feminist critiques of reason. I have also profited from her book *Reclaiming a Conversation* (New Haven: Yale University Press, 1986). Nel Noddings's *Caring* (Berkeley: University of California Press, 1984) deals with many of the same issues I discuss in these chapters and, although we sometimes disagree, I always profit from her discussion. The work of the philosophers Margaret Walker and Virginia Held have been especially helpful to me, and I am heartened by the work of Seyla Benhabib. For Held, see note 9 in Chapter 8. Margaret Walker's very helpful "Moral Understandings: Alternative 'Epistemology' for a Feminist Ethics" is available from the author, Department of Philosophy, Fordham University, New York, NY. For a sample of Seyla Benhabib's writing, see "The Generalized and Concrete Other: The Kohlberg-Gilligan Controversy and Moral Theory," in *Woman and Moral Theory,* ed. Eva Kittay and Diana Meyers (Totowa, NJ: Rowman and Littlefield, 1987). Jean Grimshaw's *Philosophy and Feminist Thinking* (Minneapolis: University of Minnesota Press, 1987) has a very useful discussion of versions of "different-voice theory." Grimshaw's work is a model of careful, respectful reading, most especially of work about which she has serious doubts — for example, my own. Much of the feminist work in literary history and aesthetics contributes to different-voice theory. I could not begin to list the many women whose work on different voices informs mine. The names in my notes offer only a hint.

CHAPTER THREE
Preservative Love

1. Julie Olsen Edwards, "Motheroath," *Women's Studies Quarterly,* vol. 12, no. 2 (Summer 1984), pp. 25–28. Because this story is short, I have not cited page references for each quotation. All quotations without a reference are to this story.
2. Jane Lazarre, *The Mother Knot* (Boston: Beacon Press, 1985), p. 85.
3. When she read this sentence, Jane Lazarre reported that what I labeled "scrutiny" a friends of hers called "vigilance." This is the kind of confirmation that I delight to receive: another mother recognizes the phenomenon I make out and names it in a way that I recognize as capturing what I intend.
4. Iris Murdoch, *Sovereignty of Good* (New York: Schocken, 1971), p. 99.
5. Murdoch, *Sovereignty of Good,* p. 95.

6. Murdoch, *Sovereignty of Good,* p. 95.

7. Spinoza, *Ethics,* Book 4, proposition, demonstration.

8. Spinoza, *Ethics,* Book 4, Proposition 42.

9. Some anthropologists have suggested that there is a cross-cultural tendency to identify women more than men with nature or at least to assign women an intermediate status between nature and culture. The debate among anthropologists begins with Sherry Ortner, "Is Female to Male as Nature Is to Culture" in *Women, Culture and Society,* ed. Michelle Z. Rosaldo and Louise Lamphere (Stanford: Stanford University Press, 1974). A second anthology, *Nature, Culture and Gender,* ed. Carol MacCormack and Marilyn Strathern (Cambridge: Cambridge University Press, 1980), makes an excellent follow-up.

   I myself am not sympathetic to the association of women or mothers with nature. The allegedly "natural" activities of women—for example, pregnancy, birth, and certainly child care—are infused with cultural meaning, dependent on technological expertise, and in many societies require women to make serious responsible choices. Conversely, if women or mothers are alienated from culture this is not because they are "natural" but because they are excluded from constructing and actively participating in cultural life. I have found Gerda Lerner's *The Creation of Patriarchy* (New York: Oxford University Press, 1986) very valuable on these points, especially her notion of "symbol systems" from which women are excluded.

10. Evelyn Fox Keller, *Reflections on Gender and Science* (New Haven: Yale University Press, 1986), p. 134.

11. Adrienne Rich, "Conditions for Work: The Common World of Women," in *Lies, Secrets, and Silence* (New York: Norton, 1979), p. 205. First printed as a preface to *Working It Out,* ed. S. Ruddick and P. Daniels (New York: Pantheon, 1976).

12. I am alluding to Virginia Woolf's statement "As a woman I want no country, as a woman I have no country, my country is the whole world" (*Three Guineas* [New York: Harcourt Brace, 1938], p. 109).

CHAPTER FOUR
Fostering Growth

1. I first heard development discussed this way in a talk by Kamla Bhasin of New Delhi, a representative of the Food and Agricultural Association of the United Nations, at a plenary session of the Third Interdisciplinary Congress of Women, Dublin, July 1987.

2. Virginia Woolf, *To the Lighthouse* (New York: Harcourt Brace/ Harvest, 1955), p. 95.

3. Tillie Olsen, "I Stand Here Ironing," in *Tell Me a Riddle* (New York: Seymour Lawrence, 1961), p. 10.

4. Ann Petry, *The Street* (Boston: Beacon Press, 1985), p. 314. The entire novel can be read as a mother's struggle to nurture as well as protect her son against overwhelming and finally defeating social conditions.

5. Tony Cade Bambara, dedication to *The Salt Eaters* (New York: Vintage, 1981).

6. Olsen, "I Stand Here Ironing," p. 13.

7. Olsen, "I Stand Here Ironing," p. 9.

8. Jean Baker Miller, *Toward a New Psychology for Women* (Boston: Beacon Press, 1973), p. 54.

9. Miller, *Toward a New Psychology,* p. 56.

10. Audre Lorde, "Manchild: A Black Lesbian Feminist's Response," in *Sister Outsider* (Trumansburg, NY: Crossing Press, 1984), p. 76.

11. Jean-Paul Sartre, *Being and Nothingness* (New York: Philosophical Library, Washington Square Press, 1956), p. 81.

12. Evelyn Fox Keller, *Reflections on Gender and Science* (New Haven: Yale University Press, 1986), p. 134.

13. When teaching Kohlberg's work I use Lawrence Kohlberg, *Essays on Moral Development,* vol. 1, (New York, Harper & Row, 1981). Kohlberg's dilemma has by now been repeated and reported in many places. A useful discussion of the dilemma with references to the literature surrounding it is Marilyn Friedman, "Care and Context in Moral Reasoning," in *Women and Moral Theory,* ed. Eva Feder Kittay and Diana T. Meyers (Totowa, NJ: Roman and Allenheld, 1987), pp. 190–204. Many of Friedman's points parallel mine. Carol Gilligan criticizes Kohlberg in *In a Different Voice* (Cambridge: Harvard University Press, 1982).

14. Gilligan, *In a Different Voice,* p. 28. In *Caring* Nel Noddings has an interesting discussion of concrete versus abstract or principle thinking that differs from Gilligan's and mine.

15. Carol Gilligan, "Moral Orientation and Moral Development," in *Women and Moral Theory.* Also personal conversations and unpublished manuscripts. Kay Johnston, "Two Moral Orientations — Two Problem Solving Strategies: Adolescents' Solutions to Dilemmas in Fables," unpublished doctoral dissertation, Harvard University, cited by Gilligan in "Moral Orientation and Moral Development." Mary Belenky, Blythe Clichy, Nancy Goldberger, and Jill Tarule, *Women's Ways of Knowing* (New York: Basic Books, 1986).

16. Sara Ruddick, "New Combinations: Learning from Virginia Woolf," in *Between Women,* ed. Carol Ascher, Louise de Salvo, and Sara Ruddick (Boston: Beacon Press, 1984), p. 138.

17. Simone Weil, "Gravity and Grace," in *Gravity and Grace* (London: Routledge and Kegan Paul, 1952), p. 1 and passim.

18. I am indebted to Lawrence Blum, "Compassion," in *Explaining Emotions,* ed. Amelie Oksenberg Rorty (Berkeley: University of California Press, 1980), pp. 507–18.

CHAPTER FIVE
Training: A Work of Conscience?

1. Grace Paley, "Midrash on Happiness," first published in *TriQuarterly,* Northwestern University, 1986, and reprinted in *Best Short Stories of 1987.* For an interesting discussion of acceptability, see Nel Noddings, "Shaping an Acceptable Child," in *Learning for a Lifetime: Moral Education in Perspective and Practice,* ed. Andrew Garrod (Hanover, NH: University Press of New England, 1989).
2. Shirley Grubka, "Out of the Stream: An Essay on Unconventional Motherhood," *Feminist Studies,* vol. 9, no. 2, p. 227. This is an autobiographical account by a mother who entrusted the care of her child, whom she still very much loved, to another woman who she believed was more suitable to the work of raising him. Anyone interested in the issues raised by my book should read this article.
3. Audre Lorde, "Manchild: A Black Lesbian Feminist's Response," in *Sister Outsider* (Trumansburg, NY: Crossing Press, 1984), p. 76.
4. Emily Dickinson, "This is my letter to the World," poem no. 441.
5. I am paraphrasing somewhat loosely what appear to me to be tenets of certain versions of psychoanalytic theory, especially in its Lacanian form as French feminists have criticized it. For an interesting account of French discussion, see Andrea Nye, *Feminist Theory and the Philosophies of Man* (London: Croom Helm, 1988). Jessica Benjamin, *Bonds of Love* (New York: Pantheon, 1988), explicates and then criticizes a similar account drawn from the version of psychoanalytic theory known as "object relations theory." The account is complicated by the fact that Fatherhood is culturally variable and often mythical. Many women mother without Fathers and many men called "Fathers" are poor, powerless, and far more the victims than the instruments of the Fathers' Laws. See Chapter 2.
6. The phrase "gaze of the other" is Sartre's from *Being and Nothingness.* It has now been appropriated by feminist film critics and theorists.
7. This phrase was used by Adrienne Rich, *Of Woman Born* (New York, Norton, 1976), p. 192. My discussion of "inauthenticity" — indeed this entire book — is profoundly indebted to *Of Woman Born.*
8. Plato, *Gorgias,* 482c, translated and cited by Hannah Arendt, *The Life of the Mind,* vol. 1, *Thinking* (New York: Harcourt Brace, 1978), p. 181.

9. I am drawing here on the work of Carol Gilligan. Of special interest is "Exit-Voice Dilemmas in Adolescent Development," in *Development, Democracy and the Art of Trespassing: Essays in Honor of Albert O. Hirschman* (Notre Dame, Indiana: Notre Dame University Press, 1986). I am also indebted to William Ruddick, "Parents and Life Prospects," in *Having Children,* ed. ONora O'Neill and William Ruddick (New York: Oxford University Press, 1979).

10. Throughout this discussion of trust, I am indebted to Annette Baier, "Trust and Antitrust," *Ethics,* vol. 96, no. 2 (Jan. 1986), pp. 231–60.

11. Simone Weil, "Human Personality," in *Simone Weil Reader,* ed. George A. Panichas (Mt. Kisko, NY: Moyer Bell, 1977), p. 333.

12. Iris Murdoch, *The Sovereignty of Good* (New York: Schocken, 1971), p. 40.

13. Murdoch, *Sovereignty of Good,* p. 67.

14. Jane Lazarre, personal communication.

15. Weil, "Reflections of the Right Use of School Studies with an Eye to the Love of God," in *Simone Weil Reader,* p. 51.

16. Murdoch, *Sovereignty of Good,* p. 65.

17. Weil, "Reflections on the Right Use."

18. Murdoch, *Sovereignty of Good,* p. 28.

19. Murdoch, *Sovereignty of Good,* p. 43. In *Philosophy and Feminist Thinking* (Minneapolis: University of Minnesota Press, 1986), Jean Grimshaw raises the question of the political import of attention. Her question, "Can attending to the 'reality' of a particular child reveal the political dimensions in which that reality is constructed?" is also relevant for the work of philosophers such as Margaret Walker. Briefly, the answer to Grimshaw's question seems to be yes and no. If, for example, a child is frightened by her mother's complicity in and submission to the physical or psychological dominance of a Father, attentiveness can reveal the source of fear. Knowledge of her child's suffering could then lead a mother to reflect on male dominance and her acceptance of it. But it is a feminist politics — not guaranteed by attention — that makes undefensive attention likely in this sort of case. Another example: if a child begins to get a sense of the race and class injustices from which he and his mother profit, his feelings will be a confused mélange, varying in the individual case but perhaps including arrogance, sadism, guilt, and fear. An attentive mother may "hear" those feelings but be unable to address them because she has not come to terms with the racial and class character of her life. She might come to terms by adopting racist views and philosophical justifications of her class privilege. In Part III I discuss sources of *antiracism* in maternal thinking and the ways in which the passionate particular loyalties of mothers can come to encompass all children.

Maternal Thinking as a Feminist Standpoint

1. Ludwig Wittgenstein, *Philosophical Investigations*, no. 19.
2. Wittgenstein, *On Certainty*, no. 204.
3. Wittgenstein, *Philosophical Investigations*, Part II, p. 226.
4. Catherine A. MacKinnon, "Feminism, Marxism, Method, and the State: An Agenda for Theory," *Signs*, vol. 7, no. 3, p. 534.
5. Mary Belenky, Blythe Clichy, Nancy Goldberger, and Jill Tarule, *Women's Ways of Knowing* (New York: Basic Books, 1986), pp. 137–38.
6. Adela Pankhurst, "I Didn't Raise My Son to Be a Soldier," in *My Country Is the Whole World*, ed. Cambridge Women's Peace Collective (London: Pandora Press, 1984), p. 100.
7. The full title of the article is "The Feminist Standpoint: Developing the Ground for a Specifically Feminist Historical Materialism." It was first printed in Sandra Harding and Merrill Hintikka, eds., *Discovering Reality* (London: D. Reidl, 1983), pp. 283–310. All of my page references are to this version. A nearly equivalent version of this article appears in Hartsock's book *Money, Sex, and Power* (New York: Longman, 1983). The entire book is relevant to my discussion here. My reading of standpoint theory emphasizes caring labor and slights the complex but important strengths of any perspective derived from the experience of oppression. There is now a considerable literature on the feminist standpoint. I am particularly indebted to Hilary Rose, "Hand, Brain, and Heart," *Signs*, vol. 9, no. 11 (1983), and "Women's Work, Women's Knowledge," in *What Is Feminism?*, ed. Juliet Mitchell and Ann Oakley (New York: Pantheon, 1986). I am also indebted to Sandra Harding's discussion of the feminist standpoint in her book *The Science Question in Feminism* (Ithaca, NY: Cornell University Press, 1986), and to Alison Jaggar's discussion in *Feminist Politics and Human Nature* (Totowa, NJ: Roman and Allenheld, 1983), and to Terry Winant, "The Feminist Standpoint: A Matter of Language," *Hypatia*, vol. 2, no. 1 (Winter 1987). In addition I have had numerous and valuable conversations with Harding about our interpretations of Hartsock and more generally about standpoint theory that have revealed the considerable differences in our readings and the ways in which standpoint theory can be variously interpreted. In my view there can be several epistemological perspectives systematically derived from experiences of women other than caring labor and transformed by feminist consciousness and politics.
8. Michel Foucault, *Power/Knowledge* (New York: Pantheon, 1985), pp. 81–82. The phrase "lost in an all-encompassing knowledge" comes from Sharon Welch, *Communities of Resistance and Solidarity: A Feminist Theology of Liberation* (New York: Orbis, Maryknoll, 1985), p. 19. I am indebted to Welch for a distinct and potentially antimilitarist reading of

Foucault. Although I am adapting Foucault's idea of subjugated knowledge to my purposes, other current notions — for example of "minority," "peripheral," or "marginal" "discourses" — are unsuitable to the points I am making. Although any variant of maternal thinking might be considered "minor" — as, for example, white middle-class, heterosexual, North American maternal thinking represents only a minority of thinkers — maternal thinking as a whole and the rationality of care of which it is a part derive from practices ubiquitous and central to the human enterprise. Hartsock has recently addressed these issues in "Rethinking Modernism: Minority vs. Majority Theories," *Cultural Critique* (Fall 1987), pp. 187–206, where she discusses and rejects the critiques of Rorty and Foucault. To adapt her current terms, maternal thinking is a "revolutionary discourse" that has been marginal and peripheral but that, as a central discourse, could transform dominant, so-called normal ways of thinking.

9. I consider myself an agnostic in respect to psychoanalytic theory. In particular, object relations theory seems a primary case of what Cixous identified as "reproduc[ing] the masculine view of which it is one of the effects." Hélène Cixous, "Laugh of the Medusa," *New French Feminisms,* ed. Elaine Marks and Isabelle de Cortivron (New York: Schocken, 1981), p. 255. Nonetheless, I believe that psychoanalytic theory, in its many versions, is the only theory of subjectivity worth serious feminist consideration and I do believe some account of the development of subjectivity is required. Among the many psychoanalytic feminist theorists, the following have been of special use to me: Dorothy Dinnerstein, *The Mermaid and the Minotaur* (New York: Harper & Row, 1976); Evelyn Fox Keller, *Reflections on Gender and Science* (New Haven, 1986), Part II; Nancy Chodorow, especially "Feminism and Difference: Gender, Relation and Difference in Scientific Perspective," *Socialist Review,* no. 46 (1979); Jessica Benjamin, *The Bonds of Love* (New York: Pantheon, 1988); Isaac Balbus, *Marxism and Domination* (Princeton: Princeton University Press, 1981); Susan Bordo, *The Flight to Objectivity: Essays on Cartesianism and Culture* (Albany, SUNY Press, 1987).

10. I am suggesting that object relations theory accounts for the characteristics and phenomena of abstract masculinity only in cultures that give excessive privilege to those characteristics, especially independence. The theory itself is a product of such cultures and, as Cixous suggests, expresses the values it explains. It is not a theory that explains male dominance, a phenomenon that occurs in societies that do not value independence in the ways object relations theory presumes. Sandra Harding's discussion of African philosophy in *The Science Question in Feminism* reveals the limits of object relations theory, at least in the form I'm using it here.

11. Klaus Thewelweit, *Male Fantasies* (Minneapolis: University of Minnesota Press, 1987), p. 364.

12. Hartsock, "Feminist Standpoint," p. 299.

13. Simone de Beauvoir, *The Second Sex* (New York: Vintage, 1974); also cited by Hartsock, "Feminist Standpoint."

14. Hartsock, "Feminist Standpoint," p. 301.

15. Hartsock, "Feminist Standpoint," p. 304.

16. Hartsock, "Feminist Standpoint," p. 302.

17. Hartsock, "Feminist Standpoint," pp. 288, 302.

18. Hartsock, "Feminist Standpoint," p. 305.

19. Alice Walker, *Meridian* (New York: Washington Square Press, 1976), p. 200.

20. Jane Lazarre, Letter to the New School for Social Research (New York City) faculty, Spring 1985.

CHAPTER SIX
Mothers and Men's Wars

1. Randall Jarrell, "The Death of the Ball Turret Gunner," in *The Complete Poems* (New York: Farrar, Straus and Giroux, 1969), p. 144.

2. Klaus Thewelweit, *Male Fantasies* (Minneapolis: University of Minnesota Press, 1987), p. 176.

3. Jarrell, "Losses," in *Complete Poems,* p. 145.

4. Thewelweit, *Male Fantasies,* p. 62.

5. Adrienne Rich, "Natural Resources," in *The Fact of a Doorframe: Poems Selected and New,* 1950–1984 (New York: Norton, 1984), p. 264.

6. Shakespeare, *Othello,* I, iii, 167–68.

7. Tim O'Brien, *If I Die in a Combat Zone* (New York: Dell, 1979), p. 52.

8. O'Brien, *If I Die,* p. 146.

9. David Marlowe, "The Manning of the Force and the Structure of Battle, Part 2: Men and Women," in *Conscripts and Volunteers, Military Requirements, Social Justice, and the All Volunteer Force,* ed. Robert K. Fullinwider (Totowa, NJ: Rowman and Allenheld, 1983), p. 190.

10. Marlowe, "The Manning of the Force," p. 191–92.

11. Marlowe, "The Manning of the Force," p. 191. Nancy Hartsock has written in a profound and illuminating way on the connections of war and masculinity. See "Masculinity, Heroism, and the Making of War," in *Rocking the Ship of State: Toward a Feminist Peace Politics* (Westview Press, forthcoming). Judith Stiehm has also written extensively and in very interesting ways on the masculinist ideology of the military. See *Bring Me Men and Bring Me Women: Mandated Change at the Air Force*

Academy (Berkeley: University of California Press, 1981) and *Arms and the Woman,* forthcoming.

12. Plato, *Republic,* 543a, 521d.

13. The phrase "techno-strategic rationality" is Carol Cohn's, and she has enunciated it in numerous talks. See "Sex and Death in the Rational World of Defense Intellectuals," *Signs,* vol. 12, no. 4, pp. 687–718. The notion of a "language of warriors" comes from Freeman Dyson, *Weapons and Hope* (Princeton: Princeton University Press, 1984). Dyson compares the language of warriors with the language of victims.

14. Jean Bethke Elshtain, "Reflections on War and Political Discourse: Realism, Just War, and Feminism in a Nuclear Age," *Political Theory* (February 1985), pp. 49–50.

15. Cohn, "Sex and Death," p. 691.

16. Cohn, "Sex and Death," p. 711.

17. Olive Schreiner, *Women and Labor* (1911; London: Virago, 1978), p. 173.

18. Virginia Woolf, *Three Guineas* (New York: Harcourt Brace/Harvest, 1938), pp. 105, 109. Woolf, however, did not deny her love for her country. Rather, she said that she would use her patriotism, "this drop of pure, if irrational emotion . . . to give to England first what she desires of peace and freedom for the whole world."

19. East German Women, *Radical America* (Jan.–Feb. 1983), p. 40.

20. Tatyana Mamanova, *Women in Russia* (Boston: Beacon Press, 1984), p. xiii.

21. Helen Caldicott, *War Resister's League Calendar,* 1981.

22. Lewis Thomas, *The Youngest Science: Notes of a Medicine Watcher* (New York: Viking, 1983), pp. 236–37.

23. Chinua Achebe, "Refugee Mother and Child," from the section "Poems on War" in *Beware, Soul Brother* (London: Heinemann, 1972), p. 12.

24. Simone Weil, *"Iliad:* Poem of Force," Pendle Hill Pamphlet no. 91, Wallingford, PA, p. 32.

25. Anne-Marie Troger, "German Women's Memories of World War II," in *Behind the Lines: Gender in the Two World Wars,* ed. Margaret Higgonet, Jane Jenson, Sonya Mitchel, and Margaret Weitz (New Haven: Yale University Press, 1987), p. 286.

26. Hiroshima survivor, cited in Bel Mooney, "Beyond the Wasteland," in *Over Our Dead Bodies: Women Against the Bomb,* ed. Dorothy Thompson (London: Virago Press, 1983), p. 7.

27. Anna Shaw, speech to Women's Peace Party, 1915.

28. Virginia Woolf, *Mrs. Dalloway* (London: Penguin Modern Classics, 1973), p. 96.

29. Toni Morrison, *Sula* (New York: Plume Books, 1973), p. 8.

30. Virginia Woolf, *Letters,* vol. 6, ed. Nigel Nicholson (London: Hogarth Press, 1980), p. 464.

31. Jean Bethke Elshtain, *Women and War* (New York: Basic Books, 1987), p. 101, Chap. 3.

32. Elshtain, *Women and War,* pp. 101–2.

33. I first read this slogan in Leila Rupp, *Mobilizing Women for War* (Princeton: Princeton University Press, 1978), p. 115. I then learned from Claudia Koonz, *Mothers in the Fatherland: Women, the Family, and Nazi Politics* (New York: St. Martin's Press, 1987), that the phrase is from a recruitment poster and that German women themselves were more reluctant than women of other industrial countries to take up war work.

34. Reported in Hilary Wainwright, "The Women Who Wire Up the Weapons," in *Over Our Dead Bodies,* p. 144.

35. Adrienne Rich, "Natural Resources."

36. I am obviously very much indebted to Sara Friedrichsmeyer's paper " 'Seeds for the Sowing': The Diary of Käthe Kollwitz," in *Of Arms and the Woman,* ed. Helen Cooper, Adrienne Munich, and Susan Squier (Chapel Hill: University of North Carolina Press, 1989). All citations in these paragraphs on Kollwitz are from this article. Claudia Koonz, in *Mothers in the Fatherland,* suggests that Kollwitz's resistance to the Nazis was only partial (see p. 317). Of various efforts to make sense of women's complex relation to militarism and war and at the same time to criticize militarism from a feminist and women's perspective, I have found especially useful Phyllis Mack, "Feminine Behavior and Radical Action: Franciscans, Quakers, and the Followers of Gandhi," *Signs,* vol. 11, no. 3, 1986, reprinted in *Rocking the Ship of State: Toward a Feminist Peace Politics,* ed. Adrienne Harris and Ynestra King (Westview Press, forthcoming), and Jane Roland Martin, "Martial Virtues or Capital Vices? William James' Moral Equivalent of War Revisited," *Journal of Thought,* vol. 22, no. 3, Fall 1987. I have also been influenced by Anne Marie Troger's discussion of women's victimization in "German Women's Memories of World War II."

CHAPTER SEVEN
Maternal Nonviolence: A Truth in the Making

1. Whatever the statistical extent of violence among mothers, maternal violence makes up only a small fraction of individual and group violence. Moreover, most mothers are women. It seems that the vast majority of violent acts — from incest to child abuse to domestic and public beatings, personal and imperialist armed robbery, and saturation bombing — are

performed by men and are often deliberately planned and officially sanctioned by men. While acknowledging statistical association of violence with men — though not of the majority of men with violence — I am here concerned with *mothers'* violence, which is primarily *women's* violence just because most mothers are women. I am also concerned with mothers', and therefore with women's, attraction to or complicity in the violence of others, including violence of lovers, public officials, Fathers, and teachers — often, but by no means always, men.

A cursory glance at Linda Gordon's *Heroes of Their Own Lives: The Politics and History of Family Violence, Boston* 1880–1960 (New York: Viking, 1988) reveals that in the records Gordon studied, fathers counted for 54%, mothers for 46% of child abusers. Gordon also says that women are more often violent with a spouse, less violent on their own. Not surprisingly, men's abusive behavior is correlated with their unemployment and with the time they spend with their children. My cursory reading has not yet revealed whether men became abusive because, as a result of unemployment, they take up mothering work (for which they were ill prepared) or whether children were targets of despair and anger (these men couldn't be Fathers) or, presumably, both.

2. Simone Weil, *Iliad, Poem of Force,* p. 3 and passim.

3. Gandhi's principal writings on nonviolence are collected in *Non-Violent Resistance* (New York: Schocken Books, 1981). A very useful book for understanding Gandhi's theory of nonviolence is Joan Bondurant, *The Conquest of Violence* (Berkeley: University of California Press, 1971). An excellent, brief, and secular discussion of nonviolence is Barbara Deming, "Revolution and Equilibrium," published, along with other essays on nonviolence, in *We Are All Part of One Another* (Philadelphia: New Society Publishers, 1984). The essay is also printed in pamphlet form published by the A. J. Muste Essay Series (New York: A. J. Muste Institute). The pamphlet is available from the War Resisters' League, 339 Lafayette St., New York, NY 10012. The political theorist Gene Sharp has written extensively on nonviolence, developing a strong tactical defense of its usefulness. See, for example, *Making Europe Unconquerable: The Potential of Civilian Based Deterrence and Defense* (New York: Ballinger Books, 1985). The War Resisters' League is a very helpful guide to the literature of nonviolence, and essays, journals, and books can be found in their small bookstore.

Throughout this chapter I invoke the words of Gandhi and King as an aid of identifying maternal nonviolence. I do not, however, believe that there is any simple translation of domestic to public nonviolence.

4. Gandhi, cited in Bondurant, p. 24.

5. Gandhi, cited in Bondurant, p. 26.

6. Gandhi, *Non-Violent Resistance,* p. 73.

7. Martin Luther King, Jr., "Loving Your Enemies," sermon delivered Christmas 1957, Montgomery, Alabama, p. 11. King's writings have been collected in *A Testament of Hope: The Essential Writings of Martin Luther King, Jr.,* ed. James Melvin Washington (San Francisco: Harper & Row, 1986). Here I use pamphlet number 1 in the A. J. Muste Essay Series (New York: A. J. Muste Institute). This pamphlet, available from the War Resisters' League, includes "Loving Your Enemies," "Letter from the Birmingham Jail," and "Why We Are in Vietnam?"

8. Gandhi, cited in Bondurant, p. 26.

9. King, "Loving Your Enemies," p. 11.

10. Gandhi, *Non-Violent Resistance,* p. 42. The march against the salt mines was led by Gandhi's followers and took place after Gandhi was arrested during his march to the sea to procure salt — a witty and effective protest against the salt tax. The event is depicted in the movie *Gandhi* and described in most accounts of Gandhi's campaigns. See, for example, Erik Erikson, *Gandhi's Truth* (New York: Norton, 1969).

11. Grace Paley, "Faith in a Tree," in *Enormous Changes at the Last Minute* (New York: Farrar Straus and Giroux, 1987), p. 85. This passage was pointed out by Jane Lazarre, a mother of black sons who, along with her husband, was determined to raise her children to resist but also feared for their safety in a hostile world. She then had to steel herself to remain calm — though she was in fact both proud and frightened — when her adolescent sons were "fresh" not only to her but, more worrisome, to authorities on whose goodwill they depended.

12. King, "Loving Your Enemies," pp. 4–8 and passim.

13. King, "Loving Your Enemies," p. 8.

14. W. B. Gallie, "Three Main Fallacies in the Discussion of Nuclear Weapons," in *Dangers of Deterrence,* ed. Nigel Blake and Kay Pole (London: Routledge and Kegan Paul, 1983). I take not only the acronym but many of my points from Gallie.

15. Quoted by Michael Walzer in *Just and Unjust Wars* (New York: Basic Books, 1977), p. 5.

16. I have in mind particularly the work of Carol Gilligan on the meaning of respectful connection and new conceptions of autonomy. See references to Gilligan throughout these notes and especially "Exit-Voice Dilemmas in Adolescent Development" in *Development, Democracy and the Art of Trespassing: Essays in Honor of Albert O. Hirschman* (Notre Dame Indiana: Notre Dame University Press, 1986) and "Moral Orientation and Moral Development" in *Women and Moral Theory,* ed. Eva Feder Kittay and Diana T. Meyers (Totowa, NJ: Roman and Littlefield, 1987), pp. 19–36. Gilligan explicitly contrasts care with justice; where she speaks of justice, I prefer egalitarian fairness — an important but subsidiary virtue in domestic life and a sometimes dangerous, though not unworthy,

public ideal. The question for different-voice theory, as I see it, is how to conceptualize, recognize, and focus on demands of "justice" from the perspective of care. Gilligan's conception of justice, like Kohlberg's, is indebted to the work of John Rawls. Gilligan herself, however, speaks of justice as it is construed from the perspective of care. "Justice in this [the care] context becomes understood as respect for people in their own terms." "Moral Orientation and Moral Development," p. 24.

17. Jane Lazarre, *The Mother Knot* (Boston: Beacon Press, 1985), p. 156.
18. Merleau-Ponty is cited in Raymond Geuss, *The Idea of a Critical Theory* (Cambridge: Cambridge University Press, 1981).

CHAPTER EIGHT
Histories of Human Flesh

1. Jane Addams, quoted in *My Country Is the Whole World,* ed. Cambridge Women's Peace Collective (London: Pandora Press, 1984), pp. 86–87.
2. Olive Schreiner, *Women and Labour* (1911; London: Virago Press, 1978), p. 170.
3. Addams, *My Country,* pp. 86–87.
4. Addams, *My Country,* pp. 86–87.
5. Schreiner, *Women and Labour,* p. 173.
6. Schreiner, *Women and Labour,* p. 172.
7. Plato, *Phaedo,* 11.65c–67d.
8. Simone de Beauvoir, quoted by Carol Ascher in "The Anguish of Existence: Remembering Simone de Beauvoir," American Philosophical Association, January 1988. The association of sexuality and birth with death is discussed evocatively and in detail in Dorothy Dinnerstein, *The Mermaid and the Minotaur* (New York: Harper & Row, 1976).
9. Throughout the discussion of birth I am indebted to Mary O'Brien, *The Politics of Reproduction* (London: Routledge and Kegan Paul, 1981), and to Dorothy Dinnerstein, *The Mermaid and the Minotaur.* Among philosophers, it was Virginia Held who first provoked me to think about birth. Her discussion and her willingness to make challenging, politically discomfiting points changed the way I thought about mothering and birthing labor. A sample of Held's work is "Feminism and Moral Theory" in *Women and Moral Theory,* ed. Kittay and Meyers. I have also been fortunate to be able to consult Held's unpublished manuscripts. I have found Klaus Thewelweit's discussion of bodies, in *Male Fantasies* (Minneapolis: University of Minnesota Press, 1987) wonderfully provocative. Among the vast and growing feminist literature on women's birthing, I should also mention Eva Kittay, "Womb Envy: an Explanatory Concept" in *Mothering: Essays in Feminist Theory,* ed. Joyce Tre-

bilcot and Carolyn Whitbeck, (Totowa, NJ: Rowman and Allenheld, 1984), and Carolyn Whitbeck, "The Maternal Instinct" also in *Mothering: Essays in Feminist Theory*.

10. Plato, *Symposium*, 11, 208e–209a, 209d.

11. The classic example here is de Beauvoir, *The Second Sex*. Other feminists have explicitly or metaphorically connected intellectual and artistic creation with — not against — birthing labor. For an interesting discussion of these women, see Susan Stanford Friedman, "Creativity and the Childbirth Metaphor: Gender Difference in Literary Discourse," *Feminist Studies*, vol. 13, no. 1, Spring 1987, pp. 49–82.

12. I take the phrase "the Big Dichotomies" from Alice Jardine, *Gynesis* (Ithaca, NY: Cornell University Press, 1985), p. 71, who attributes it to Meaghan Morris. Many writers have criticized these dichotomies. Among them, V. Spike Peterson of American University has developed a critical argument centering around the public-private dichotomy that is relevant to maternal thinking. See her "Historicizing the Public-Private Dichotomy," paper delivered at the Berkshire Conference on the History of Women, Wellesley, MA, June 1987. Manuscript courtesy of the author. Although variants of the Big Dichotomies recur in *contemporary* feminist and other critical readings of Western philosophy, the interpretations of them vary within historical contexts. My own — and I believe others' — readings are undoubtedly influenced by contemporary consciousness of the assaults to which female bodies are subject and by the threats posed by reproductive technologies. The medieval historian Carolyn Bynum has persuasively argued that in late medieval cultures women were not only burdened but also were considered and considered themselves gifted by their association with fleshliness. The flesh was a medium for union with the divine, and Christ was often depicted maternally, including as a birthing woman. This conjunction of burden and giftedness seems a fruitful avenue for contemporary secular exploration. See Carolyn Bynum, *Jesus as Mother: Studies in the Spirituality of the High Middle Ages* (Berkeley: University of California Press, 1982) and, on women's bodies, *Holy Feast and Holy Fast: The Religious Significance of Food to Medieval Women* (Berkeley: University of California Press, 1987).

13. Even when "the body" is celebrated by Western philosophers, as it often is in this century, it is still usually defined with reference to adult, purposive projects. Philosophers reject a dualistic separation of mind from body as Spinoza did or, like Merleau-Ponty, make embodiment a defining condition of perception, without acknowledging birthing labor, let alone according it a central role in their representation of the bodily. Or worse, a philosopher like Sartre (and to a lesser extent de Beauvoir) makes embodied being-for-others integral to human nature but then attributes to social-sexual relations an essential hostility. The anxious

competitiveness of bodily interconnection exaggerates rather than challenges Reason's fear of the sensual immersion and dependencies crystallized in birth.

14. Wilfred Owen, "Dulce et Decorum Est," *Collected Poems* (New York: New Directions, 1963), p. 55.

15. The phrases "techno-strategic rationality" and "rational world of defense intellectuals" are from Carol Cohn, "Sex and Death in the Rational World of Defense Intellectuals," passim.

16. A compelling discussion of the discipline of the body, particularly the military body, occurs in Michel Foucault, *Discipline and Punish*, trans. Alan Sheridan (New York: Vintage Books, 1979).

17. Elaine Scarry, *The Body in Pain* (Oxford: Oxford University Press, 1985), p. 73.

18. Cohn, "Sex and Death in the Rational World of Defense Intellectuals," p. 711 and passim.

19. Marlowe, "Manning the Force," in *Conscripts and Volunteers*, p. 190.

20. Cohn, "Sex and Death," pp. 692–96.

21. In the United States, Black male bodies have been the principal targets of sexual and racial projection. For a detailed rendition of American racist projection onto male Japanese bodies during the second world war see John W. Dower, *War Without Mercy: Race and Power in the Pacific War* (New York: Pantheon, 1986).

22. Elaine Scarry, *The Body in Pain*, Chap. 2.

23. For the philosophical celebration of the male soldier's identification with the universal see Genevieve Lloyd, "Selfhood, War and Masculinity" in *Feminist Challenges*, ed. Elizabeth Gross and Carole Pateman (London: Allen and Unwin, 1987). See also Nancy Hartsock, "Masculinity, Heroism, and the Making of War," in *Rocking the Ship of State*, ed. Harris and King (Westview Press, forthcoming).

24. For a poignant discussion of this fantasy among soldiers in the first world war see Eric Leed, *No Man's Land: Combat and Identity in World War I* (New York: Cambridge University Press, 1979). For a peculiarly innocent account of an American rebirth away from home in the same war, see Willa Cather, *One of Ours* (New York: Vintage Books, 1971).

25. J. Glenn Gray, *The Warriors* (New York: Harper & Row, 1970), Chap. 3. See also John Keegan, *The Face of Battle* (New York: Viking Press, 1976), Chap. 5.

26. Nancy Huston, "The Matrix of War: Mothers and Heroes," in *The Female Body in Western Culture*, ed. Susan Suleiman (Cambridge: Harvard University Press, 1985), pp. 119–36.

27. Cohn, "Sex and Death," p. 700.

28. Cohn, "Sex and Death," pp. 699–702. For other interesting discussions of birth imagery in war and nuclear armament, see Brian Easlea,

Fathering the Unthinkable: Masculinity, Science and the Nuclear Arms Race (London: Pluto Press, 1983) and a paper by Evelyn Fox Keller, "From Secrets of Life to Secrets of Death," which highlights fantasies of anal birth. Manuscript courtesy of the author.

29. Jane Lazarre, *The Powers of Charlotte* (Trumansburg, NY: Crossing Press, 1987), p. 189.

30. Phyllis Chesler, *Women and Madness,* cited in Huston, "The Matrix of War."

31. The phrase is from Mary O'Brien, *The Politics of Reproduction,* passim. What are the actual and desirable meanings of paternity? This question is very much under discussion, partly because of radical changes in at least middle-class sexual-domestic mores in conjunction with the increasingly widespread use of artificial insemination — including self-insemination by women in settings of their choosing. Although I stand by my distinction between Fathers and fathers, look forward to men's increased participation in mothering, and certainly want mothering to be considered as "masculine" as it is "feminine" (for all these points, see Chapter 2), I feel I am only at the beginning of understanding the meaning and future of paternity. I see hard times ahead for both women and men as men come to terms with changing social conditions and reproductive practices.

32. The phrase "right to a fertile body" is from Hilary Rose from a talk given at the Third Interdisciplinary Congress of Women, Dublin, Ireland July 1987.

33. Hannah Arendt, *The Human Condition* (Chicago: University of Chicago Press, 1958), p. 247, cited in Jean Bethke Elshtain, "Reflections on War and Political Discourse," *Political Theory,* February 1985.

34. Elshtain, "Reflections on War and Political Discourse," p. 53. Although Arendt writes about natality, in my view her account is more transcendent and removed from actual birthgiving than Elshtain suggests. Conversely, because she is indebted to Arendt, Elshtain takes a distance, not typical of her writing, from the woman who gives birth.

35. Representations of madonna and child reinforce this sentimentalization. They also assimilate mothering to birthgiving by concentrating on those few months of infancy in which a child is still on his mother's lap. Kristeva's fascinating explorations of the infant-mother, then child-mother, relation also suffers, in my view, from an implicit acceptance of the powerful cultural fantasy of mothers as primarily physically immobile encirclers of tiny, quiet infants. See Julia Kristeva, "Motherhood According to Giovanni Bellini," in *Desire in Language* (Oxford: Basil Blackwell, 1980) and also in *The Female Body in Western Culture,* ed. Susan Suleiman (Cambridge: Harvard University Press, 1985). In *Women of Brewster Place* (New York: Viking Penguin, 1983), Gloria Naylor con-

siders from a young mother's point of view the fantasy of mothering as consisting primarily of giving birth to and mothering infants (passim; see especially the chapter "Cora Lee").

36. Margaret Walker, "The Concept of the Erotic," unpublished manuscript.

37. Emily Martin, *The Woman in the Body* (Boston: Beacon Press, 1987), p. 164.

38. J. Glenn Gray, *The Warriors,* Chap. 6.

39. Celeste Schenck, "Feminism and Deconstruction: Re-Constructing the Elegy," *Tulsa Studies in Women's Literature,* April 1986, pp. 13–27. Schenck cites "Even the Dead are bored with the whole thing" from Anne Sexton; "More Crazy mourning, more howl more keening" from Adrienne Rich; and "Mourning without End" from May Sarton.

40. Schenck, "Feminism and Deconstruction," pp. 15–16, 19.

41. Toni Morrison, *Beloved* (New York: Knopf, 1987), pp. 84–85.

42. Simone Weil, "Human Personality," in *The Simone Weil Reader,* p. 315.

CHAPTER NINE
Notes Toward a Feminist Maternal Peace Politics

1. Alicia Ostriker, *Stealing the Language* (Boston: Beacon Press, 1986), p. 212.

2. Jane Lazarre, *The Mother Knot* (Boston: Beacon Press, 1986), p. 156.

3. For a discussion of women's participation in (and occasional resistance to) the Nazi German government, see Claudia Koonz, *Mothers in the Fatherland: Women, the Family, and Nazi Politics* (New York: St. Martin's, 1987). Among the many virtues of this fascinating book is its tracing of the complex interconnections between women's separate spheres, the Nazi and feminist use of women's difference, and women's participation in but also disappointment in the Nazi state.

4. Dorothy Dinnerstein, *The Mermaid and the Minotaur* (New York: Harper & Row, 1976), p. 226.

5. Christa Wolf, *Cassandra* (New York: Farrar Straus & Giroux, 1984), p. 53.

6. Dorothy Dinnerstein, "The Mobilization of Eros," in *Face to Face* (Greenwood Press, 1982). Manuscript courtesy of the author. For an intellectually sophisticated and high-spirited account of an American women's politics of resistance, see Amy Swerdlow's work on Women's Strike for Peace, forthcoming from the University of Chicago Press. For an example of her work, see "Pure Milk, Not Poison: Women's Strike for Peace and the Test Ban Treaty of 1963," in *Rocking the Ship of State:*

Toward a Feminist Peace Politics, ed. Adrienne Harris and Ynestra King (Westview Press, 1989).

7. The title of a well-known essay by Adrienne Rich in *Lies, Secrets and Silence* (New York: Norton, 1979), pp. 275–310.

8. Hegel, *The Phenomenology of Mind,* part VI, A, b, "Ethical Action: Knowledge Human and Divine: Guilt and Destiny" (New York: Harper, 1967), p. 496.

9. Julia Kristeva, "Talking about *Polygoue*" (an interview with Françoise van Rossum-Guyon), in *French Feminist Thought,* ed. Toril Moi (Oxford: Basil Blackwell, 1987), p. 113.

10. Marjorie Agosin, "Emerging from the Shadows: Women of Chile," *Barnard Occasional Papers On Women's Issues,* vol. 2, no. 3, Fall 1987, p. 12. I am very grateful to Temma Kaplan, historian and director of the Barnard College Women's Center, whose interest in "motherist" and grass-roots women's resistance movements inspired this section. Temma Kaplan provided me with material on the Madres and discussed an earlier draft of the chapter.

11. Nathan Laks, cited in Nora Amalia Femenia, "Argentina's Mothers of Plaza de Mayo: The Mourning Process from Junta to Democracy," *Feminist Studies,* vol. 13, no. 1, p. 10. The Argentinian Madres protested until the fall of the military regime and still exist today, though they are now divided in their political aims.

12. Marjorie Agosin, Temma Kaplan, Teresa Valduz, "The Politics of Spectacle in Chile," *Barnard Occasional Papers on Women's Issues,* vol. 2, no. 3, Fall 1987, p. 6.

13. Simone Weil, "Human Personality," in *Simone Weil Reader,* p. 315.

14. Agosin, "Emerging," p. 18.

15. Simone Weil, "Human Personality," in *Simone Weil Reader,* p. 315.

16. Phillip Hallie, *Lest Innocent Blood Be Shed* (New York: Harper & Row, 1979), p. 104. (Italics added.)

17. Agosin, "Emerging," p. 16.

18. Agosin, "Emerging," p. 14.

19. J. Glenn Gray, *The Warriors* (New York: Harper & Row, 1970), pp. 21, 23.

20. Agosin, "Emerging," p. 21.

21. Patricia M. Chuchryk, "Subversive Mothers: The Women's Opposition to the Military Regime in Chile," paper presented at the International Congress of the Latin American Studies Association, Boston, 1986, p. 9.

22. Rene Epelbaum, member of the Argentinian protest, in an interview with Jean Bethke Elshtain, personal communication.

23. Agosin, "Emerging," p. 18.

24. The phrase "partisans of women" is Terry Winant's in "The Feminist

Standpoint: A Matter of Language," *Hypatia,* vol. 2, no. 1, Winter 1987.
25. Sandra Lee Bartky, "Toward a Phenomenology of Feminist Consciousness" in *Feminism and Philosophy,* ed. Mary Vetterlin-Braggin, Frederick A. Elliston and Jane English (Totowa, NJ: Littlefield Adams, 1977), pp. 22–34.
26. My discussion here is directly indebted to Bell Hooks's discussion of solidarity in *Feminist Theory: From the Margin to the Center* (Boston: South End Press, 1984).
27. I take the idea of an "imaginative collective," which I have found valuable in several contexts, from a conversation with Helen Longino following reading an article by Valerie Miner where Miner used the term: "Rumors from the Cauldron: Competition Among Feminist Writers," in *Competition: A Feminist Taboo?* ed. Valerie Miner and Helen Longino (New York: Feminist Press, 1987), pp. 183–94.
28. Dower, *War Without Mercy* (New York: Pantheon, 1986), p. 12.
29. I am indebted to the idea that we live under nuclear siege and therefore are already at a quite particular kind of war and to the detailed military history and philosophical analysis of Helena Knapp, dissertation in progress, Union Graduate School.
30. "The Challenge of Peace: God's Promise and Our Response — A Pastoral Letter on War and Peace," National Conference of Catholic Bishops, May 1983, Part 2, Section 128.
31. The notion of a "firebreak" between nuclear and conventional weapons is both contested and insisted on in nuclear discourse. I am simply asserting what I elsewhere would argue — that nuclear and conventional weapons are inextricably connected technologically, strategically, and, as important, in the theories and fantasies that shape common thinking about war.
32. Arthur Danto, "Gettysburg," *Grand Street,* vol. 6, no. 3, Spring 1987, p. 111.
33. East German Women, in *Women in Russia,* ed. Tatyana Mamanova (Boston: Beacon Press, 1984). For full and other references see notes to Chapter 6 in this book.
34. Virginia Woolf, *Three Guineas,* p. 142.
35. Christa Wolf, *Cassandra,* p. 66.
36. Wolf, *Cassandra,* p. 73.
37. Wolf, *Cassandra,* p. 74.
38. Leslie Marmon Silko, *Ceremony* (New York: Viking Penguin, 1977), p. 8.
39. Silko, *Ceremony,* p. 246.
40. Simone Weil, "Iliad, Poem of Force," p. 29, in *Simone Weil Reader,* p. 177.

Index

Credits

Portions of Parts I and II originally appeared in "Maternal Thinking," *Feminist Studies* 6, no. 2 (Summer 1980). Portions of Chapter 7 originally appeared as "Remarks on the Sexual Politics of Reason" in *Women and Moral Theory*, ed. Eva Kittay and Diana Meyers (Totowa, N.J.: Rowman and Littlefield, 1987).

The following material has been reprinted by permission: Randall Jarrell, "The Death of the Ball Turret Gunner," in *The Complete Poems* (New York: Farrar, Straus and Giroux, 1969), p. 144; Randall Jarrell, "Losses," in *The Complete Poems*, p. 145; Adrienne Rich, "Natural Resources," in *The Fact of a Doorframe: Poems Selected and New, 1950–1984* (New York: Norton, 1984), p. 264; Chinua Achebe, "Refugee Mother and Child," in *Beware, Soul Brother* (London: Heinemann, 1972), p. 12; Wilfred Owen, "Dulce et Decorum Est," in *Collected Poems* (New York: New Directions, 1963), p. 55.